self and soul

self and soul

A Defense of Ideals

MARK EDMUNDSON

Harvard University Press
Cambridge, Massachusetts
London, England
2015

First printing

Library of Congress Cataloging-in-Publication Data

Edmundson, Mark, 1952–

Self and soul : a defense of ideals / Mark Edmundson.

pages cm

Includes bibliographical references and index.

ISBN 978-0-674-08820-7 (alk. paper)

1. Conduct of life. 2. Ideals (Philosophy) 3. Ideology. 4. Self (Philosophy)

5. Soul. I. Title.

BJ1521.E36 2015

170'.44—dc23

2015004974

To my Grandmother: Frances Benton,
To my Godmother and Aunt: Shirley Shine,
And most of all to my Mother: Eileen Edmundson.
They made my childhood a paradise.

Contents

Main Sources Cited in the Text

CHAPTER 1   Homer. *The Iliad.* Trans. Robert Fagles. New York: Penguin, 1998. Cited by book and line number.

CHAPTER 2   *The New Oxford Annotated Bible.* Ed. Bruce M. Metzger and Roland E. Murphy. New York: Oxford University Press, 1989. Cited by gospel, chapter, and verse.

CHAPTER 3   Emerson, Ralph Waldo. *Essays and Lectures.* New York: Library of America, 1983. Cited by page number.

CHAPTER 4   Shakespeare, William. *The Riverside Shakespeare.* Ed. G. Blakemore Evans. Boston: Houghton Mifflin, 1997. Cited by act, scene, and line numbers.

CHAPTER 5   Blake, William. *Complete Poetry and Prose of William Blake.* 2nd ed. Ed. David Erdman, with commentary by Harold Bloom. Berkeley: University of California Press, 1982. Cited by page number.

CHAPTER 6   Freud, Sigmund. *The Standard Edition of the Complete Psychological Works of Sigmund Freud.* Trans. James Strachey et al. 24 vols. London: Hogarth, 1953. Cited by volume and page number.

self and soul

Polemical Introduction
The Triumph of Self

This is a book about ideals—and about their potential disappearance from the world.

It is no secret: culture in the West has become progressively more practical, materially oriented, and skeptical. When I look out at my students, about to graduate, I see people who are in the process of choosing a way to make money, a way to succeed, a strategy for getting on in life. (Or they are, in a few instances, rejecting the materially based life, though often with no cogent alternative to pursue in its stead.) It's no news: we're more and more a worldly culture, a money-based culture geared to the life of getting and spending, trying and succeeding, and reaching for more and more. We are a pragmatic people. We do not seek perfection in thought or art, war or faith. The profound stories about heroes and saints are passing from our minds. We are anything but idealists. From the halls of academe, where a debunking realism is the order of the day, to the floor of the market, where a debunking realism is also the order of the day, nothing is in worse repute than the ideal. Unfettered capitalism runs amok; Nature is ravaged; the rich gorge; prisons are full to bursting; the poor cry out in their misery and no one seems to hear. Lust of Self rules the day.

Maybe the departure of ideals from our lives is all to the good. Surely ideals are dangerous: those who commit their lives to ideals sometimes find untimely ends; they can die violent deaths. When they do survive they often do so in poverty and neglect. And perhaps what the past called ideals are substantially based upon illusions. Perhaps there are no authentic ideals, only idealizations. Maybe the quest for perfection in thought, in art, in war, and in the exercise of loving-kindness only leads to trouble. It's possible that ideals are what Freud (all the time) and Nietzsche (most of the time) said they are: sources of delusion. But then again, maybe they are not.

Commitment to ideals may be passing from the world, but this should not happen without chance for second thought. Young people, who have traditionally been the ones most receptive to ideals, should be able to make the choice themselves. Do they want to live a practical life in a practical culture? Do they want to seek safety and security and never risk being made fools of? Or do they perhaps want something else? Every generation should be able to hold its own plebiscite on the issue of ideals. But many in the West, coming of age now, have never had the chance to hear the debate. (And many of their elders have forgotten or suppressed the issue.) Young people have been born into a world where the most pinched version of middle-class values—success, prosperity, safety, health— seems to stand supreme. Some have never encountered alternatives, except in misplaced or disguised form. Every man and woman should have the chance to ponder the question of the ideal.

The first ideal that arises in the West, as it does in most cultures, is the heroic ideal. There are two main versions of the Western hero, and we owe them both to Homer. One version is embodied by Achilles, the other by Hector. Achilles, the protagonist of *The Iliad,* is the warrior who seeks the first place; he yearns to be recognized as the best of the Greeks. He is beyond fear. There is no risk Achilles will not take, no deed he will not attempt, to attain what he hopes for: immortality. Achilles does not wish to live forever on earth or in some agreeable afterlife. Though he is the son of a goddess, he knows that he will someday die; and the afterlife according to the Greeks is a gray and dismal state. Homer's Achilles wants to attain eternal life in the minds and hearts of other men, warriors in particular. What matters to him is his reputation as a fighter, and he will risk anything to enlarge it. When Agamemnon challenges Achilles in open council and tells him that he is not, as he believes, the best of the Greeks, Achilles faces a crisis. He must prove that he is the warrior he takes himself to be.

Hector, the greatest of the Trojan warriors, seeks reputation too, but it is not the most important goal in his life. Hector is the model for what later generations will call the citizen soldier. His first aim is the defense of his city and his people. Though he is a formidable warrior, Hector is also an accomplished statesman and a loving husband and father. At one point in *The Iliad*, Hector confesses that he had to "learn" to step out onto the battlefield and go face to face with his enemies. To Achilles the spirit of war came naturally. Hector must acquire it—which to many only makes him more human and more sympathetic. In the entire city of Troy there are only two men who treat Helen, the ostensible cause of the war, with kindness. One is Hector's father, King Priam, the other Hector himself.

Do we as a culture still respect the two Homeric archetypes, the citizen soldier and the fearless warrior who seeks the first place? Respect, perhaps; but how few young men and women with real choices in life are now ready to emulate either one of them? Some members of the service academies no doubt understand the Homeric standard. But even for some of them, the military is a career path, a source of steady, secure employment. And the sons and daughters of the middle class generally refrain from volunteering to serve. They have other goals on their minds: prosperity, security, a family. There are still true warriors in our culture, still men and women who would emulate Hector or Achilles, but there are not many of them, and there are probably fewer all the time.

It is not that contemporary culture is willing to surrender contact with the heroic ideal. Contemporary individuals seek such contact all the time, but they do so through violent movies, action-filled TV shows, and shoot-em-up video games. Current culture is ambivalent about ideals; we cannot embrace them (that's far too dangerous), but we cannot quite abandon them either. So we live in an entertainment culture that counterfeits ideals. We can all be simulation warriors with no risk to our safety and our middle-class aspirations.

Homer does not flinch at showing the hardships and grief that come with being a warrior. But the lives of the Homeric heroes are full of meaning: they live in danger, yes, but they live with a fullness and intensity of purpose that it is not possible to match in the everyday world. In action, they are united within themselves and, at least in their own minds, united with the natural world, which (they believe) values what they embody: strength, courage, and beauty. Though the lives of the Homeric heroes are often short— Hector and Achilles both die young—they are replete with meaning. There is no danger that the true warrior will die feeling that he has never lived. The middle-class man, it's been said, is the man who desires to live as long as possible. But is what he experiences in that quest really life—at least when you compare it to what Hector and Achilles enjoyed?

The second great Western ideal emerges as an ambivalent attack on Homer and Homeric values. Plato repeatedly expresses his admiration for the Homeric poems; he seems to admire Homer above all literary artists. But to Plato there is a fundamental flaw at the core of Homer's work: Homer values the warrior above all others. For

Plato the preeminent individual is the thinker, and the best way to spend one's life is not in the quest for glory but in the quest for Truth. Plato introduces the second of the great ideals into Western culture: the ideal of contemplation.

There are no philosophers in Homer. Odysseus is a master strategist; his thinking is pragmatic and tactical. Nestor has rich experience and a long memory, but like Odysseus his mind turns naturally to results: What must we do to get what we want? To Plato, thought is something else entirely. Plato is not concerned with what we need to know to navigate practical difficulties. He does not care about short-term plans and military schemes. Plato seeks a Truth that will be true for all time. He is not looking for truth that applies exclusively to Greeks, or to men and women who live in city-states, or to those who exist at the same point in time that he does. Plato seeks Truth that will apply to all men and women at all times.

When Plato asks what beauty is, he is not asking what beauty might be in a certain culture, under a certain political dispensation, within a particular history and set of aesthetic assumptions. He wants to know what beauty is, period. When Plato speaks in *The Republic* about how the spirit is composed and how best to cultivate it to achieve happiness and to do as little harm as possible, he is not talking about the spirit under capitalism, or under communism, or under Catholicism, or after the Protestant Reformation. He is talking about the Spirit, and that is that. If Plato's account cannot illuminate the human condition in America in the year 2020 as well as it did the human condition in Greece when he was teaching and writing, Plato fails.

Others have followed Plato in his quest for the Truth—or rather they have followed him and parted from him at the same time. To quest for ultimate Truth after Plato is to believe that Plato, great as he was, did not settle matters. Comprehensive thinkers like Aristotle and Schopenhauer, thinkers who touch almost every area of human experience, have got to believe that Plato was not quite correct, even if on some level they probably must admit that all philosophy, theirs included, is a footnote to his work.

But the quest for philosophic Truth, on the scope and scale that Plato pursued, has all but disappeared. It is virtually gone from the academy, where philosophers are engaged (often brilliantly) in deciding what makes a true sentence or a valid argument. Passionately addressing such issues, they have no time to ask the crucial Platonic questions. What are good and bad? What are right and wrong? What is justice? What is beauty? "This is not any chance conversation," Plato's Socrates says, "but a discussion about how we ought to lead our lives."

Nor does current popular culture care much about philosophic Truth. The average citizen now is a reflexive pragmatist. Though he may not have read William James or John Dewey, he believes implicitly that truth is whatever is best in the way of belief. Truth is embodied in the way of looking at the world that will help get him what he wants. The intellect is a practical organ, like a hand, that guides the individual toward the fulfillment of his desires. The mind isn't best used to seek eternal Truth: that is impractical, a waste of time. The mind is a compass to get bearings in life; a calculator to ascertain profit and loss; a computer to plan one's next move in life's chess match. What the Frankfurt School calls Instrumental Reason rules the day. And anyone who graduated from college and took a course in anthropology, or history, or sociology, knows that there is no Truth, only truths. These truths are dependent upon historical context, group affiliation, tribal mores—and of course upon race, class, gender, and sexuality.

In our culture, the philosopher has been eclipsed by the disseminators of information. Knowledge now is information with immediate practical value. The philosopher demands too much. His books are hard to read, and what he asks of us by way of a virtuous life is likely to be inconvenient. So we replace the Platonic philosopher with the philosophy professor, scrambling after minute distinctions, and with the public pundit, full of fleeting information and half-knowledge. But as to wisdom—that is another matter. Maybe detractors of the philosophic ideal, from the brilliant Jacques Derrida to the brusque investor on the floor of the stock exchange, are right, and the philosophical ideal is a rank deception. It hides a drive for power; it feeds into fascism. But maybe the primary function of the deconstructionists, inside the academy and out, is defensive. They deliver the middle class from a major source of disruption—which might also be a source of insight and illumination—the philosophical ideal, the quest for Truth. We owe it to all to pose the question of the ideal thinker—of what Stevens called "the impossible possible philosopher's man"—for every generation.

There is a third ideal that stands next to the heroic and the contemplative: the compassionate ideal. The ideal of compassion comes into the Western tradition definitively with the teachings of Jesus Christ. But the compassionate ideal is older than Jesus; it is manifest in the sacred texts of the Hindus, in the teachings of the Buddha and, less directly, in the reflections of Confucius. Did any of these teachings have an impact on Jesus? We will probably never know. What is certain is that the Gospels swerve profoundly from the Hebrew Bible. There are intimations of Jesus' teachings on compassion in the Psalms and in the books of the prophets, but what he says about love and forgiveness and kindness for all is radically distinct from the ethos of the Hebrew Bible, which, at least in the Pentateuch, the Bible's first five books, is often a warrior ethos. From the start, Yahweh is a loving creator god and a god of justice—but he is also a war god.

There is no affirmation of revenge or retribution in the teachings of Jesus of Nazareth. His gospel is the gospel of forgiveness, a gospel that the poet William Blake summarized in an inspired piece of doggerel: "Throughout all Eternity / I forgive you[,] you forgive me / As our dear Redeemer said / This the Wine & this the Bread." Blake suggests, and the great philosopher Arthur Schopenhauer actively argues, that the gap between the Old Testament and the teachings of Jesus is so wide that what Jesus offers is in significant ways a new religion. It is a religion, Schopenhauer argues, much closer to the wisdom of the Upanishads and the teachings of the Buddha than to the lessons of Abraham or Moses, profound as those lessons may be.

Compassion is the core of Jesus' ministry. Compassion is the new ideal, the good news that Jesus brings, displacing the ethos of justice that dominates the Hebrew Bible. Love your neighbor as yourself. Who is my neighbor? the lawyer asks Jesus. Jesus answers with a story. A man is beaten and robbed and left in a ditch. Members of his own group pass him by, leaving him to suffer. But a Samaritan comes along, and he lifts the poor man from the side of the road. He binds the man's wounds and mounts him on his own beast. He takes the suffering man to an inn and pays his bill and says that he will return to visit the wounded man and also to settle accounts. Then the Savior's question: Which of these was a neighbor to the unfortunate man?

Every man is my neighbor. Every woman is my neighbor. This is the central teaching of Jesus, and though it is not an easy teaching to put into practice (Jesus himself seems to fail it on at least one occasion), it may confer on living men and women a sense of wholeness, presence, and even joy. No longer is one a thrashing Self, fighting the war of each against all. Now one is part of everything and everyone: one merges with the spirit of all that lives. And perhaps this merger *is* heaven, or as close to heaven as we mortals can come.

Who takes seriously the gospel of love, the love that Paul called agape, in the present? Surely there are some. A monk here, some nuns there, a collection of lay workers in Africa or Asia: there are still magnificent exemplars of the teachings of Jesus throughout the world. But in our culture of the Self, religion is often merely a Sunday affair, or a way of life that affirms the rule of the Father and his list of stiff prohibitions. Often when people say the name Jesus, what they mean is God the Father, God the commanding patriarch. But Jesus brought something new into the Western world, though it was already old in the East: the gospel of mercy.

The wager of the Gospels is that compassion can make life worth living. Perhaps this is so, perhaps not. Maybe Nietzsche is right when he says that Christian values invert heroic values and leave us all weaker, prizing sickness of body and spirit when we once prized strength and health. Freud says, pragmatically, that he could not imagine loving everyone equally because most people simply do not deserve his love. He adds the Darwinian point that the basic attitude of one human to another is competitive hostility. But Freud and Nietzsche, geniuses though they were, may be wrong. Compassion may be an ultimate standard, a time-transcending ideal. Each generation of men and women ought to have the chance to review the evidence: they ought to be able to decide for themselves.

Courage, compassion, and serious thought: these are the great ideals of the ancient world. And though their lights are dimming in the pragmatic, Self-seeking West, there is still time to revive them, to examine them, and, if one is so moved, to bring them to one's own life. These ideals are available to almost all of us. Though their first exemplars tend to be male, the ideals are there for men and for women alike. (What could feminism be if not the struggle to give women and men both fair access to the best chances that existence offers to us?) The ideals are there for members of all races and for every class. The warrior needs strength, yes; the thinker needs the chance to develop intellect, certainly. These facts may eliminate certain individuals, though not as many as one might imagine. But the life of compassion, perhaps the most consistently rewarding of the ideals, is available to all of us, beginning now.

This study considers the ideals in their purest, most intense forms: courage in Hector and Achilles; compassion in Jesus, the Buddha, and Confucius; contemplation in Plato and Emerson; imagination in Blake. The objective is to offer visions of the ideal that leave as little as possible in doubt. Few are those who will be able to adopt an ideal without reserve. There will almost always be some need for the protective armor of Self. (Though in the very best and most exemplary of lives, the Selfhood barely exists.) Even those of us most enclosed in Self can expand our beings with the simplest acts of courage or compassion, or with a true effort at thought. And after that initial expansion, who knows what might befall?

Perhaps too there are those who ought to have nothing to do with ideals, and will still manage to live lives of deep satisfaction—at least to themselves. Even Thoreau says that he has no desire to convert the ones "who find their encouragement and inspiration in precisely the present condition of things, and cherish it with the fondness and enthusiasm of lovers" (58). Strong idealist that he can be, Thoreau even reckons himself to be to some extent in their number.

Naturally the ideals have had their detractors, including one even more potent than Freud and Nietzsche. At its halfway point, this book takes on a historical dimension with reflections on William Shakespeare. Why Shakespeare? Harold Bloom tells us that Shakespeare "invents the human." It is a provocative observation though finally not quite an accurate one.

Surely Shakespeare brings extraordinary psychological insight to the stage: Bloom says that he gives us characters who overhear what they say and, based on that overhearing, change. They are both therapist and patient to themselves. It's not certain that this is comprehensively true of Shakespeare's heroes. What is true is that

Shakespeare helps change our sense of human life and human promise through an *almost* complete rejection of ideals. Like his contemporary, Cervantes, Shakespeare has only contempt for the heroic ideal. It is not only that his martial heroes—Titus, Hector, Othello, Hotspur, Macbeth, and more—perish on the stage; heroic warriors often perish on stage. But in Shakespeare, they and the values they uphold become objects of deep skepticism and sometimes of contempt. Nor is Shakespeare terribly friendly to the religious ideal or the ideal of contemplation. His depiction of Hamlet offers an exception from his pervasive distrust of ideals, which is part of what makes the play as fascinating (and anomalous) as it is. But overall, Shakespeare is our great de-idealizing writer.

Shakespeare does not create a comprehensive turning away from ideals in the West. Larger factors are involved. But Shakespeare senses the impending anti-idealist turn, by and large endorses it, and helps bring it to pass. Shakespeare, as Arnold Hauser argues, is a poet of the dawning bourgeois age, who has little use for chivalry and the culture of heroic honor. One might add that Shakespeare does not seem terribly well disposed to the burgeoning culture of wealth and comfort, the culture of Self that is on the horizon. His ambivalence about the rising class is perceptible in *The Merchant of Venice, Twelfth Night,* and a number of the other plays that feature the rising middle class and the aristocrats who have integrated themselves into the new order.

The great shift from a feudal world to a modern one would have taken place if William Shakespeare had never lived. But Shakespeare does his part to urge the transition forward, much as Cervantes does. And Shakespeare allows us to see some of the dynamics of the transition. We are now prone to believe that Shakespeare had no palpable convictions. To use Keats's famous term, Shakespeare is to most of us the ultimate poet of negative capability. He is capable of abiding in uncertainties, mysteries, and doubts without driving forward to conclusions. But in fact, Shakespeare's work is alive with values—they simply echo the anti-idealist values of his current audience and of the current world almost perfectly and, so, are nearly invisible.

Sigmund Freud, we sometimes hear, is Shakespeare's heir. And in this there is a dose of literal truth. Freud read Shakespeare (in English) throughout his life and refers to him many times in his letters, essays, and books. There's no doubt that reading *Hamlet* helped Freud develop the theory of the Oedipal Complex. Freud's central idea, that character is conflict and that the individual does not always know the realities of his own inner struggles, is surely Shakespearean. Freud might also have looked to Shakespeare to inspire (or to confirm) his intuitions about the human penchant for bisexuality, about the role of ambivalence in love, and about the determining force of family life.

But Freud's kinship with Shakespeare is deeper and more significant. Freud takes the enmity with ideals implicit in Shakespeare's work and renders it explicit. Freud is a relentless enemy of the warrior ideal, the religious ideal, and the ideal of transcendent philosophy. He is a worldly pragmatist, who tries to guide his patients and readers to hard-won and often precarious inner equilibrium and to measured satisfactions. To ask for more from life—to seek contact with the ideal—is to fall to illusion and in time, probably, to find ruin. Ideals simply will not sustain the level of investment that humans bring to them; they betray us repeatedly. The unity that ideals confer on the subject is temporary: it is better to learn to live with anxious internal conflict than to succumb to delusion. After the idealization there inevitably comes disillusionment, the hangover that follows the bout of intoxication. The suffering can last a long time. Why waste life on courage, compassion, or the quest for Truth? The exhilaration is brief, but the aftermath protracted and painful.

Freud, we are often told, is obsolete. Yes and no. The war he enlisted in against ideals seems all but over. Freud's middle-class morality has won. Almost no one seeks ideal perfection; almost no one seeks the sublime. The culture of Self is virtually unchallenged, so why go to the trouble of reading and pondering a difficult thinker? Freud demands too much. And his ultimate verdict on the life of the Self—a life based on desire rather than on hope—is not sanguine. He seems even less pleased than Shakespeare does about the life they both help usher into being. Both sometimes seem inclined to perceive it as Nietzsche does, as the life of the Last Man, the man who hops and blinks and has his little poisons for the day and for the night. Yet after ideals, what else is there?

Love, maybe. On the subject of love, Freud and Shakespeare seem to part. In the comedies, which as Doctor Johnson observed, Shakespeare wrote with natural ease, there appears to be some hope for human happiness. The depictions of Eros there are bittersweet, not brutally dismissive. Shakespeare does not seem inclined to want to rid the world of romantic love the way that he does of chivalric pretensions.

Freud is an enemy of romantic love and, accordingly, of Romanticism, the faith in the redemptive power of Eros. Between the time of Shakespeare and of Freud what may be a fresh ideal enters the Western world. The ideal of Romantic love, manifest in Shelley and Blake, Whitman and Crane, and many others, hinges on a belief that by joining with the beloved, the Soulmate, the individual will reach his or her highest promise. Romantic love is not a form of satiety in itself. Blake calls the state of erotic complacency Beulah, the place where all contraries are true. Genuine Romantic love is a state from which one attempts to remake the world (or some small portion of it) for the better. To Shelley, love is the source and soul of inspiration. To Freud, who believes he has seen too many patients delude themselves in love, Eros is another ideal bound to fail. Like the ideals of courage and compassion, the ideal of love is a source of stunting illusions.

In the early twentieth century, Freud defends the integrity of the Self against the blandishments of another state of being, which we might call the State of Soul. Freud stands in the tradition of Montaigne, affirming the belief that the life of skeptical, humane detachment is the best of possible lives. This anti-idealist ideal remains a moving one. In what's perceived to be an age of rampant war, poverty, terror, and uncertainty, it is not surprising that men and women gravitate to a life of what one might call enlightened Self. They prize decency, justice, and economic opportunity for all. In Freud, in Montaigne, in Orwell, we encounter the lineaments of a life of humane Self. And it must be respected. In this book's final chapter, I hope to say what can be said on behalf of such a life. Surely the life of ideals can devolve into delusion. (Maybe ideals are nothing but delusions.) Yet the question remains. How quickly can a life of Self collapse under pressure into a life of self-centeredness and greed?

Freud is an impressive polemical enemy of all the Soul States. He deploys his intellectual energy and insight against Compassion, Romantic Love (and the creative acts that might rise from it), Heroism, and (with reservations) the quest for Truth. Freud, we might say, is the great champion of Self over Soul.

William Blake, Walt Whitman, and William Butler Yeats all write with visionary acumen about the tensions between Self and Soul, though the meanings they impart to the terms vary somewhat. For Blake we habitually exist in the State of Self. We live for our personal desires; we want food and sex, money and power and prestige. We aspire to health; we want to live forever in the flesh, or for as long as possible. But we can also pass into another state, the State of Soul. Then we live not for desire but for hope. We live for the fulfillment of ideals. The State of Soul, when perfectly realized, is united, fully present, and in a certain manner exists outside of time.

Blake thought of the Soul State as preeminently associated with poetry and the imagination. But this book expands his view to associate Soul with compassion, courage, and the quest for Truth. The Soul State serves not only the individual who enters it, but also others who gain from loving-kindness, protection, inspiration, and the paths opened by true thought. But the State of Soul is, as Blake also knew, a dangerous state. Those who pursue it are sometimes victims of ridicule, neglect, persecution, and even of violent death. And not all claimants to higher states are to be believed and trusted— no end of deception has gone on in the name of ideals.

Maybe we are best off without ideals. Perhaps there can even be something bleakly noble in affirming ourselves as fundamentally Darwinian creatures who live to sustain our existences with as little pain and as much pleasure as possible. But is that all there is to life? The question of the great States of being, Self and Soul, is in danger of dropping off the map of human inquiry. In its place there opens up an expanse of mere existence based on desire, without hope, fullness, or ultimate meaning. We can do better. This book seeks the resurrection of Soul.

I

Ancient Ideals

1

The Hero

What is better: a short heroic life that brings glory or a long peaceful existence full of humane contentment? For the majority of people living in the civilized West, this is not a difficult question; it is barely a question at all. They seek wealth and longevity. They want to be respected by their neighbors and be secure—and they want the same for their children. They live within the borders of Self. Self can be greedy and grasping, though it can also be civilized and highly responsible. (There are more and less enlightened forms of Selfhood.) Yet ultimately Self puts its own interests first. Health and money, an occupation, a place in the world, success: these are the goals Self establishes and pursues. Self exists within the sphere of its own desires. Even in its most expansive moments, Self has a difficult time imagining that there could be other ways to live, other States.

But there are. Self is not the only state of being that a human can enter: there is also the State of Soul. Soul is unified, joy bringing, and fully present to experience. Yet it's also a dangerous State, both to the individual who enters it or strives to do so and to those he encounters in the world. If from the beginning of history the great majority have been people who would choose a long life of civilized contentment over a life of glory, there have been others—a few—who dissent. Some of them want to live for the joy that seeking honor can bring. They want their names to live forever on the lips of men. They prefer death to dishonor and vow never to do anything that will undermine their reputations. Such individuals will not let an insult from an equal pass; they will never let a genuine quarrel drop.

In the West, the archetype of the heroic warrior, Achilles, faces the choice that everyone who has a hunger for the heroic life faces. Early in his life Achilles learns that two destinies lie before him. In the first he goes to war, where he will do astonishing deeds and achieve everlasting fame. In the second, he stays home and lives a prosperous long life. All his worldly desires are satisfied. It is up to Achilles to make the choice, and he chooses the short and heroic life. Most sons and daughters of the educated middle class cannot imagine making such a choice today. But there are still those—though perhaps there have never been so few—who are willing to risk their lives for fame, camaraderie, and the horrible, exhilarating intensity of being that war can bring.

What constitutes the heroic spirit? The hero is proud. Even those who aspire to heroism and have not yet proved themselves exude a confidence far above the common measure. David stepping up to Goliath with his sling in his hand; Lancelot unsheathing his sword against a foe; Odysseus stringing his bow to take revenge on the suitors: all of them feel that victory is assured in advance. Their confidence in themselves is absolute.

When we first meet Achilles in *The Iliad*, he possesses warrior's pride in the highest measure. The war against Troy has been going on for nine years, and he has been fighting against the Trojans and their allies on the plains in front of the city. He's also stormed fortified towns, always in the forefront of the fighting. He has leapt ahead of the other men to confront danger. His achievements along with his extraordinary beauty and physical prowess have given Achilles an enhanced sense of self. He feels a fullness and unity of being because of what he is and what he has done.

Before Achilles left for the war in Troy his father Peleus gave him simple and daunting advice. He told Achilles that he must always achieve the first place. He must be the bravest of the warriors, taking risks and doing deeds that no one else can match. It wouldn't be enough for Achilles to do his duty. He has to seek out opportunities to achieve remarkable feats. He has to put himself constantly at risk. Peleus wanted his son to be the best man in the army, first among the Greeks, and that's what Achilles strives to be.

At the opening of *The Iliad*, Achilles clearly believes that he is the best of the Achaeans. No warrior means more to the army than he does, and this fact fills Achilles with pride. But then everything changes. Agamemnon, the king and leader of the Greeks massed at Troy, demands that Achilles surrender the slave girl, Briseis, to him after the god Apollo has forced Agamemnon to give up his own prize, Chryseis. Agamemnon makes his demands not privately in a conference with Achilles or in a meeting with the most important princes, but publicly, when the entire army is massed. It's not clear exactly what Achilles' feelings are for the slave girl. At one point he cries out that he deeply loved her, at another he says it would have been better for all if one of Apollo's arrows had struck her down after she was captured.

Achilles is enraged by the king's demand. His first thought is that he can end the dispute immediately by killing Agamemnon. Agamemnon is a formidable warrior, perhaps the best spear thrower in the army, but he couldn't stand for an instant against Achilles. In a flash, Agamemnon would be lying dead in the sand. Yet the gods will not tolerate the killing of Agamemnon. Hera sends Athena down to stop Achilles, and it is clear that Hera speaks for Zeus, the king of all kings in the Greek cosmos. Zeus is nearly always sympathetic to rulers and invariably distrusts rebels. Achilles puts his sword back into its scabbard and gives way to Agamemnon—he will hand over his prize.

He is humiliated in front of the troops. Now Achilles can no longer confidently claim to be what he thought he was, the best of the Greeks. The fullness of pride he maintained up to this moment is broken—he's suffered a wound to his sense of being and withdraws from the armies into his tent. To the modern reader (the reader who, in all probability, lives within the circumference of Self) Achilles' behavior can look childish: he seems to be suffering from what the psychologists would call wounded narcissism. But heroic pride and modern-day narcissism are different conditions. In the Homeric poem, pride depends not only on one's sense of self but also on the judgment of one's peers and on the sanction of Nature and of the gods. It is the result of having done great deeds. To the hero, pride is *necessary* for victory in battle—perhaps even for survival. When one possesses an epic unity of being, mind and heart and body have merged completely. One does not need to think, per se; after a certain point, one does not even need to plan. One goes out onto the battlefield and acts. The warrior does with superb grace and brutal instinct what he has been made to do.

When inner fullness disappears, the warrior is in danger. He's no longer one being united for action, but two: the man who acts and the man who observes. After the encounter with Agamemnon, Achilles' unity of being, the warrior's necessary grace, is broken. He begins to doubt himself and to question his heroic destiny. He begins, in short, to think. Homer renders this state by presenting a dialogue between Thetis and Achilles in which Achilles expresses his fears and frustrations. He has already chosen the short glorious life—he's already made his bargain. Will the gods betray him and deprive him of the glory that's rightfully his?

　　Mother!
You gave me life, short as that life will be,
so at least Olympian Zeus, thundering up on high,
should give me honor—but now he gives me nothing.
Atreus' son Agamemnon, for all his far-flung kingdoms—
the man disgraces me, seizes and keeps my prize,
he tears her away himself!

(I, 416–422)

Achilles is legitimately confused. How could events have come to this pass? He does not understand it, try as he might. If he were to go onto the battlefield in this state he would be a far less effective fighter. Self-consciousness in war can be fatal when it reaches too high a degree, and the true hero learns to be wary of it, much as the athlete does.

The athlete, like the warrior, must become one and not, at least in competition, split into two. In Homer, when you *speak* with a god, as Achilles does to his mother, Thetis, you are often entering the realm of self-consciousness.

The Homeric warrior believes that he lives in a cosmos that reflects his values. He affirms courage and beauty and so does the natural world around him. He is committed to a life of striving for preeminence and so is every other form of life he encounters. In his fragment "Homer's Contest," Nietzsche notes that in the heroic Greek world envy can be a virtue. It is possible to say that a man does not strive hard enough, is not sufficiently eager for the first place, that he lacks the power of envy to goad him forward.

Homer corroborates the heroes' vision of the world in a number of ways, most immediately through his depiction of the gods. *The Iliad* begins with the quarrel between Achilles and Agamemnon, but on Mount Olympus gods are quarreling, too. Hera and Zeus are on different sides in the war between the Greeks and Trojans, and matters come quickly to the point where Zeus threatens to throttle his wife there on Olympus, in front of all the gods. The gods are quarreling, yes, and like the mortals that they simultaneously love and disdain, the gods are quarreling about power.

The gods in Homer value what the mortals do—strength, beauty, renown, amazing deeds, and power: power most of all. They contend with each other for position much as the Greek and Trojan warriors do. Zeus appears to be preeminent, and for the time being he is, but it's clear that the gods have rebelled against him at least once in the past, and it's likely they could again. (Thetis saved Zeus during the rebellion and so can beseech him now to help her son in return.) Achilles is at home in this cosmos, at least until the quarrel with Agamemnon. The gods he worships worship what he does. They act as he would if he were as powerful as a god and destined to live forever.

How different is the relation between the God of the Hebrew Bible and his worshippers. The God of the Old Testament is radically removed from his mortal creations; he is of another order of being entirely. Humans cannot understand his ways. On what seems a whim, he makes a wager with Satan on whether or not Job, his loyal servant, will turn against him if his fortunes change. Yahweh visits every kind of degradation on Job, until the unfortunate man is sitting alone in a pigsty, his family dead, his wealth gone. He is covered in sores and scraping himself with a piece of broken pottery. When he protests his fate, and asks what he has done to deserve it, the Lord answers that Job cannot know his ways. Yahweh is of a different order of being. Where were you when I created the foundation of the earth? he asks Job. Can you put a hook through Leviathan's lip and raise him from the sea? "Can you bind the chains of the Pleiades, or loose the cords of Orion?" (Job 38.31).

The existence of Yahweh in his sublime otherness is an ongoing statement about the limitations (and the inadequacy) of mankind. Men and women are made in his *image,* but he far exceeds them in every other way. Yahweh is not different from men in degree but in kind. When the Jewish believer meditates on God he must invariably feel the distance between what he is and what a being can be. Achilles and his fellow warriors feel little of such sentiment. The gods of the Greeks are not always kind or generous or just, but they are comprehensible. Their existence makes the world luminous, its meanings clear. "Happy are those ages," Georg Lukács writes, "when the starry sky is the map of all possible paths—ages whose paths are illuminated by the light of the stars. Everything in such ages is new and yet familiar, full of adventure and yet their own. The world is wide and yet it is like a home, for the fire that burns in the soul is of the same essential nature as the stars" (29).

Warriors since Homer have sought to live in a similar state of fullness. Fighters tend to think of themselves as beings who live with primary, natural values. They embody qualities—courage, endurance, strength—that Nature endorses. Though their lives may be harsh and short, they feel at home in the world. They are (or believe themselves to be) primary men and women. This is no less true now than it was when Homer wrote—at least for those few who believe in the warrior ethos. But their kind may be dying out. They are being replaced by middle-class men and women whose central aspiration is to endure and who seek not honor but respect, not ascendancy but stable existence.

Homer reinforces the symmetry between the heroic worldview and the world of Nature through many of the poem's similes. The men coming to muster are like bees flying 'round and around their hive. The generations of men who breed on the earth are like leaves. They burst into green life in the spring, but by autumn are dead and brown. Achilles in his wrath is like a lion, being hunted by the men of a village, feeling his might and about to spring on his first victim. These similes and others like them establish congruence between what happens in the natural world and what is happening in the war on the plains of Troy. The fighting men are not doing anything unnatural by fighting. In making war they are not defying the order of things. War is as natural as the flight of bees, the passing of the generations of leaves, the hunger of a virile lion for his prey.

The lives of the Greek warriors are full of meaning, and not because they are subtle philosophers and engage in ongoing dialectical exchange about war and its values. There is no place for philosophy at Troy. To the heroes the only form of thinking that matters is strategic. How shall we ambush the enemy? How can we bring the walls of the city down? The warriors do not have to think about what kind of life is best, for they *know* that theirs is: Nature corroborates them constantly. The Greeks take obvious pride in their conviction that they have created a culture that is as close to Nature as any human beings before have done or (presumably) will do. What Nature loves, the warriors love; what Nature despises, they despise as well—or so they believe. Nature loves beauty and strength; the warriors camped on the beach at Troy and those enclosed within the city's walls love the beautiful and the strong. And it is on earth as it is in heaven.

Most currently existing individuals cannot claim to value what Nature values. (Describing human beings now through analogy with lions or bees would probably sound absurd: we are too much the products of our culture to be rendered in natural terms.) At their most humane, people today endorse fairness, equality, decency, democracy, and one law for all. However admirable these standards may be, no one thinks of them as natural. The animal kingdom is not a realm of equals; survival is not won by the judicious and fair. Most people feel a disjunction between what they value and what

Nature endorses, and this causes an ongoing sense of dislocation. The contemporary individual is not at home in the world. The warrior senses himself to be an integral part of all he sees around him, as disturbing and even horrifying as that may be. The warrior is at home in the world, though there is little that is kindly, generous, or sweet about the world in which he dwells.

The scene of heavenly strife in the first book of *The Iliad* ends with the intervention of the blacksmith, the god Hephaestus, who begs his mother Hera not to defy the king of the gods. He reminds Hera and the assembled gods of the time that Zeus became enraged at him and tossed him from the height of Mount Olympus— Hephaestus fell for days and landed finally on an island where the men nursed him back to health. But the quarrel between Zeus and Hera only really ends when the smith rises to take up his task serving the gods their nectar and ambrosia. He comes grunting and limping from place to place, and the gods cannot help themselves, they are overwhelmed with mirth. It is hilarious to watch a cripple stump his way across a room. "Uncontrollable laughter broke from the happy gods / as they watched the god of fire breathing hard / And bustling through the halls" (I. 721–723). It is not only that beauty is a delight to the Greeks and worthy of worship, but also that ugliness is appalling, a crime against Nature.

The Greeks and Trojans share the gods' veneration for beauty. The war is about Helen, the most beautiful woman in the world— "the face that launched a thousand ships," in Marlowe's phrase. In a moving scene, the old men of Troy, Priam's counselors, look down from the battlements and see Helen. They speak to each other in the thin, reedy voices of cicadas. They are so old that they are like children again and do not know desire. Yet Helen awakens them. And for a moment, they can imagine that the war has been worthwhile—all the slaughter, all the suffering, all the mourning—because of the sheer beauty of this woman. "Who on earth could blame them?

Ah, no wonder / the men of Troy and Argives under arms have suffered / years of agony all for her, for such a woman. / Beauty, terrible beauty!" (III, 187–190).

Homer, the ancient author, burns through time and challenges the contemporary reader with difficult questions. Do you too not value courage and beauty above all things—just as the heroes in the poem do? Wouldn't you love to be an Achilles, or a Helen? (Or at least to strive to be?) Isn't settling for anything else a shrinking away from human promise? "The earth has become small," says Nietzsche's Zarathustra, "and on it hops the last man, who makes everything small. His race is as ineradicable as the flea-beetle; the last man lives longest" (*Thus Spoke Zarathustra*, 17).

Achilles is surpassingly beautiful; he is among the strongest of warriors, the swiftest of runners. Though he will not live long, he should be enjoying his being to the hilt, living in a world where values are clear and he embodies every form of excellence. He is the paragon of all that the Greeks prize, but after the encounter with Agamemnon he is cast down. How could this be? After his quarrel with the king, the perfect harmony between his being and the world disappears. The fire in the stars is no longer quite identical with the fire in his soul. He feels cast away from his godlike being and robbed of his proper destiny. The fullness in which he began the poem is lost, and now he must find a way to restore it. Achilles' quest to re-establish inner plenitude and to heal the wound of Agamemnon's humiliation is the central drama of *The Iliad*. In this quest Achilles will lay down the pattern for heroes to come, from the time of the Greeks to the present moment.

The hero keeps his word. When Zeus nods his head, all he has promised will come to pass. When the warrior assents to any great commitment, he is bound to it. Achilles' speech is dramatic, impassioned, and headlong—yet whatever he promises, even in his highest moments of passion, he will try with all his might to do. He is at Troy for a simple reason: he promised he would fight. He gave his word, swore an oath, and now he is in Asia Minor, rather than back home in Greece. At the beginning of the poem he again makes a promise, and this time it is *not* to fight, at least until Agamemnon makes amends.

Agamemnon does try to make an apology when, after Achilles leaves, the predictable happens and Hector, greatest of Trojan fighters, goes raging through the Greek lines. Agamemnon now understands that without Achilles the Greek army is not half what it was. So Agamemnon calls his advisors together and tells them what he will do. He will make restitution to Achilles; he will give him treasure now: horses, gold, and armor. Later when Troy falls, Achilles will have his pick of the plunder. Anything he wants he can have, beginning with twenty women to serve in his house and join him in his bed. When the troops return to Greece, Achilles can marry any one of Agamemnon's three daughters that he chooses and she will bring an incomparable dowry. More than that, Agamemnon makes a solemn promise: he will return Briseis to Achilles immediately. And he swears that he has left her untouched: "I never mounted her bed, never once made love with her—/ the natural thing for mankind, men and women joined" (IX, 160–161).

But Agamemnon adds a final clause. He will give Achilles all these gifts and signs of respect, but Achilles must do something too. He must bow down to Agamemnon as his lawful king. He must be willing to recognize that Agamemnon is superior. "Let him bow down to me! I am the greater king, / I am the elder-born, I claim—the greater man" (IX, 192–193).

When the ambassadors led by crafty Odysseus (the first pragmatist) go off to speak to Achilles, they show him due respect, and they list for him the gifts the king is ready to give. They tell him about the stallions and the gold and the marriage to one of the king's daughters and the dowry to follow. But Odysseus, being Odysseus, does not mention Agamemnon's final, rather anguished demand, that Achilles recognize him as the greater man.

It does not matter. Achilles holds the entire offer in contempt. Heroes (like saints, like true thinkers) have no deep concern with wealth. Treasure to them is tantamount to trash, except as it testifies to their preeminence. They receive it as tribute; they give it away to others as a form of largesse and recognition. But material wealth does not mean very much to true warriors. They live for other goals. There is one gift that Achilles wants from Agamemnon and it is very simple. Agamemnon could get Achilles back into the fighting immediately if he called the troops together, stood up, apologized to the hero, and announced to everyone that Achilles is by far the better man, the best of the Achaeans. With Achilles the Greeks were victorious, without him they are being decimated by Hector and the Trojans. But Agamemnon will not say what he needs to say, and so Achilles is bound in his tent.

Every true hero must have an adversary worthy of him. The figure must be formidable, but in literary renderings of the hero at least, the adversary often illustrates something essential about the hero himself. In the adversary, we often see what the hero overtly is not—and what he, rather secretly, might be. Beowulf becomes as ferocious and even monstrous as Grendel in order to defeat him; Goliath, the giant, may adumbrate some of the excesses that David will indulge when he is king. Part of what grieves Achilles while he is keeping to himself in his tent is that he must postpone his ultimate encounter with his great adversary Hector.

Hector is a remarkable hero—strong, courageous, daring—but he is a very different being from Achilles, something we see with clarity in one of the most moving scenes in the poem. Hector has come in from the battlefield and his armor is covered with dust, grime, and blood; he's exhausted from fighting, though he will soon return to the war. He meets his wife Andromache, and there in the arms of a servant is Astyanax, his son, the boy the Trojans call "lord of the city." Astyanax is "in the first flush of life, only a baby . . . the darling of [Hector's] eyes and radiant as a star" (VI, 473–475). Hector and his wife come together and talk in a humane, understanding way. They share a remarkable intimacy. Andromache tells Hector how frightened she is for him. She has lost her father and her mother and also her seven brothers, all of whom were killed in a single day by Achilles, who now threatens to rob her of her husband as well. You are my father and my mother now, she tells Hector, and you are my brother, too. You are all of my family.

Hector doesn't resort to bragging or lordly indifference in response, as Achilles might do in similar circumstances. He says that all this weighs on him as well. He too is distressed about what will become of his family. But he is the leading warrior in the city, the best of the Trojans, and he has no choice but to do all he can to defend his people. He says he believes that there will come a day when Troy will fall and his father Priam and his mother Hecuba will die, but still he will fight on as hard as he can. The thought of the fall of the city gives Hector great pain, he says, but nothing like the pain that comes when he contemplates Andromache being captured by the Greeks, dragged from the city, sold into slavery, and made to serve another woman, hauling water and washing clothes in some faraway place.

Hector reaches out to the nurse to take Astyanax, but the boy draws back and begins to cry. He is terrified of his father dressed in his dazzling filth-splattered armor and wearing the massive helm with its horsehair crest.

> And his loving father laughed,
> his mother laughed as well, and glorious Hector,
> quickly lifting the helmet from his head,

set it down on the ground, fiery in the sunlight,
and raising his son, he kissed him [and] tossed him in his arms.
(VI, 562–566)

The boy recognizes Hector, laughs, and cries out with delight. This is his father, the large-hearted man who adores him.

The scene dramatizes Hector's dual nature. Hector is two men. He is the valiant warrior who stands against the Greeks on the plains, but he is also the man beneath the helmet, the loving pater familias. "I've learned it all too well," Hector says, "To stand up bravely, / always to fight in the front ranks of Trojan soldiers, / winning my father great glory, glory for myself" (VI, 528–530). Hector had to *learn* to be a hero. It did not come naturally to him. (As David Mikics observes, the verb *didaskein* is not used in the sense of learning warfare for Achilles or for anyone else in the poem.) By nature, he is probably closer to being a statesman than a warrior, a man who would in time become a just and temperate king, like his father, Priam. He is a loving father and a loyal friend, tolerant and generous. Helen says that there are only two men in Troy who treat her with kindness: one is Priam, the other Hector.

Hector may not have been born to be a warrior, yet he has forged himself into a superb one, a match for any of the Greek fighters with the exception of one. Achilles is from a different order of being than Hector. Achilles is part god, the son of Thetis; Hector is entirely mortal. Achilles may have had to acquire some of the technical arts of war when he was very young, but he never needed to *learn* to be a warrior, in the way that Hector did. The life of battle came naturally to Achilles—he was made for the camp and the assault. Hector is two men, the one who wears the helmet and the one who lives his life without it. Achilles in his full pride is one man: Achilles might be less menacing when he takes his helmet off, but not much.

We know Achilles first through his quarrel with Agamemnon, when his pride has been gored. We know Hector best as a man in the midst of his family. He is the one who loves and protects Andromache and Astyanax and the rest of the city too, which is like an extended family to him. Achilles speaks often of his family, and particularly of his aged father, Peleus, whom he fears he will never see again. But he has traded the life of the hearth for the life of the camp; he has exchanged intimate life with a woman, like the one Hector has with Andromache, for a life with men. His closest bonds are with other males. His friend Patroclus may or may not be his homosexual lover—in Homer's text there is no evidence that he is. But their relations are intimate and warm. Patroclus serves Achilles, lays his fire and cooks his food with a wife's tenderness, yet Patroclus is, in his own right, an accomplished warrior. Achilles has jettisoned the pleasures but also the tedium of life at home for a life in the out of doors away from family and from women and children.

The hero does not stay at home. Like the saint and like the thinker, who travels in his mind, the hero doesn't have much patience for the domestic circle. You need to leave your father and mother and follow me, Jesus says, and those who choose Soul over Self usually choose a life in the open air, or at least a wandering life. Domesticity means repetition, custom, and convention to the man or woman who wants to achieve the unity of being that the Soul State promises. The life of the home pulls the individual in too many directions: he has multiple obligations, a multitude of tasks. The hero and the saint want to unify their beings around one ideal only—be it glory or compassion. (You think of many things, Jesus tells one of his followers, but there is really only one thing.) Once one has consecrated oneself to an ideal, home and family become irrelevances. Family is a point of piety in the life of the Self—it is the basis for self-justifications. One must work, thrive, and get ahead—all for the family. The pure hero often sees family as an impediment and is always suspicious of it, if not hostile. As the critic George Steiner puts it, "Homer knows and proclaims that there is that in men which loves war, which is less afraid of the terrors of combat than of the long boredom of the hearth" (180).

Those who have quested after ideals have frequently understood that family is the terrain of the Self. It is where one functions as a biological being, sending one's genes into the future, attempting to assure the safety and success of one's children. So strong though is the ideology of Self that all must claim to put family first at all times. The soldier in the field may well feel that life is at its best when he is with his comrades even in the midst of danger. But publicly he cannot say as much. Family comes first. When fighters come home from war, and are clearly in a state of distress, we assume that they have been scarred by what they have experienced, and often this is so. But is it also possible that they are dispirited precisely because they miss their proper element, war? Are they perhaps, sometimes without knowing it, longing for the life they had under arms? When Achilles makes his choice for a short glorious life, what he is rejecting is the life of home—and this on some level is what every pure warrior must do.

Hector is an extremely admirable man—to many he is more admirable than Achilles. But he does not concentrate the heroic essence, which is single-minded devotion to the ideal. He cannot achieve unity of being, though this is so for the most persuasive of reasons: he was not really born to be a warrior. He fights for his city and for his family, but not ultimately for the reason that the true Homeric hero fights, to be the best of his kind. The true hero wants to be someone who will be sung about forever and whose name will never disappear from the lips of men. Hector may want fame, but he wants life for himself, his family, and his people more. He would surely sign away any claim he might have for glory in exchange for the safety of Troy. Hector wants to live a long time. Achilles would not give up the prospect of glory for anything; Hector might be content to die a relative unknown if he could see Astyanax grow to be a man, and be able to imagine that his dear son would someday fill his father's place as he, Hector, has filled Priam's. If the Trojans decided to launch an expedition to reclaim a wayward princess who had eloped beyond the seas, it is entirely likely that Hector, tempted as he might be with the prospect of glory, would stay home.

Northrop Frye says that part of Homer's achievement lies in his ability to depict an enemy of his own people, the Greeks, with full humanity. Hector is Achilles' antagonist, yet he is an admirable figure—and not an image of Selfhood at its worst. But Homer does include an image of Self in his poem, and it is one that will travel through time, most saliently into the work of the individual who may be the greatest single enemy of ideals, William Shakespeare.

Early in the poem, Homer allows the ugly misshapen soldier Thersites to cry out in front of the troops against Agamemnon. What Achilles has been saying about the king is right, Thersites proclaims. And there's more. Agamemnon is nothing but a thief, appropriating the goods that other men have fought and died to win. After a battle, he takes all the best: he grabs a lion's share of the treasure; he claims the sons of wealthy Trojans to ransom; he gets the most alluring girls to take back to his bed. The common soldiers ought to rebel. "Abandon him here in Troy to wallow in all his prizes" (II, 276), Thersites says. The common soldiers should rise up, take to their ships, and leave Agamemnon on the beach.

Thersites is ranting, but the rant is eloquent enough. To the foot soldiers should go the spoils, to the laborers the fruit of their work. Thersites speaks out against the presiding ideology that keeps the princes in command. That he is ugly is not beside the point. "Bandy-legged he was, with one foot clubbed, / both shoulders humped together, curving over / his caved-in chest and bobbing above them / his skull warped to a point / sprouting clumps of scraggly, woolly hair" (II, 251–255). The ugly man cannot participate in the Greek quest for excellence: heroes are healthy and handsome. Thersites is a cur, a castaway and an outsider. But as an outsider, he can see in ways that the others cannot. Like Socrates, the most famous contender against common opinion, Thersites is ugly—pushed from the midst of common life, such men observe from the edges. Detachment is forced upon them. They are compelled to think, to interpret what appears before them. Obliquely, strangely, in Thersites Homer shadows forth the contemplative ideal.

Thersites must be dealt with, and Odysseus steps forward to do it. He strikes the man across the shoulders with his marshal's baton and tells him that if he ever rails against the leaders again it will go even worse for him. Odysseus will strip him nearly naked and beat him like a dog, chasing him up and down the beach. The commander draws the scene of Thersites' future punishment with such graphic élan that the men can all but see it. They envision the misshapen soldier scuttling like a wounded crab along the beach and they break into ferocious laughter. But Thersites has had his say, in the fashion of Socrates, who is willing to pay to expose others to his truth. He has spoken, in what will be the fashion of Marx, about how the upper orders steal from the lower. No matter how brightly the armor shines and how grandly the horsehair plumes wave, Thersites (and Marx) proclaim that theft is still theft.

It does not matter much that Thersites sides with Achilles against Agamemnon. What matters is that he challenges the heroic code. He mocks it in the way that the alienated philosopher or the egalitarian economist might. Thersites is absurd to the men in the poem and, presumably, to Homer. He is the negative inverse of all they value, the heroic code's version of the Selfhood—ugly, common, and cowardly.

Achilles is in love with war in a way that Hector (and of course Thersites) never could be, and as a rule he fights with a brutal integrity—which makes what happens to him at the hands of Nestor disturbing. The Greeks are in disarray, being driven toward their ships by the raging Hector, and Nestor, the aged counselor and warrior, who is decades older than even the oldest fighters at Troy, begins to fear that the Trojans will overrun the camp and burn the ships. So he approaches Patroclus and offers a plan. Achilles will not enter the fray—there is nothing to be done about that. But suppose Patroclus were to put on the armor of Achilles and go to battle in his place? It might inject some confidence into the flagging Greeks. The Trojans might believe that Achilles had returned and fall back. Patroclus could put on some of Achilles' valor with the hero's arms and work wonders on the battlefield.

It's surprising that Achilles agrees to the stratagem. Clearly he loves Patroclus and wants to give him the chance to win glory. Clearly, too, Achilles is disturbed by what's happening to his fellow Greeks in his absence. Achilles assents because he thinks that he can have it both ways. He can help the Greeks and perhaps, by proxy, he can even save them. Anything Patroclus accomplishes in his armor will accrue at least partly to Achilles, and Achilles is feeling bereft of distinction. (Who is he when he is not fighting?) But even while Achilles enters the field of battle through his double, he can maintain his grudge against Agamemnon and stay sequestered in his tent. It seems a perfect plan.

But it is not the sort of plan that the true hero employs. The true hero opposes his body and his fighting spirit—his essence—to the bodies and fighting spirits of the foes. He arrives on the field as himself and he fights as himself. His armor is of major importance to him—it is his identity. It signifies his fierce, highly defended warrior essence. Nestor's plan is pragmatic. The plan demotes essential and idealistic considerations in favor of techniques to solve the problems at hand. Pragmatism is not about maintaining honor or creating the perfect work of art or living entirely for others: pragmatism is about getting the job done. We might say that Nestor is one of the first pragmatists in Western literature, though it is Odysseus who embodies the type most thoroughly.

In both *The Iliad* and *The Odyssey,* Odysseus is the man who does what he has to do in order to survive and win. No piece of cunning is too low, so long as it achieves the desired results: he tricks Polyphemus, tricks Circe, tricks the suitors. There is nothing he favors less, it sometimes seems, than fair and open fight. He is, as Max Horkheimer and Theodor Adorno suggest in *Dialectic of Enlightenment,* the precursor of middle-class man. The true hero is an essentialist: he believes in eternal values—the value of honor preeminent among them. The pragmatist believes in getting what he wants. When Achilles hears the plan, he stops thinking as an essentialist and he becomes pragmatic—he tries to solve the problem at hand, rather than trying to live up to enduring standards.

Achilles warns Patroclus to save the ships from being set on fire by the Trojans but not to push his advantage too far. Patroclus must not try to force Hector and his troops back to the walls of Troy. But in battle, wearing the armor of Achilles, Patroclus clearly begins to think that he *is* Achilles. He fights gloriously. He saves the Greeks and rallies them, and at the critical moment, he cannot pull back. He leads the Greeks in a furious counterattack against the Trojans and pushes them toward the walls of the city. But then the temper of battle shifts. The god Apollo slams Patroclus with the flat of his massive hand; the Trojan Euphorbus wounds him with a spear thrust. Finally Hector comes on to finish him. He strikes Patroclus down and jeers at the fallen hero. "The vultures will eat your body raw" (XVI, 976), he cries. But Patroclus has a final word to say. You think you've won a great victory, he tells Hector. But you only delivered the third blow. If I could have fought you myself, you would not have stood a chance. But you've won now—enjoy your triumph. "One more thing," Patroclus continues:

> Take it to heart, I urge you,
> you too, you won't live long yourself, I swear.
> Already I see them looming up beside you—death
> and the strong force of fate, to bring you down
> at the hands of Aeacus' great royal son . . .
> Achilles!
>
> (XVI, 996–1000)

Patroclus has the prophetic power of a man on the threshold of death. Soon Hector will have to meet his unbeatable enemy.

When Achilles learns what has happened to his friend he explodes with grief and with rage. He blames himself for letting Patroclus go into battle, and he rages against Hector, who must pay for what he has done—even though Achilles knows well that once Hector dies, he himself does not have long to live. Hector has taken the armor of Patroclus, Achilles' old armor, and this is surely an act of hubris. Hector is not Achilles—and forgetting that helps put him on the path to destruction. Meanwhile, Achilles must wait, grieving and fasting in his tent as Hephaestus, the smith god, forges him another suit of armor and a magnificent shield.

In the world of strife that is *The Iliad*, the hero who seeks the first place knows that one obligation eclipses all others: when provoked, he must take revenge. He is a creature of retribution. The hero never lets an insult pass, never endures a slight from an equal or a near equal. When his reputation is threatened in words, he will boast of his accomplishments, and do so without shame. When someone harms him or one of his friends or allies, the hero must repay as quickly and ferociously as he can.

This is one of the most difficult aspects of the heroic ideal for the modern middle-class man or woman to accept. Virtually everyone believes that it is wrong to take revenge. When pressed, they may claim that it is against the laws of Christianity to do so. The Savior taught forgiveness, we hear. When struck, we must turn the other cheek. But the fact is that war is always based in retribution: one nation outrages another and the insulted nation must retaliate. In war, on the ground, payback is necessary. If you let a defeat go un-avenged, the enemy will believe that you are beaten and demoral-ized, and then be flooded with fighting confidence. But one might ask: Is the current antipathy to revenge really based in Christian values? Or is it based on timidity?

Hector has killed Patroclus, now Hector must die. And he must die in a thoroughly humiliating way. The hero needs an act of dra-matic retribution to make up for the death of Patroclus but also to restore his wounded warrior's pride. For without that pride, both he and the fighting men who depend on him are in danger. Achilles makes of the death of Hector a spectacle, a piece of theater that un-folds with a vast audience watching, the Greeks in joy, the Trojans horrified.

Armed and returned to battle, Achilles begins his onslaught, and soon the Trojans are driven back to the walls of their city. Achilles slaughters so many Trojans, dumping their bodies in the River Scamander, that the river god rises up in outrage and tries to kill the hero. But Achilles escapes the furious water god and the slaughter continues. It looks as though Achilles and the Greeks might over-whelm their enemies and end the war with a grand victory. But at a critical moment, Apollo diverts Achilles and the Trojans stream into their gate to safety—all but one. Hector is left standing on the field. He knows that he could follow his fellow warriors back into the city, but he feels it would be cowardly. The men he has urged on during the Trojan onslaught, before Achilles retook the field, would mock him. So he decides to try to stand his ground against the deadly Achilles.

Virtually all the Trojans seem to be massed along the walls of their city looking down at the action. The Greeks too have come together, as if in assembly, to watch the fight. Achilles has surely made it clear to them that they are not to intervene, for this moment is his. The gods too are present, looking down from Olympus.

Staring from the parapet, Priam puts aside his massive dignity and begs Hector to relent and come back into the city. The king conjures up a terrible image of Troy falling in defeat after Hector is gone. He himself will be murdered, cut down by a Greek sword or run through with a spear, and his own dogs will lap his blood from the floor. They'll gorge on his aged body, tearing at his gray head and at his genitals. "Yes, the very dogs / I bred in my own halls to share my table, guard my gates— / mad, rabid at heart they'll lap their master's blood / and loll before my doors" (XXII, 80–83).

Hecuba, mother of Hector, stands forward on the wall and exposes her withered breasts, reminding Hector that she has given him life, and telling him that he must preserve himself for the sake of all of Troy. "Pity your mother too, if I ever gave you the breast / to soothe your troubles, remember it now, dear boy" (XXII, 98–99). Priam and Hecuba are genuinely horrified, but there is also a sense in which they seem to be playing a part in a terrible dramatic ritual.

Three times Achilles chases Hector around the walls of Troy, with all the spectators looking on, feeling the full force of Hector's humiliation. He is a warrior. He is not supposed to *run*. Zeus watching from Olympus is distressed. He remembers all the thighbones that Hector has burnt in his honor, he recalls the man's piety and courage. And the king of the gods nearly relents and reverses

Hector's fate. But not quite. At the point of decision, Zeus raises his celestial balance beam on high. In one pan is the fate of Achilles, in the other the fate of Hector. "And down went Hector's day of doom" (XXII, 253).

Athena descends to preside at the killing; she takes the form of Hector's friend and brother Deiphobus and tells Hector that he should stand and fight, for who knows who may win the contest? Deluded, Hector stops running and faces his attacker. From then on nothing is in doubt. Achilles approaches his prey with ferocious confidence. Hector, ever the man of reason and decency, begs for some humane pact between them. He says that if he dies—and on some level he knows he will—he wants his body returned to his parents so they can perform the funeral rites and mourn him properly. He will do the same for Achilles if he should lose the fight and perish. But Achilles laughs. There are no pacts between men and lions, or between wolves and their prey, he tells Hector. The full restoration of his honor is going to require not only victory in direct combat: Achilles will need more.

Hector fights with all he has, but he cannot withstand the force of Achilles, who overwhelms him. With his dying words, Hector reminds his great foe that soon he, Achilles, will be dead, cut down by Paris outside the Scaean Gates. But Achilles is not moved. Let death come when Zeus and the other deathless gods will it, Achilles says—as long as I have my glory, as long as I have due revenge.

Every true warrior is willing to make the crucial trade: he will die early in order to achieve glory. He will perish young in the body so that his fame can live on and on in the future. There is only one kind of desirable immortality for Achilles. Heroes do not live to ascend to heaven—in Homer the afterlife is dismal. The hero wants to be remembered as a person who does deeds that others cannot; he wants to live on in the minds of men as someone who did not fear death.

When Hector is finally dead, Achilles pierces his ankles and runs a rawhide thong through them. He yokes the body to his chariot and in bitter triumph rides away, dragging Hector's head in the dust. Later, after Patroclus in buried and the body of Hector is in the Greek camp, Achilles will perform a ritual that recalls his triumph. Again, he pierces Hector's ankles and again yokes his body to the chariot. He drags the corpse around Patroclus' tomb three times, the number of times that Hector ran around the walls of Troy in terror (XXII, 198; XXIV, 19). Achilles wants as protracted, public, and complete a triumph over Hector as he can possibly achieve.

For Achilles, it would be deeply unsatisfying to fight Hector alone, or with only a few witnesses, one man against another in the manner of a nineteenth-century duel. No, the scene in front of Troy repeats and enlarges the scene of Achilles' humiliation at the beginning of the poem, when Agamemnon takes his slave girl. All the Greeks are there to watch Achilles reclaim what is his by right, his full honor. The Trojans are there, too, and they must see. Honor is won and lost in public—with all looking on. The restoration to full stature for Achilles is a theatrical event, almost ceremonially religious in its inclusion of men and gods, presided over by Zeus who, with his balance beam, takes on something like the role of the high priest at a sacrifice.

Is Achilles' restoration of pride, fullness of being, a horror to the civilized reader? It may be. But for Achilles the restoration of pride is necessary—without it he will not be able to fight with full force. Without it, he will not be able to lead the troops to victory and protect them when they're besieged. Achilles is the Greek bulwark against defeat, which means death and slavery. He owes it to his fellow soldiers and himself to restore his brilliant and terrifying fullness of being. To fight as he must, Achilles needs to believe he is the best of the Greeks, and that all of his comrades concur—and after defeating Hector, he has achieved precisely that.

But there must be limits to the true hero's rage. When he has taken his retribution—and war is always based in some measure on retribution—he must know how to arrive at equanimity.

After he defeats Hector, Achilles still will not dismiss his Myrmidons, for Patroclus has not received proper funeral rites. Fighting must stop until Achilles' dear friend has what he deserves. There follows the burning of the body, along with the sacrifice of horses and also of twelve Trojan young men, whose throats Achilles cuts at the funeral pyre. But after the ceremony come the funeral games, and here Achilles takes another step toward his restoration.

There is boxing, running, a chariot race, and Achilles presides over them all, making the final judgments and offering prizes from his store. He determines who will compete and passes out the trophies to the victors. Achilles is monarch of the scene. He is ruler here, not Agamemnon.

The final match is in spear throwing, and Agamemnon is to be one of the contestants. Against him will be matched at least one other expert in the art. Stop, says Achilles. It is unnecessary to go further. We all understand that no one can throw a spear like Agamemnon. "Atrides—well we know how far you excel us all; / no one can match your strength at throwing spears" (XXIII, 986–987). Agamemnon is the winner by my decree, Achilles declares. He will have the prize, the prize I have set aside. The act is one of aggressive deference. Agamemnon wins, but he wins only at the pleasure of Achilles. He does not get to demonstrate his excellence to the army. He doesn't have the chance to regain some of the prestige he has sacrificed to the slayer of Hector. As it is now, Agamemnon could have lost the contest. No one really knows. The king is honored, yes, but the honor is received at the hands of Achilles, the monarch of the moment. It is a brilliant stroke. By exalting Agamemnon, Achilles humiliates him. But this is what a man can do who has restored himself to the full glory of his fighter's pride.

Achilles reaches the pinnacle of his proud magnanimity in the encounter with King Priam, when Priam, guided by Hermes, makes his way to Achilles' tent to beg for the body of Hector. The meeting between Priam and Achilles is one of amazing grandeur and pathos. The old king enters the hero's tent, past his many friends and retainers, and throws himself at Achilles' feet. And there he does the nearly unthinkable. He kisses the hands of Achilles: "kneeling down beside Achilles, [Priam] clasped his knees / and kissed his hands, those terrible, man-killing hands / that had slaughtered Priam's many sons in battle" (XXIV, 560–562). He begs the hero for mercy. He entreats Achilles to give up the body of Hector so that Hecuba and Andromache can see him again and so that the Trojans can mourn their champion with a fitting burial.

Achilles is shocked at Priam's daring. He cannot believe that the old man would risk his life this way. Though he still is mourning for Patroclus, Achilles softens. Looking on Priam, he is compelled to think of his own father, far away, at home. Achilles is Peleus' only child and Achilles feels certain that his father will never see him alive again. The hero breaks into tears, mourning for his lost friend and for his father, a grieving old man, much like the one before him grasping his hands.

One still cannot quite say that what Achilles feels is empathy. He feels sorrow for himself and for his own father, and that connects him to Priam. Yet Achilles is still where we always have seen him—at the center of his own world.

But then something moves within the hero. He looks upon Priam and he says, "Poor man, how much you've borne—pain to break the spirit" (XXIV, 605). For a moment, hardly more than that, Achilles seems to leave himself and to enter the life of another man, the suffering old king who is his mortal enemy. "Poor man, how much you've borne—pain to break the spirit! / What daring brought you down to the ships all alone, / to face the glance of the man who killed

your sons, / so many fine brave boys?" (XXIV, 605–608). For a long
time Achilles has inhabited only his own mind and heart. The force
of his perceptions and the focused intensity of his speech arise in
part from his dwelling firmly within himself and seriously entertaining no perspective but his own.

Now though, there is another way of being and of suffering in the
world—that of old king Priam. The state will not last: Achilles will
soon be the shining center of his cosmos again. But for an instant
he—and Homer—have been open to an alternative mode of being,
one that values not strength or beauty or even shining intellect, but
compassion. As time unfolds, the idea that we are all brothers and
sisters and that we bear a kinship to every creature that lives and
suffers on the earth will become manifest in dramatic ways. With
Buddha, Confucius, and Jesus the idea will at times seem to dominate the world. Here, passingly, it appears that Achilles tastes the
spring of human benevolence; for an instant he is not a hero, not an
individual, not a power, but simply one with another suffering being
within a universe of pain. Here Homer shadows forth the compassionate ideal, just as, more indirectly, his depiction of Thersites
shadows forth the ideal of contemplation.

Yet just after he touches on the experience of compassion, Achilles
also finds a way to reaffirm his own priority. Priam tells Achilles that
the Trojans will want a protracted period of mourning for Hector.
The Trojans will need eleven days, Priam says: nine to mourn him
in their halls, the tenth to hold a public feast, and the eleventh to
build a barrow and burn the corpse. The Trojans will also need to
be able to leave their city to gather wood for the pyre—so they will
be vulnerable to Greek attack.

Achilles answers immediately. "All will be done, old Priam, as
you command. / I will hold our attack as long as you require"
(XXIV, 787–788). Before making this promise, Achilles consults no
one. Shouldn't he talk with Agamemnon? Shouldn't he bring the

other princes together for council? He does not need to do so now. He has shown himself to be the superior man, the best of the Greeks.

Something else remarkable happens in the final book of the poem: the Trojans begin to take their farewell of Hector, and we listeners and readers do so with them. We hear the stunning laments of Hecuba and Helen and Andromache. With them we recall what Hector meant to the Trojans. Andromache's lament comes first: she cries out about all she has lost with the death of her husband. He has been her savior; her father and mother and brothers are gone, and now her husband is dead. She pictures herself in slavery, serving another woman; she imagines her son in a life of misery. She recalls to us Hector the husband, the man who adored his wife and child. We remember him removing the flashing helm with its horsehair plume to calm crying Astyanax. We hear him again talking to Andromache with a firm intimacy that no two other people in the poem demonstrate. Hecuba recalls Hector the fighting man who stood before Achilles and did all he could to save Troy, against even the will of Fate. This is the warrior we remember, leading the charge and pushing the prideful Greeks back to their ships, the man full of daring and hungry to share glory with Achilles. Last, Helen remembers his amazing kindness, reminding all how generous Hector could be. He and Priam were the only Trojans who treated her with dignity, and when others rose against her it was Hector who quieted them.

The great poem ends with the burning of Hector's corpse and with the magisterial last line: "And so the Trojans buried Hector, breaker of horses." The last book of the poem dramatizes the triumph of Achilles and his momentary transformation into a way of being that he himself can probably barely comprehend and that is foreign to almost all the rest of the life of the poem. A man-god feels compassion—not condescending pity, but compassion for a hated enemy.

But the final book also returns us to Hector and asks us to consider again his status in the poem. He is a man and not a god—he lives the way we do; he is not born to war as Achilles is. He *learned* to be a warrior. In another world he would perhaps be a man of peace, a superior minister and a just king. But in this world, the world of Greek and Trojan strife, Hector must bring himself to the fore and fight against impossible opposition. Unselfishly, brilliantly, most often bravely, he is compelled by duty to strive against a godly man. By the end of the poem another version of the heroic individual may be emerging. Here is a man not entirely unlike ourselves, who achieves vast dignity fighting not primarily for glory or prizes but to defend what he loves. Achilles fights to capture the first place and to keep his word. He said he would go to Troy and fight for victory—being a man of honor he will do so. His father Peleus insisted that he be first in all endeavors and he strives to be. As a warrior, at least, he is supreme and he will set the standard not only among Greeks and Trojans but for all time. He becomes what Shakespeare's Cleopatra calls "the soldier's pole." Hector is the citizen soldier. He is the man who fights a defensive struggle for what he loves, even though the will to fight is probably not primary in his nature.

The Iliad seems to touch on the universal. Past cultures from all over the world lived with values similar if not identical to those Homer dramatizes. Men and women seem always to have stood in awe of what Emerson, in a late life essay on courage, calls "the perfect will, which no terror can shake, which is attracted by frowns or threats or hostile armies, nay, needs these to awake and fan its reserved energies into a pure flame, and is never quite itself until the hazard is extreme; then it is serene and fertile and all its powers play well" (229). The Roman legions fought under the sign of Achilles, as did Alexander's Macedonians. But so much is obvious. What is less readily perceived is that what Achilles valued and what he achieved would be immediately comprehensible to the Viking warriors, to the Mongol horsemen, to the Samurai, and to the fighters in pre-Columbian Mexico and Central America, the Inca and the Aztec. The nobleman fighting from his chariot in Confucian China is a cousin of Achilles. The Sioux warrior, the Maori, and the Zulu would have no trouble comprehending the vision of the Homeric poem. One is tempted to think that there is something intrinsic to human beings that loves courage and beauty and that can only turn away from that love with great effort.

But now both of the ideals of *The Iliad*—Hector's and Achilles'—are fading from us. Self has no time for them. Now one wishes to live as long as possible and as well as possible, which is to say as richly and securely as one can. One wants to be diverted and entertained. One wishes above all to be happy. (Warriors do not care very much for happiness—they care for glory.) One has one's pleasures for the day and pleasures for the night, but health is always paramount.

Health and wealth used to be means to an end. Health let the warrior enter the battle at the peak of his powers. Wealth made certain that he was well armed and provisioned. To have the material necessities of life and to possess physical well-being put one in a position to do remarkable deeds. Now health and wealth have become ends in themselves. One lives to amass treasure. One lives—what does one live for? One lives to go on comfortably living. The idea of consecrating oneself to some great task is now patently absurd to many. The goals of the Self are not in themselves ridiculous. One must sustain life, at least for a while. One must eat. But when the Self's priorities become the only priorities known to men and women we risk growing absurd. We invest the acts of staying alive and staying healthy, of eating good food and getting the right kind of exercise, with a level of meaning they will not sustain. One wants to live forever! What for—what will the goal of such a life be? The goal of living forever is exactly that—to live forever. But what is worth doing in such a life no one any longer can tell you. "One still works," says Nietzsche, "for work is a form of entertainment. But one is careful lest the entertainment be too harrowing" (*Thus Spoke Zarathustra*, 18).

When the goals of the Self are the only goals a culture makes available, spirited men and women will address them with the energy that they would have applied to the aspirations of the Soul. The result is lives that are massively frustrating and not a little ridiculous. People become heroically dedicated to middle-class ends—getting a promotion, getting a raise, taking immeasurably interesting vacations, getting their children into the right colleges, finding the best retirement spot, fattening their portfolios. Lives without courage, contemplation, compassion, and imagination are lives sapped of significant meaning. In such lives, the Self cannot transcend itself.

But the Self seems to hunger for such transcendence. There is an allure to the states of the Soul. How do we now deal with it? Culture throws up an array of what we might call substitute satisfactions. Culture, we might even speculate, may be dominated by the fabrication of Soul. We will not go to war, no not us. But we will play war in our video games; we will watch it on the screens—large, small, and microscopic. We'll become oafishly obsessed with sports, a safe simulacrum of war. We will read about heroism, imagine it, pine for it. We will dream of Hector and Achilles but fear the dream.

There is much to be wary of in the warrior ideal. One legitimately fears that the aspiring hero will turn into the brute, the sadist, the killing machine. One fears that the hero will not always pause long enough to ponder whether his cause is just. But these are not the main worries that keep the culture of Self disposed against heroic ideals. Self respects the will to live more than anything: one must live long; one must live well. Self fears the life of the hero. For the hero, through the force brilliant in his soul, is someone who is always ready to die.

2

The Saint

The Iliad is a great poem of aristocracy—natural aristocracy, Homer's heroes believe, and overall the poem confirms them. Homeric man values beauty and prowess, and Nature, at least as Homeric man sees her, does as well. Force rules in Nature as it does on the plains of Troy; beauty shines forth in the natural world and in the human world launches a thousand ships. The Homeric gods are aristocrats and love what the heroes love. They too are fascinated by beauty and courage. Mortal men are dear to the gods when they show their bravery in the face of the one terror that the gods will never have to encounter, Death.

Yet it is from aristocracy that one of the most profound rebuttals to the heroic ethos arises. Gautama, the one who will in time become the Buddha, descends from a noble lineage. He comes from a region of South Asia where the Aryans have not achieved domination and where the caste system has not taken full hold. His father is a potentate; his family is known for its power and its independence. Shortly after Gautama's birth, his father summons Brahmin soothsayers to predict the boy's future.

The soothsayers concur on one matter: Gautama has a remarkable destiny before him. This is an extraordinary child. But it is not clear what the destiny will be. Two roads open before him, not entirely unlike the roads that opened before Achilles. Gautama may become a great warrior king, unite India, and bring an age of peace, justice, and prosperity. Or he may take another route, and become a spiritual quester. Perhaps he will go on to carry enlightenment to all humanity.

It is immediately clear to Gautama's father which destiny he wants his son to fulfill. He hopes for temporal greatness for his boy. He wants Gautama to be a king, like himself but greater. So he sequesters Gautama in the palace. There the young man has everything he wants: he has a lovely wife; he has a son, Rahula—whose name means the weight, the shackle—and all earthly delights. Gautama has exquisite music, fine food, dancing girls, and art. He has every advantage that Self lives to acquire. His life is perfection—or, from another vantage, his life is the perfect metaphor for the suppression of Soul. Gautama in the pleasure palace is an image of a Self that is enclosed within itself.

But into the hallowed world of the prince comes disquiet. Or—the legend tells us—disquiet is sent by the gods who themselves live in sorrow waiting to be set free. One day Gautama, in company with his servant, takes a ride outside the palace. There the prince encounters an old man, bent double, weak, tottering, nearly blind. "What is that?" Gautama asks his servant. "That is a man in the throes of old age, sir." The prince is stunned. "Does everyone grow old? Will I too become such as he is?" Yes, in all probability you will, the servant tells him. Gautama is full of grief and confusion. He returns to his father's pleasure dome in distress.

But Gautama's education in human suffering continues. Soon the prince meets a sick man, a being like himself in every way except that his body is being eaten by disease. The man seems to be disintegrating before the eyes of the prince and his servant. Is that too my destiny? Will sickness befall me as well? Yes, in all likelihood it will, the servant admits.

And there is worse. Not long afterward, on another foray outside the palace of enchantments, the palace of Self, the prince sees an unmoving human form by the roadside. And what is that? It is a corpse, your highness. The man is dead. He lives no more. And this too—the prince knows the answer himself by now, no doubt—this must happen to me? Indeed it will, since your life too must come to an end, and if your end is like that of most, it will be bitter, terror-filled, and riven with pain.

The last of the prince's four encounters takes a different form. Together with the servant, the prince sees a lean man with a shaven head, an alms bowl in one hand, a staff in the other, wearing a saffron-colored robe. He encounters a man who has *voluntarily* assumed some of the attributes of the old man, the sick man, and even of the corpse. This individual, who could have sought pleasure, as the prince has done, has apparently sought something like the reverse. He has turned away from the satisfactions of the stable life in pursuit of other goals, and he seems to have made this turn of his own volition.

And who is this? Gautama wants to know. Why does he look the way he does? Where has he come from and where is he going? It is a monk, the servant tells him. He lives without a secure roof overhead, in an unhoused state, far from the comforts (and the conflicts and limits) of family. He wanders in the forests and he begs for his meager food. He is practiced in the art of something called meditation. He seeks wisdom.

What sort of wisdom does he seek? Gautama asks. He seeks some way to deal with—perhaps to *overcome*—the sorrows of old age, sickness, and death. He is searching for a way of living that passes beyond earthly sorrow and delivers him, and perhaps in time will

deliver others, from the frustration of human life. Gautama resolves that he will take up this quest. He decides that he will leave
the palace. (That is, he will leave the Self's life of pleasure and ease
that we know in youth, and he will do so voluntarily, through the
strength of his own will.) His parents weep when he tells them he is
leaving. He does not have the heart to wake up his wife and his son
(his darling shackle), who will surely oppose his going and maybe
with their tears keep him at home. At the crest of a hill, Gautama
changes clothes and horses with his servant (who, some say, returns to the dwelling of the gods, his errand done) and goes off in
search of his destiny. He leaves not as Achilles does, to become
the renowned warrior of his father's hopes, but to develop through
harsh adversities into one of the most profound spiritual teachers
yet known to mankind.

Different as they are, Achilles and Gautama are also brothers of
the spirit. Both reject the easy life that fate offers them. Achilles will
not stay at home with his family and possessions and live to serene
old age; Gautama cannot abide inside the walls of the pleasure dome.
He leaves to contend with old age, sickness, and death, and in a
sense Achilles does too. Achilles deals with old age and sickness by
his willingness to depart from the world before those evil states descend upon him. He will never be anything but young and brimming with health and surpassingly beautiful. As to death, Achilles
seeks to overcome it by rushing toward it. By bravely dying young,
he will gain the only kind of immortality he can believe in—
immortality on the tongues of men through time. Both Achilles
and Gautama rebel against a safe predictable life—the kind of life
we associate with the prudent Self. Both act against their own "happiness" and the happiness of their families. Both go off to transform the world. Both are aristocrats. The day a certain Indian potentate meets Gautama, he says that he wants to make the young man
his heir. He knows he has met one of his kind. But Gautama says

no—he is off to found an aristocracy of spirit, an aristocracy that all may join.

Gautama's spiritual quest does not occur in a void. The forests that he enters to seek the answer to the riddles of old age, sickness, and death are full or people, mostly male but not all, engaged in spiritual quests. Everywhere there are monks who have taken vows of poverty and chastity. When one group of monks passes another, they call out to each other: "Who is your guru?" "What is your dharma?" "Who is your teacher?" "What is your doctrine?"

There is a sense abroad in the world that an old spiritual order is breaking down. Hinduism, with its manifold gods and its stunning poetic texts, has been for centuries the heart of spiritual life in India. But the Hindu high priests, the Brahmins, have become hierophants, who hoard their knowledge. They have degenerated into spiritual entrepreneurs. If you want holy teachings, you must pay for them. In the eyes of young questers like Gautama, the Brahmin priests are not unlike what the Sophists, who teach dialectical skill for pay, are to Socrates or what the Pharisees are to Jesus. A new way has to be found, Gautama sees, a way that is plainer, purer, more rational, and can be proved on the pulse of experience. Gautama will become a practical visionary. No mysticism, no enigma, little poetry—only what is useful and conducive to peace here, in this life.

But first Gautama explores the forms of knowledge available among the wanderers, the "vagrant dwellers in the houseless woods." Gautama finds two potential masters. Both are formidable teachers and both recognize in the young Gautama a superbly promising student. He quickly assimilates their teachings. Nothing puzzles him about their thought, yet he sees that neither teacher offers the way to freedom. Neither can deliver him from his obsessions with the sorrows of old age, sickness, and death.

In time, Gautama becomes an ascetic, and one of a particularly uncompromising sort. There comes a time, the Pali Text tells us, when by pressing on his belly, he can feel his backbone behind him. He subsists on six or seven grains of rice a day. He mortifies his flesh in the way that only a man of the most ferocious—that is perhaps to say "aristocratic"—strength of will can do. Yet the transformation that he seeks is still not to be had: old age, sickness, and death, followed by birth back into the world of suffering, continue to loom.

Lost, unable to break through, Gautama does something surprising. He sits down. He begins meditation under a Bo tree, and as the hours pass and he drops more deeply into his spirit's life, remarkable events take place. He comes to see that suffering is not accidental. Suffering is essential. It is the fundamental condition of being. Suffering is life / life is suffering. In the unenlightened state there is no remainder. And yet—the second of the Buddha's truths—the source of suffering is discernible. Gautama's meditations reveal it to him. The reason for suffering is desire, selfish desire, the desire for private fulfillment. The hungers for primacy, possession, safety, security: these strivings lead to inner turbulence, which is the core of human unhappiness. Can such desires be overcome? The third of the Buddha's truths proclaims that they can. There is in this world the prospect of overcoming suffering, because there is the possibility of overcoming desire. And how is this overcoming possible? It becomes not a possibility but a reality when one follows the eightfold path: right views, right intent, right speech, right action, right livelihood, and the rest.

Gautama believes he has broken through. He has found the way to redeem the life of suffering. It is nonattachment to the things of this world, the admission of impermanence, and the cessation of selfish desires. The way to enlightenment is through overcoming ego—destroying the misleading fiction of Self.

Is all this an affront to the warrior ethos of Achilles? Yes and no. Achilles strives always—he hungers for the first place. But he is not obsessed by most forms of worldly desire—possession, prosperity, security, long life—these goals mean virtually nothing to him when he pursues and embodies the warrior ideal. The violence that is at the center of the heroic quest is an affront to Buddhist thinking, yes. But Achilles, who refuses to stay home and live the comfortable life of the domestic king, is also an enemy of certain sorts of striving, the striving that will in time become the middle class's reason to exist.

The Buddha makes his breakthroughs, and his spiritual way is revealed. But perhaps his greatest moment of trial is ahead of him. Much like Jesus in the desert, the Buddha under the Bo tree undergoes temptation. Demons spin toward him from out of the air and they offer him their bounties. He can have temporal power, be a lord of this world, much as his father hoped he would be. He can lead a life of erotic bliss: no end of women and intoxicants, no end of pleasure. These possibilities Gautama waves aside—just as Achilles would, just as Socrates and Jesus would. But the demon Mara, Lord of Death, has something more appealing to offer. Why not depart from this world? Mara asks him. Now you can enter into the sublime State of being called Nirvana and leave all the difficulties of earthly life behind. Abandon this sad world afflicted by death and desire.

But the Buddha, having reached enlightenment, is determined to spread his wisdom. He is committed to bringing his four noble truths to other beings who need deliverance. Gautama has resolved to reenter the world and to reveal what he has learned.

Will you? Is that truly wise? The demon Mara, whom we might think of as the Buddha's version of the Selfhood, asks him. Don't you know what will happen?

Then the demon spits out the most daunting words. No one will listen to you, he says. You will be mocked. You will be taken for a fool. No one will understand you. People will laugh.

What a blow is public mockery to the aristocratic spirit. Shakespeare's Cleopatra prefers death to being ridden in a cage through the streets of Rome in Caesar's triumph. She imagines herself being parodied on the stage, by a prepubescent male. They'll "boy my greatness," she says. For Gautama to imagine being mocked—it is as though Achilles had to imagine being reduced to the condition of Thersites: ugly, misshapen, and absurd. All residual aristocratic pride will evaporate in the dismissive glare of the crowd. It is the temptation to escape mockery, to leave the world without the divine teachings and ascend to another sphere of being that shakes Gautama. He is indecisive. He weighs the alternatives: heavenly calm forever against living on in a world of pain and grief and, maybe most disturbing of all, of ridicule.

They will not listen. They will laugh at you. The people will not care.

For a long time Gautama pauses—then the glowing words. Perhaps some of them will not care, perhaps some will laugh, the great teacher says. But not all of them will. No, not all! "There will be some who will understand." There are some who will listen to what I have to say and take what I have to give, and they will be transformed.

This is the decisive blow. The evil god disappears like dust and the heavens open and rain down lotus blossoms. Nature sings in joy. Even the gods join in the elation.

So the Buddha begins his life as a teacher. For close to forty-five years, he tramps through India enduring the sun and the hard rains. Nine months of every year Gautama preaches, gives counsel, and offers comfort. For three months he withdraws for extended periods of meditation and thought. Yet he does not disappear forever. He is a moon that draws clouds around him like protective covering. Time after time he returns to his task.

People hold him in awe. They gather to him to hear his words. He will speak on large topics to be sure, but he will also address the most personal and minor difficulties. Should I marry? What profession should I take up? Shall I move from the country to the town? He is renowned for having a cool head; he has the prowess of a logician. But his heart is warm. He shows genuine love and concern.

People do not know what to make of him. He does not remind them of anyone that they have known. So they ask him not, Who are you? Rather they ask him, What are you? Are you a man or are you a God? On this matter the Buddha does not equivocate. I am just like you, he tells them. I am a man. I was born and in time will die. And then they ask, Are you truly enlightened? Have you achieved the apogee of spiritual knowledge? Enlightened? the Buddha is prone to reply. Say rather, simply, that I am Awake. He is, more precisely, the *awakened* one, which suggests that in the past he was asleep. He was a somnambulist, sleepwalking his way through existence in the vale of Self. So virtually all of us, men and women, are asleep in the inner and the outer being. We are not truly alive and will not begin to live until we take the first step down the road to knowledge by conceding that life is, at its core, suffering.

What is it to be awake? First, it is to be attuned to the truth of pain. The awakened individual refuses to shut out the sufferings and terrors of life. He says no to all anesthesia, whether the anesthesia be alcohol, sex, entertainment, consumption, or travel. (He has his little poisons for the day and his little poisons for the night, says Nietzsche of the man who lives only in the State of Self.) The awakened one is responsive to suffering and does not turn away from it in himself or in others. He does not try to pretend it is something other than what it is. He escapes from his palace of pleasure and leaves the life of non-awareness behind him. All false cheerfulness, all hearty embrace of Self, he distrusts. He sees life's sorrow for what it is, yet he is not brought to despair by it.

The Buddha teaches tranquility through the acknowledgment of suffering and through detachment from selfish desires. And he has other, perhaps more subtle, teachings to dispense. Buddhism is essentially a godless religion, if it is a religion at all. There is no supreme being. There is no transcendent figure that one is obliged to worship. The gigantic statues of Gautama that dot the East and draw worshippers with their flowers, incense, and prayers for well-being and prosperity are a manifestation of error. They ought not to exist. Buddhism does not revolve around worship. Meditation is not prayer. If one gives thanks as a Buddhist, one does so in the spirit of paradox. One is grateful, even though there is no One—no divine originator—to whom one is grateful. There is joy in Buddhism. But it is the joy that comes from clearing the mind and achieving uninhibited being in the moment. To be awake and present is to experience marvels. But joy does not come as a result of contact with a deity. Gautama is an exemplar, not an incarnation. Buddhism is a post-religious faith.

The Buddhist sense of time is radical. Gautama teaches that all stability—except perhaps for the apparent stability of the noble truths and the divine path—is illusory. Nothing abides; everything passes. Human beings impose stability—or seek to—to obscure what inevitably awaits. The world of human culture teems with illusions. Love is an illusion, family is an illusion, friendship, the same. Perhaps the most pernicious of the illusions, because the most desperately maintained, is the illusion of Self. Self, to Gautama, is a defensive bulwark. It is conducive to errors about stability and control. Jacques Lacan says nothing new when he announces that the ego is a paranoid structure.

To Gautama, virtually all humanly conceived structures are paranoid, betraying fear of the inevitable even as they work to suppress the fear. All is mutability; nothing endures but time and change. And since all beings live on the wheel of time and of suffering, there is only one right attitude to assume toward them: the attitude of compassion. Human beings must proceed gently with each other, as they should with all living things. For everyone's road is a hard one. A latter-day Buddhist teacher recommends that when one approaches another being, one must remind oneself in a subliminal whisper of a simple fact: the person before me is suffering; he is suffering and he desires happiness. She suffers. She wishes to be happy. He suffers. He wishes to be happy. Achilles will forever be known as the apogee of courage; Plato embodies the free exercise of the mind in quest of Truth. The Buddha helps bring another quality to the center of the world's consciousness: compassion.

People continue to converge reverently on a figure they conceive of as the compassionate Buddha. And compassion is inseparable from the Buddha's vision. But one must add that the Buddha's teachings begin with the individual being and *his* hopes of overcoming the life of suffering. It is a simple fact but a salient one. The Buddha's great legend is the legend of one person in search of enlightenment. It is an individual story. What the Buddha achieves, he by and large achieves alone: the path he opens is a path for single beings. Others matter, of course; but this is not a story of collective change. "Be lamps unto yourselves," the Buddha says. Work out your salvation for your own being. Envy, anger, competitiveness, malice: all these flaws are associated by the Buddha with selfish desires—as is the desire to have and to be a Self. Yet it sometimes seems that the chief objection to the vices of the Self is that they bring disquiet to the *individual* spirit. They distemper the mind. They cause agitation and so undermine the quality that Gautama seems to treasure above the rest, which is peace. Inner peace dies on the blade of strife and anger. Inner peace requires the doctrine of loving compassion. Disquietude is the primary enemy. And in this too some of the old aristocratic spirit may persist. The aristocrat is beyond agitation. He is regally calm, Gautama-like.

The traditional Hindu values persist beneath the Buddha's vision. The sense beautifully delineated in the Upanishads—that there is one life for all, that we live in the midst of one miraculous being, and that to harm another being is to harm oneself—all this undergirds Gautama's gospel. But it is not always at the center. An enemy of the Self, Gautama nonetheless affirms the life and acts of the individual, the one who is to become his own lamp.

What Gautama brings to the world is preeminently his person. He provides a doctrine, yes, but also an incarnation, a breathing and walking instance of the spiritual discipline he propounds. And this person begins to change the world so that it looks to compassion as a Soul value—a value that can create unity of being and joy—and not just to courage.

Suppose, contra Nietzsche, that compassion is not a resentful rebuttal to the ethos of courage. Suppose compassion is a second Soul State, a second great ideal, always potentially present, latent in men and women, always already possible. It is a State we may enter from the State of Self, to think again of Blake. Suppose compassion is a second Soul virtue, no less potent, though later in its full disclosure to the world, than courage. Suppose a new possibility for a life that is whole and filled with meaning has received embodiment in Gautama and becomes available in time to virtually all human beings?

It is now not only aristocrats and godly males like Achilles and Hector who can live from and for the Soul. Compassion is a virtue open to everyone. The promise of full, unified life unfolds flowerlike. And it is to be encountered not only in India, but more and more throughout the world.

In China, not far from where the Buddha achieves wakefulness and puts Mara to rout, a teacher not entirely unlike him begins his career in failure. Confucius wants what many thinkers—both honest and nefarious—have wanted. Confucius wants a post with significant public responsibility. He wants to do something for the suffering masses of China. The countryside around him is violent, and in time it will grow much more so. The noble chariot-fighters who have pledged themselves to abide by a code not unlike the one sustained by the warriors in *The Iliad* have lost humane bearing. On some days entire cities are slaughtered, men and women and children, all, not sold into slavery, but butchered. No one can live safely. When an embassy goes off to treat with a duke, all the ambassadors are killed, their bodies mangled horribly, then sent back to their ranks. The crime is repaid and repaid again. The common people are animal creatures, often slaughtered freely by their supposed betters.

Confucius, a man of relatively humble origins whose parents died when he was young, cannot bear what he sees around him. The "heroic" excesses sicken the genial, gentle, humorous, and above all modest man who, though sometimes a severe teacher, takes pleasure in drinking some wine, reciting poetry, talking and laughing with his friends. "In the late spring," he says, "after the spring clothes have been newly made, I should like, together with five or six adults and six or seven boys, to go bathing in the River Yi and enjoy the breeze on the Rain Altar, and then to go home chanting poetry" (XI.26).

He loves his pupils: Yen Yuan, virtuous in conduct; Tsai Wo, adept in speech; Jan Yu, accomplished in the art of government; Tzu-yu and Tzu-hsia, true men of learning (Confucius XI.3). And they love the master, each in his way. When one of his pupils dies or must leave him, the master is stricken. Yen Yuan dies and he is irreplaceable in the master's heart. "When Yen Yuan died, in weeping for him, the Master showed undue sorrow. His followers said, 'You are showing undue sorrow.' 'Am I? Yet if not for him, for whom should I show undue sorrow?' " (XI.10).

What does the master teach? He teaches one quality above all others: he teaches benevolence. Benevolence, which is something other than compassion, though not unrelated to it, is the constant theme of Confucius. Compassion is the most antihierarchical of religious concepts. In it, there is nothing of ancient Greece, with its love of order and degree. Each human being is the equal of every other. Each human being? Yes, but it is not foolish here to include the animals and even the plants. They too are part of the one life that is in us and abroad (as Coleridge put it). The Buddha's commitment to reincarnation is a way to affirm this—spirit passes into different forms of matter in a sequence that ends only with enlightenment, if it ends there. (One may take Bodhisattva vows, refusing to accept enlightenment until every being is enlightened.) All creatures suffer: all beings are, in this way—and it may be the only way that matters—equal.

To Confucius, matters are a bit different. He is devoted to bringing into existence a class of—how far can a paradox stretch?—saintly bureaucrats. Surely, Confucius believes, there are at least two classes of men, the leaders and those who must be led. From the latter not a great deal can be expected. From the leaders much has been asked, but over time too little has been given. The best lack all conviction, except about their own needs for wealth and power. The best are becoming the worst. This situation Confucius is devoted to changing.

Who is the benevolent man? Who is the *gentleman* that Confucius prophesies and attempts to embody? He says that surely there are many who are as well intentioned as he is, many who possess equal or greater intelligence. But how many are there who are as eager to learn what it takes to become a gentleman? Few, he suggests. Perhaps none at all.

The man of benevolence is the one who always puts others before him. Though he is not immune to the lure of success, he constantly subordinates success to the pursuit of higher ideals. He places the welfare of the common people first. He works unceasingly for them, struggling for their interests. And in this, he is practical.

Asked what he would do as a ruler, Confucius says that first he would feed the people and then he would make them prosperous—and then, only after the primary needs have been taken care of, would he initiate them into the Way.

The man who genuinely works for the common people does not stand a great chance of success. The world is corrupt. Leaders do not want to hear the Truth. (When Confucius finally becomes a prince's advisor, he is quickly dismissed for his candor.) Those in power are almost always greedy and disdain to share what they have. So the benevolent man is unlikely to win approval in their eyes. He will be passed over for promotion. He will see his most thoughtful plans for the betterment of the masses ignored or ridiculed. Yet still—suffering the wounds that patient merit always takes from the unworthy—he strives on, not thin-lipped but cheerful, affable, both sweet and tough, like the Master himself.

At the heart of the Master's teaching is a central principle: filial piety. One reveres the past, and in particular one reveres the past as it is embodied, exemplified, and transmitted by one's parents. What is the appropriate mourning period for a deceased mother or father? Three years is correct. Less is an affront. How far should a child, even a grown child, stray from a parental home? He must stay as close as possible. When he does journey he must do all he can so as not to inflict disquiet on his parents. Surely a dutiful son or daughter will give a parent the choicest bits of meat at dinner and will cede the place closest to the fire. This goes without saying. But if he is a truly dutiful son, she a dutiful daughter, this will be done with a smiling face. To serve the parents is a blessing.

To the Romans, religion—*religare*—meant being tied back to the past. One lived to emulate glorious ancestors, those who had risen to the level of minor deities. The oldest Romans, founders of the Republic, were men and women held in awe for their virtue, probity, endurance, and courage. One sought, at best, to relive their lives.

In Confucius' thinking, veneration for the past and for the virtuous ancestors may be even stronger. To live well, one must repeat the best of what has come before. A man who wishes to be remembered with respect comes as close as possible in character and action to his most virtuous forebears. He merges with them; his identity becomes indistinguishable from theirs. How far this is from the hero's wish to shine as no man ever has before. The hero wants to be peerless, beyond compare. Achilles is little like Peleus, little like Thetis. The only apt comparisons for Achilles are with Olympian gods. Some few men may for a moment remind one of Achilles. But Achilles reminds us of no other man.

Confucius fails—or rather Confucius succeeds by failing. He finally finds the office he desires, advisor to a prince, but it does not go well. The Master is far too candid. He will not tell the noble lord what he wants to hear. If the noble lord demands a rationale for increasing his wealth at the expense of the common people—if he requires self-justification or propaganda—then Confucius cannot oblige him. He, like Socrates, believes that man's first obligation to other men is to tell the truth.

Reflective though he is, Confucius has no overt investment in another, transcendental world. (Though some scholars have suggested an *implicit* investment.) It is hardly possible to imagine him propounding a myth of the cave. There is no pure sunlight, no pure contemplation: for Confucius, only practical knowledge, tactics, resilience, modesty, filial piety, and grace.

But from these quiet virtues arises an ideal that shines through Chinese culture and beyond for twenty-five hundred years, the ideal of the gentleman. The gentleman is sweet in temper and does not seek his own advancement at the expense of others. He abjures war except under conditions of the greatest necessity, and rather than seeking—as Achilles' father told him to do—for the first place, he compounds his honor by modesty. He lets others take the credit that belongs to him; he watches serenely as his inferiors are promoted beyond him. He simply does his best, and if his highest hopes for improving the lives of the common people do not come to fruition, then he accepts matters with tranquility. He knows—the idea is at the heart of much of the East's wisdom—that we must judge ourselves by our intentions and not (as the pragmatic West often insists) by results.

His reward? The reward of the gentleman is an unblemished reputation and the most desirable state of spirit, the state of serenity. The Confucian gentleman achieves peace. He arrives at the inverse of the burning turbulence in which the warlords live. He is one with himself and he is whole. For he has found the secret of the Soul: kindliness, generosity, thoughtfulness, a life dedicated to others. However agitated the world around him may be, the gentleman, like the Master who showed him the way, is perpetually at peace.

How does the ideal of compassion arise in the West? How does the conception of human beings as being equally worthy of love and kindness arise in Palestine after it emerged in India and China five hundred years before? Surely Jesus, a spiritual genius of the highest order, may have arrived at the compassionate ideal on his own. Throughout the Gospels he displays almost unflagging originality and an often fiery independence of mind. Based on experience and reflection, Jesus may have come to celebrate compassion above the other virtues without the influence of any teacher or set of doctrines.

But it's also possible that some practical form of transmission took place. Maybe merchants or warriors or itinerant scholars wandering the world, as the Greek Herodotus did, somehow traversed the great stretches between India and what the West now calls the Holy Land. Perhaps whole religious groups—call them cults if you like—made the journey West over the Silk Road seeking freedom to pursue their spiritual disciplines or to express ideas of their own about the world and how to live in it. And of course the great Hebrew tradition is not without references to the compassionate ideal. The ideal is not absent from the Psalms, the Book of Deuteronomy, and the teachings of the prophets. But the compassionate ideal does not have nearly the centrality in the Hebrew tradition that it has in the teachings of the Buddha and Confucius—and in the teachings of Jesus of Nazareth.

During the humiliating days of the Roman occupation, the Jews pined for the long-promised Messiah. The Jews were, not for the first time in their history, under domination by an alien power. They were hungry for liberation from the oppressions of Rome. But some were clearly hungry to be liberated from what they perceived to be a faith that had become stiff and over-ritualized. They were as oppressed by their priests, it seems, as the people of India had been by the Brahmins when the Buddha began to teach.

Perhaps there was some practical transmission of the soul-wisdom of the East to Jerusalem and its environs. But perhaps too it was the singular genius of Jesus of Nazareth that brought the ideal of universal love and benevolence to the Jews and the Romans—from whom it passed in time to the entire Western world. The Buddha had the spiritual tradition of the Hindus behind him. In the great texts—the Upanishads and the Gita—much of the Buddha's wisdom is hinted at, suggested. It is for the Buddha to complete the vision. Jesus is not born into a spiritual tradition—a soul-tradition—that is comprehensively akin to the vision he unfolds. Jesus never stops being a Jew, but what is freshest and most vital in Jesus is often in tension with his native tradition.

The Jews of the Hebrew Bible were a warrior people. David and Sampson and Saul are figures with distinct affinities to the heroes in *The Iliad*. They are men of force and prowess, who seek preeminence. They clearly want their names to echo through time in recognition of their deeds. Though service to their people—Hector-like service—is surely more important to them than the quest for glory that Achilles undertakes. David—as beloved by the Lord as any figure in the Hebrew Bible, perhaps more beloved even than Moses—begins his ascendancy as a fighter. He is the champion who brings Goliath to the ground in an instance of that ritual so esteemed by the ancient Greeks, single combat. Throughout his life, David fights and wins, fights and wins, loses, wins again. His many victories set him apart from his fellow Hebrew warriors who, despite the assistance of Yahweh, are often unsuccessful on the battlefield. Yet the ancient Jews aspire to be warriors. At least in the early phases of the Hebrew Bible, Yahweh is a war god—though not always an effective one. The archetype of the Hebrew warrior is perhaps Sampson, who is victorious, then undone, and who finally ends his life in self-destroying triumph. The Jews of the Old Testament fight constantly. They fight for survival and they fight for victory. And their God Yahweh is their god of battle.

Yahweh is more than that, of course. In his first manifestation he is a creator God. He is the generous bountiful deity who makes the sun and the stars and the teeming earth. He creates man in his own glorious image, by molding a piece of red clay and sending his generous breath into it. When he finds his first creature to be lonely—despite his own grand eternal isolation, he quickly understands Adam's plight—he creates for him a helper and friend in Eve. Yahweh is the maker of the heavenly garden, the creator of blissful earthly perfection. (The lines that Milton offers in *Paradise Lost* to describe the creation are among the most memorable in the poem, dramatizing God's bounty and largess.) Yahweh creates, and he creates out of love.

But Yahweh can be violent too. In a burst of rage he drowns the entire earth, leaving only Noah, his wife, and his sons and daughters alive, along with the animals, two by two. He destroys Sodom and Gomorrah and everyone residing there, except Lot and his wife.

The Lord turns her into a pillar of salt for daring to defy his command and look over her shoulder at the destruction that he's brought. He murders the firstborn male of every Egyptian family. When the Egyptian forces pursue the Jews across the desert, goaded on by the Lord, who wants to demonstrate his powers, a particularly horrible end comes their way. Says the Lord: "I will harden Pharaoh's heart, and he will pursue them, so that I will gain glory for myself over Pharaoh and all his army; and the Egyptians shall know that I am the Lord" (Exodus 14.4). The Egyptian army is lured into the Red Sea, which has parted to let the Jews cross. But when the Egyptians follow, the waters close and every one of them drowns. (There are presumably no pleasurable ways to die, but drowning, though brief, is surely one of the most bitter.) In warfare Yahweh is disposed to give no quarter.

It is illuminating to recall how King Saul fell out of favor with the Lord. Through the prophet Samuel, the Lord tells Saul that he must attack a city called Amalek and punish the Amalekites for what they did to oppose the Israelites when they came out of Egypt. But Saul must do more than capture the city. Every man and woman and child has to die. Every beast has to go down to the sword. No living, breathing creature can be left. "Now go and attack Amalek," says the Lord, "and utterly destroy all that they have; do not spare them, but kill both man and woman, child and infant, ox and sheep, camel and donkey" (Samuel 15.3).

And Saul complies—almost. He murders numberless men and women and children. But he does not kill enough to satisfy Yahweh. He leaves Agag, king of the Amalekites, alive, and he spares a handful of animals, sheep and cattle and lambs. And so he infuriates the Lord. The prophet Samuel approaches Saul in a rage: "You have rejected the word of the lord," he says to Saul, "and the Lord has rejected you from being king over Israel" (Samuel 15.26).

After the slaughter of the Amalekites, Saul is no longer holy in the Lord's sight. He is not the valiant slayer of men and women that Yahweh requires. Soon David will take his place in the affections of God.

Like the culture of the Romans, the culture of the Jews is not a truly conducive site for the new soul-doctrine of universal love to flourish. The Jews conceived of themselves as a nation and a race. They are God's chosen people. God shows them his particular favor. He confers his blessing upon them, though often he is compelled then to retract it. Much is asked of the Chosen People. They must rise to ethical standards that set them apart from their neighbors. They must obey the commandments and worship a harsh but bountiful invisible god who will tolerate no graven images and no other gods. Much is given to the Jews as well. Manna appears every day in the desert (unless and until the people take up more than a day's rations); the trumpets blow the walls of Jericho down; Daniel survives the lion's den; Jonah lives on in the belly of the whale; David takes down the giant Goliath; Sampson smites legions of Philistines with the jawbone of an ass. Everywhere Israelites wander they find opposition, sometimes violent. But they are steadied by the knowledge that there is one God presiding above other gods, and that God has chosen them over all peoples on the earth.

In his most central and fresh teachings, Jesus seems closer to the Buddha and to the Hindu sages, and even to Confucius with his ideal of the sainted civil servant, than he is to any prominent figure in the Hebrew Bible. Yet for all of his originality within the context of the Romans and the Jews, Jesus takes pains to bind himself to the Old Testament tradition, at least overtly. Despite all the tension involved in his relation to the Hebrew past, Jesus does not want to break completely with it. Jesus seeks to maintain continuity, even as he embodies disjunction. This traditional antitradition is not extraneous to the work of Jesus. The paradox lies at the center of his achievement.

And there is more complexity to Jesus and his teachings. Once the Buddha makes his breakthrough under the Bo tree he never turns back, at least as far as we know. We do not commonly hear of him expressing doubts about the four noble truths or the eightfold path. Confucius famously said that as he grew older his fundamental desires—his basic set of wants—became fully consonant with his teachings. There was no gap for him between is and ought. He had no tendency to waver. But Jesus struggles. At certain key moments the Gospels dramatize his difficulty in living out the compassionate ideal. His own provincialism and lack of imagination seem to get in his way. And Jesus—at least Mark's Jesus—is afflicted with doubts. He wavers about who (and what) he truly is.

Like the Eastern sages, Jesus is a prophet of compassion—the ideal is at the core of any number of the events that orthodox Christian take to be his miracles. The famous story of the loaves and fishes, as it occurs early in the gospel of Mark, is a salient example. A crowd has been following Jesus for days, listening to his teachings. Jesus calls his disciples to him and says, "I have compassion for the crowd, because they have been with me now for three days and have nothing to eat. If I send them away hungry to their homes, they will faint on the way—and some of them have come from a great distance" (Mark 8.2–3). His disciples are puzzled, as his disciples frequently are. How can they feed so many people out here in the desert where nothing is growing? Jesus asks them what food they have with them. It turns out that they have only seven loaves of bread. Jesus gathers the loaves and blesses them and asks his disciples to distribute them to the crowd. There are also a few fish on hand and Jesus blesses those and gets his disciples to pass them out too. The members of the crowd, which Mark tells us numbered about four thousand, eat their fill. When the disciples gather what's left over, there are seven baskets. Then Jesus sends them away. "And immediately he got into the boat with his disciples and went to the district of Dalmanutha" (Mark: 8.10). This is the miracle of the loaves and the fishes.

What happened? From the orthodox perspective, from the perspective of those who demand miracle, mystery, and authority, the Son of God has performed a miracle. He has used his supernatural powers to create abundance where there was scarcity. He's defied the laws of physics and shown what a powerful figure he is: truly the Son of God.

But there is another explanation for this event, more naturalistic, less tied to what one might call superstition. What happens with the loaves and fishes may still be a miracle, but a miracle of a more earthly and, perhaps ultimately, a more profound sort. When Jesus sees that the people are hungry, he asks the disciples how much food they have. The answer is that Jesus and his entire party has seven loaves and a few fish among them. And then they do something remarkable. They give all the food they have to the crowd. That's it— after the loaves and the fishes are gone, there is nothing left for them. Maybe they will not starve to death because of their charity, but it's likely that they will go hungry for a while. Jesus and his friends feel enough compassion for the crowd to give them all that they have to eat. They don't hold anything back. What is ours is yours. Take it.

Is it possible that the crowd is moved by this act? Is it possible they are touched by the compassion of the teacher? He'll give them what he has and leave nothing for himself. He doesn't love them in some abstract way; he loves them immediately and viscerally, the way a mother loves her children and will give them the last food that she has. Is it possible then that the people in the crowd, the four thousand, follow suit and reach into their cloaks and their sacks and take out what food they have? What was stored away and hidden

for themselves and themselves alone is now for everyone. They
share. The people in the crowd are no longer a gathering of sepa-
rate and distinct selves. For now, in their act of compassion for each
other, they are one body. What was once a crowd is now a community. The prison-house of individuality breaks down. They have im-
itated the Savior in his generosity.

And what precisely does the Savior save one from? He saves you
from Self. He delivers you from the horrible illusion that you are
alone in the world and that no one can ever care for you and love you
and sustain you. That crowd, through sharing, becomes a node of
universal being, and the people in it are finally, if temporarily, free.
Some of them, perhaps, will spend their lives seeking this feeling
in which Self melts away and the Soul becomes ascendant. They
will do so by following Jesus, not in the literal sense of trooping after
him, but in the deeper sense of trying to do as he would do, trying
to be compassionate, trying to be kind.

How different this world of sharing is from the Homeric world.
In Homer, the protocols of dining are of central significance. It's a
matter of real consequence who carves the meat, who is served first,
who gets the choice pieces. When Andromache laments the future
of her son Astyanax in a world without his father Hector, her synec-
doche for his sufferings is a scene at a future meal. There other
young men whose fathers are alive thrust Astyanax away from
the table. He gets no choice cuts of meat. He barely gets a drink
from the golden cup. "Years ago," says Andromache, "propped on
his father's knee, / he would only eat marrow, the richest cuts of
lamb . . . / Now what suffering, now that he's lost his father" (XXII:
588–589, 593). At the table that Jesus sets no one is thrust away and
no one is compelled by rank, age, or gender to eat last. This is the
meal in which all become one and feel themselves free from the
burden of identity—the social armor of Selfhood.

Jesus came to deliver the gospel, which means the good news. What is this good news? It is, to speak very broadly, that the kingdom of heaven is at hand. Or, to put it more provocatively (and probably with more accuracy): the kingdom of heaven is *Now*. And what is this kingdom of heaven? It is life free from the Self. Time and again, Jesus comes forward to save us from ourselves and teach us to live in heaven. Now.

We have multiple ways of sustaining slavery to Self, and Jesus is out to expose them all—even the forms that can sometimes grip the Savior himself. The Self grows strong in isolation, when we are unable to surrender ourselves to the community of sharing. We think of ourselves only and not of the rest. We hide our resources away so that we can use them privately. We believe that if we do not rely on ourselves and only ourselves, we will not survive.

But the Selfhood has other devices too. Earlier in the Gospel according to Mark there is a scene where people come to Jesus bearing a paralyzed man. The crowd around Jesus is so dense that they cannot get him into direct contact with the sufferer, so they take the roof off the dwelling where Jesus is teaching and they lower the man down. Jesus sees the faith of the man and of those who have brought him and he says quite simply, "Son, your sins are forgiven" (Mark 2.5). The scribes—professional priests—who are present are angry. Who is this man to forgive sins? Only God can forgive sins.

Jesus feels their disquiet and he says to them, "Which is easier to say to the paralytic, 'Your sins are forgiven' or to say 'Stand up and take your mat and walk'?" He continues, "But so you may know that the Son of Man has authority on earth to forgive sins, I say to you, stand up, and take your mat and go to your home" (Mark 2.8–9). And the man does. All who witness the event are amazed.

They believe that they have seen a miracle and in a sense they have. But the miracle is in all probability a miracle of perception and humane generosity. Jesus has unparalleled ability to read people. He can look into their faces, observe their postures, note their gaits, and know them with an uncanny accuracy. Walking down the road one day, he sees a tax collector named Levi. Who is more detested than a tax collector, who grinds the people to serve the authorities in the temples and to enrich the imperial power of Rome? Yet Jesus passes by Levi and sees something in his face. (From what we can tell, the two exchange no words.) "Follow me," Jesus says to him, and Levi drops what he is doing and he follows (Mark 2.14). "Follow me," is Jesus' great expostulation. It doesn't simply mean drop what you're doing right now—stop working your account books or going to market—though it does mean that. It means follow me for life. Live as I do, out in the open air; believe as I do, in the promise of human beings to break loose from what confines them; be kind and gentle to those who need it and stand up to the various intellectual bullies and oppressors who dot the path.

Follow me. Levi takes Jesus to his home and holds a banquet in his honor. The guests are Levi's friends, not the most pious or respectable crowd. When detractors criticize Jesus for consorting with the likes of Levi, he replies that physicians consort with the sick and not the well, and that he is here to save the sinners and not the pious. (The conventionally pious are often beyond hope. They think too well of themselves to change.) Jesus reads Levi accurately—as he reads so many others—and Levi has the chance to live as a better man (Mark 2.13–17).

Jesus apparently reads the paralytic rightly, too. Perhaps what he sees is that this man is—as many of us have been and will be—paralyzed, not so much by some physical malady as by guilt, fear, or anxiety. He is frozen by his sense of unworthiness. Stand up, says Jesus, start again: your sins are forgiven. You and those who brought you here, and who clearly love you, have faith that you can overcome the forces impeding you—all you need is a brisk shove. Jesus is happy to administer the shove. What Northrop Frye says about the miracles of Jesus is often true: they "depended on the belief of the recipient. A real miracle is an imaginative effort which meets with an imaginative response. Jesus could give sight to the blind and activity to the paralyzed only when they did not want to be blind or paralyzed; he stimulated and encouraged them to shatter their own physical prisons" (81–82).

Granted, the Gospels show Jesus performing miracles that seem supernatural. He walks across the water with equanimity. He raises Lazarus from the dead. But around such a figure, it is inevitable that legends will accrue. Jesus' most revealing miracles are miracles of perception and love. What do they reveal? They reveal a new way of being in the world, based on compassion, love, and the forgiveness of sins. One emphasizes Jesus' miracles of spirit, rather than of matter, under the belief that they open the door to a State of Soul. To this way of thinking, the miracles of matter lead only to more superstition and to the closing off of human possibility. The objective of these reflections is not to identify the true and only Jesus, but to focus on the Jesus that leads us from Self to Soul, the Jesus who is the spiritual brother of Buddha and Confucius.

Does Jesus literally turn water into wine when he attends the wedding in Galilee? Maybe. Maybe he does. But it's also true that when one is stimulated by the company of a young man about to bring the good news to the world, the water may taste more than a little like wine.

When Jesus sees a group of men about to stone to death a woman supposedly caught committing adultery, he doesn't resort to magic to stop them. He simply tells them to look into their own hearts and know themselves as the sinners that they (and we all) are. We can dissolve guilty feelings in ourselves by transferring them to another, then punishing her. But that gives us only temporary reprieve and creates more guilt in its turn. Better to face our own reservoir of guilt and do something about it. Stop and think: examine yourself. Let him who is without sin cast the first stone. Does stopping a blood-hungry group of men with a simple expostulation qualify as a miracle? If not, what does?

Guilt is one of the deadliest weapons in the Selfhood's arsenal. It cripples men and women, both in the body and in the spirit. One of Jesus' central messages is that no sin is unforgivable if the sinner is truly sorry. He tells individuals to throw off the griefs of the past and start again, try to be a good man or a good woman. Go and sin no more, Jesus says repeatedly in the Gospels. At that moment, the ones who hear him are born anew if they have the strength to be. How many of us are in some measure disabled by the burden of past sins? We can't get beyond our guilt or regret, or our anger about what happened in the past. Nietzsche said that one of the most disabling human maladies is resentment against time and time's It Was. We want to turn back time and correct the past. Or we spend our days wishing that the past had never been what it was. The kingdom of heaven is now, Jesus tells us—throw off the old inhibitions, throw off guilt and live in the present. Pick up your bed and walk.

William Blake, who idolized Jesus and disliked Yahweh, at least as he is conventionally imagined, thought that the forgiveness of sins was at the center of Jesus' teachings. "Throughout all Eternity" Blake says, "I forgive you[,] you forgive me / As our dear Redeemer said / This the Wine & this the Bread" (477). Jesus is the power in us that wants to learn from the past but not be suffocated by it. It's the part that is always ready for a new beginning, in which we cast off the Selfhood like a suit made of rotten rags and live. For Blake, the heart of the Gospels is not the crucifixion or the last supper, the suffering and death that Yahweh seems to require as a sacrifice to redeem the sins of man. It is the doctrine of forgiveness. Jesus is asked how often a man should forgive the crimes of someone who has sinned against him. Once, twice, seven times? Of course, the

Savior says. For nothing curdles the heart as much as the spirit of revenge. "Not seven times," Jesus says, "but, I tell you, seventy-seven times." (Matthew 18.22).

Jesus' capacity to read people—to sense where it is they stand with the Selfhood—is often thoroughly kind, as it is with the paralytic, frozen in his misery. But it can have an edge as well. A young man approaches Jesus and asks him what he needs to do to inherit eternal life. Jesus looks into the man's face, listens to his voice, and clearly perceives that he is rather conventionally pious—though maybe he desires to be more. Keep the commandments, he tells the young man. Don't murder, don't bear false witness, don't commit adultery, and don't steal. Honor your father and your mother. "Teacher," says the young man, "I have kept all these since my youth" (Mark 10.20).

Surely Jesus sees a glint of something promising in the young man, something that might help him pass beyond the standard, often passive, virtues. "You lack one thing," Jesus says. "Go, sell what you own, and give the money to the poor, and you will have treasure in heaven; then come, follow me" (Mark 10.21). Jesus, out of compassion for this questing young man, who lives with the conventional virtues, opens up a new way of life. Sell what you have and give it to the poor. Then the great injunction: Come, and follow me. Throw the Selfhood off and live fully in the present, above time. But the young man cannot do it. He is unable to crack the crust of his conventional goodness. "When he heard this," the Gospel says, "he was shocked and went away grieving, for he had many possessions" (Mark 10.22).

But Jesus has given him the chance to know himself, even if the self-knowledge he achieves is harsh. The young man thought he had a stronger spiritual drive than he did. He thought he was ready to enter the heaven that Jesus offers: the heaven of the Soul here and now. It's a heaven that brings unity and fullness of being and a presence in this world but not of it, a presence that exists above time—for time is simply the medium in which we hope to achieve our desires. Sell your goods and give them to the poor—the man cannot do it. But now, thanks to Jesus, he knows what separates him from eternal life. And maybe in time he will change. Northrop Frye, speaking from the vantage of Blake, observes that "sensible people will tell us that it is foolish to throw everything to the winds, to give all one's goods to the poor and live entirely without caution or prudence. But they will not tell us the one thing we need most to know: that we are all born into a world of liquid chaos as a man falls into the sea, and that we must either sink or swim to land because we are not fish" (80). Sensible people will not tell us this, but Jesus will.

When the young man leaves, Jesus broods aloud to his apostles. "How hard it will be," he says, "for those who have wealth to enter the kingdom of God" (Mark 10.23). There is little if anything in the Hebrew Bible that declares against wealth—to grow rich honestly is a sign of favor from the Lord. What Jesus says is shocking. But all he means, one might assume, is that money is a medium of desire. If you have money, and money to spare, you can spend your time imagining what you will buy with it: houses, land, livestock, and brides. You can buy those things and wish for more and maintain your being inside time. The man without money is less tempted to spend his life imagining what he will acquire, enjoying his new acquisitions, and guarding the goods he already possesses. He can think about the one thing the young man lacks—the one thing that is everything. That one thing is freedom from the bonds of this world—the getting and spending by which, as Wordsworth has it, "we lay waste our powers." "Martha," says Jesus at another moment, talking to his friend, "you are worried and distracted by many things; there is need of only one thing" (Luke 10.41–42).

Why is Jesus such an inspired reader of others? How is he able to look into the heart of the young man who wants eternal life and see his strength but also sense his limits? Jesus sees clearly, one might conjecture, because he has elevated himself above desires. He does not want or need anything from anyone else. If people will feed him and his disciples, very well. If they will give them shelter, good. Jesus is grateful. But if these gifts do not come readily, well then they will come in time. If people want to listen to what Jesus says, he is not displeased. He is confident that he offers the key to joy. But if they do not care to listen to him that is their affair; they can go their ways. To any number of people he utters what may be the most beautiful words in the Gospels, come and follow me. But if they do not follow, he seems un-distressed. He wants joy for them, not elevation for himself. Because he is beyond desire and committed to hope, Jesus can see into the hearts of those who are tormented by desire, or who, having spent a life desiring the paltry things of this earth, now hunger to break free.

Jesus deals with the Pharisees and the other high priests of what he feels has become a hierophantic religion by laughing at them. He shows repeatedly that he can outsmart them in debate, while at the same time demonstrating that debate doesn't matter much. An excessive reliance on the mind makes men ignore the spirit and ignore the needs of their fellow men and women. When they criticize him for healing on the Sabbath because it breaks the commandment to "keep holy the Lord's day," Jesus seems to become genuinely angry. "Is it lawful to do good or to do harm on the Sabbath, to save life or to kill?" (Mark 3.4). Jesus is here in behalf of life and the restoration of life, and they matter every day of the week.

Jesus has a particular affinity for those who have not been overcome by the full force of the Selfhood. In the spiritual philosophies of Confucius and of Buddha, there is no salient place for the child. The ideal there is the adult who has evolved to a high degree of intellectual prowess but has also developed (or sustained) a capacity for humane feeling. For Jesus, the child is a crucial image of enlightenment. To be saved, we need to make ourselves open and receptive in the manner of a child. We need to have faith that if we risk loving our neighbors, we will receive love in return. When the disciples try to keep children away from Jesus, he reprimands them. "Let the little children come to me, and do not stop them" he says, "for it is to such as these that the kingdom of God belongs. Truly I tell you, whoever does not receive the kingdom of God as a little child will never enter it" (Luke 18.16–17). He is supremely protective of them. "If any of you put a stumbling block before one of these little ones who believe in me, it would be better for you if a great millstone were hung around your neck and you were thrown into the sea" (Mark 9.42). The gospel of Jesus is a song of innocence—one must throw off the false garb of experience and then struggle, often fiercely, to maintain an open heart. Innocence has to be reclaimed.

It is not inconsequential that the Gospel relates the infancy of Jesus. The man who turns up at the age of thirty spreading the good news is, in his generous innocence, directly related to the child born in the unprotected manger. The child is father to the man, says Wordsworth, and, at least in the case of Jesus, it is so. In the Gospels, the babe is the holy teacher's true progenitor. Jesus will always be directly related to the child visited by shepherds and magi. In Eliot's wise poem, "The Journey of the Magi," the sages from the pagan east, returning home, are never happy again in the old dispensation, with their summer palaces, their sorbets, and their dancing girls, having seen what they have in the stable. Their decadent world of Self has been disturbed by a child.

Jesus often surrounds himself with women—people who possess no substantial power in patriarchal Rome or Jerusalem. And he takes their part. When men are about to stone the women caught in adultery, he utters the famous words: Let him who is without sin cast the first stone. Jesus understands that whatever the women may or may not have done, it is not nearly so heinous as the righteous pleasure that the men clearly would take in murdering her. After Jesus issues his rebuttal the accusers walk away. He looks up at the woman and asks: "Has no one condemned you?" She tells him that no one has. "Neither do I condemn you. Go your way and from now on do not sin again" (John 8.11). Women and children are not overt images of Soul in the Gospels; only Jesus at his most imaginative and generous fills that role. But the life of the modest, mild, and innocent is a gateway to the eternal life that Jesus promises.

Rome is another presiding image of Selfhood in the Gospels—it bears down on Jesus in much the way that the teachings of the Pharisees do. (So the sophists, and eventually the state, bear down on Socrates, who teaches young men without pay and urges them to question all matters on the earth.) Jesus' attitude to Rome is anything but simple. It can, in fact, be rather surprising.

The Romans are in one sense the enemies of Jesus, as they are the enemies of all the Jews. The Romans are the conquerors, the Jews the conquered. By refusing to assimilate themselves to the Roman religion, keeping their rituals and their faith in the Lord, the Jews have become a "stiff necked people" in the eyes of their conquerors. The Jews have a history of being conquered and oppressed, but they have a historical memory of freedom, too. They sought and found it and for a while thrived in the Promised Land.

The story of Jesus and the centurion is well known. A Roman centurion, commander of a company of a hundred men, has a dear servant who is sick and on the border of death. He sends messengers to Jesus and asks him to help. As Jesus approaches the house where the servant is lying ill, the centurion comes out, meets Jesus, and tells him that he is not worthy that Jesus should come under his roof. Speak but the word, the centurion says, and my servant will be healed. Jesus marvels at the man's faith, which is greater, he says, than that of many of his own people. The man's servant is immediately made whole.

What matters most here is that Jesus is ready to extend his teaching to the conquerors. His message about the way to enter heaven now is not only for the Jews, it is for the members of the imperial army should any of them choose it. This ministry is not about strengthening the Jews at the expense of anyone else; it contains wisdom for all. Of course, should all Romans take Jesus' teachings to heart, the Jews would no longer be a subject people. For Jesus preaches equality among men, not domination of one race or people over another. For him all people have been chosen for the possibility of a joy that arises when they overcome the Selfhood. The way to end Roman supremacy isn't through armed rebellion—the Jews will try this and fail twice, shortly after the death of Jesus—it is to open up the gospel of peace to all.

In time, Rome will be overtaken by the message of the Gospel, Constantine will convert, and the Roman Empire will become—with multiple contradictions involved—a Christian empire. Gazing at the cross, Constantine will famously say: Under this sign I shall conquer. How much and how little the so-called Christian empire actually was Christian—that is, steeped in the teachings of compassionate Jesus—is, to say the least, an open question.

Perhaps the best known of Jesus' encounters with Rome comes when Pharisees approach him and ask if it is right to pay taxes to the Roman overlords. If Jesus says it is not correct to pay the taxes, he is a rebel and the Romans can suppress him. If he says it is right, then Jesus is an imperial lackey and Jews will be more likely to ignore him. Bring me a coin, Jesus says to them. They bring him a Roman token. Now whose picture is on it? It is the picture of the Roman emperor, Augustus, adopted son of Julius Caesar. Then from the Savior the famous lines: Render unto Caesar that which is Caesar's. Render unto God that which is God's.

Jesus draws a stark dividing line through experience. There is that which belongs to the emperor and that which belongs to God.

There is the life of Jesus and there is the business of the world. Soul exists and must exist in relation to Self. It behooves every individual to understand the difference between these states. The living man or woman must fully comprehend his relation to worldliness. All of us may not be able to live like Jesus. His own distance from worldly matters is signified by the fact that he must ask one of his questioners for a coin. "Bring me a denarius," he says, "and let me see it" (Mark 12.15). He is apparently not carrying one himself. This fact, as much as Jesus' answer, conveys his relation to the question. If you are as pure as Jesus, you owe nothing to Caesar and everything to your conception of God. Others may be compelled to set the terms of the equation differently. But what matters here is that they stop and think, as Jesus does, and then set those terms. How much must I give to Caesar and Selfhood—if anything? What do I have left for the Soul?

At the center of Jesus' gospels is compassion, loving-kindness. He shows it to his own people, he shows it to the Romans. But compassion is sometimes a difficult virtue to sustain even for the teacher himself. In Mark's Gospel a Gentile woman, a Syrophoenician, comes and bows down before Jesus and begs him to cast a demon out of her daughter. Jesus says to her: "Let the children be fed first, for it is not fair to take the children's food and throw it to the dogs" (Mark 7.27). Jesus' language is shocking. Because this woman is a Gentile, not a Jew, he calls her and her daughter dogs. But the woman is undaunted. "Sir," she says, "even the dogs under the table eat the children's crumbs" (Mark 7.28). We've heard your teachings, the woman all but says, and there's nothing in them that applies to Jews and Jews alone. The good news is for all of us. Jesus is surprised by her resolve. "For saying that," he replies, "you may go—the demon has left your daughter" (Mark 7.29).

The story may well dramatize Jesus' own clinging to the old ways. He is still able to think of himself as a member of a tribe that is in conflict with other tribes. The sense of his universal mission is not always fully with him. And if this broadly loving view is hard for Jesus to sustain, it can only be more difficult for other men and women. Here Jesus is willing to be taught by another, a woman, and set again on the path of compassion. Like most of us he is tempted by the belief that only those who look like us and speak our language and follow our customs are genuinely human. The rest are Gentiles, the rest are, perhaps, dogs. The struggle to attain the Soul State of compassion is great—great for us, and at least on one occasion, it is a challenge for Jesus himself. "Do not give what is holy to dogs," Jesus says in Matthew, "and do not throw your pearls before swine, or they will trample them underfoot and turn and maul you" (7.6). The passage is interpretable in many ways. But after the encounter with the Syrophoenician woman, it surely evokes Jesus' occasionally wavering view of who is permitted to hear the gospel of compassion and who is not.

Jesus does not always act in a conventionally pious way. He doesn't always live in perfect tune with his own teachings. In the temple he picks up a whip to chase the moneylenders away. He blasts the fig tree because something about it offends him. What it is we do not really know. He tells his disciples that when people refuse them hospitality, they need to shake off the dust from their feet on the offenders' doorsteps, and retribution will follow. Jesus apparently has a willful, wayward streak with which he struggles. Like the Buddha he is human and heir to the sorrows and temptations attendant. Like the Buddha, he is not unlike ourselves.

In the Gospel of Mark, Jesus makes his own confusion about his role manifest. Pious commentators tend to believe that Jesus is posing a rhetorical question when he asks his followers: "Who do men say I am?" But there is more than a small chance that Jesus is being quite sincere. His own teaching is so original, even while being potently traditional, that it would be no wonder if he were inclined to be confused about his identity and his mission. He may also be afraid—Jesus is afraid more than once in the Gospels—that if he is manifest to others as the Messiah, they will expect what he cannot deliver and in time turn against him in disillusioned rage. Jesus is a complex and imperfect figure, which can make his commitment to the ideal all the more moving.

We must love our neighbor, Jesus says. But who is our neighbor? A lawyer asks him this question, and Jesus answers with one of the most memorable stories in the Gospels. A traveler is beaten and robbed, thrown into a ditch, and left to die. Past him go two members of his own group who see him and do nothing. They simply continue on their ways. But there comes another man, a Samaritan, someone from another tribe. He sees the suffering man in the ditch and he does not pass him by. He gathers the man up, mounts him on his own beast, and takes him to an inn. There he binds the man's wounds and sees that he is bathed and made comfortable. He gives the innkeeper money and promises to return to settle the rest of the ailing man's bill. Now which of these, the Samaritan or the man's own tribesman, was a neighbor to the Samaritan? "The one who showed him mercy," the lawyer says. To which Jesus responds: "Go and do likewise" (Luke 10.37).

Love your neighbor as yourself: this is the central teaching of Jesus. It can seem hard, almost impossible to do. But Jesus indicates that it is the way to liberation. Loving your neighbor as yourself can free you from competition and strife. It can bring you into the community of men and women and help you feel that you belong. Loving your neighbor as yourself, or trying to, you can breathe more calmly. You can feel that you are at home in the world. The great phrase—love your neighbor as yourself—occurs famously in Leviticus: "You shall not take vengeance or bear a grudge against any of your people, but you shall love your neighbor as yourself" (Leviticus 19.18). But here "your neighbor" is one of "your people." Jesus seeks to expand the dictum to encompass everyone who lives; he seems to be both respecting and radically revising the Hebrew Bible.

Through his example and his teachings Jesus cultivates a new way to live, one based not on justice but on loving-kindness. ("Use every man after his desert," says Hamlet "and who shall scape whipping?") But he does something else almost as significant. He works to change the established conception of God. He works to bring his followers' idea of God the Father progressively further into line with the new teachings. For between Jesus and the God of the Hebrew Bible there is a gap. Writing in his notebooks, André Gide says: "I should note down at once the main lines that I see becoming clear, with greater sharpness and vigor than ever—of the antagonism between Christ and God—of Christ's *error* . . . of claiming that he was closely associated with God" (440). This is extreme: there are potent continuities between Christ and the faith of Yahweh. But there are major disjunctions as well.

When Jesus begins his ministry, the Jewish conception of God is well in place. The God of the Old Testament is a war god yes, but preeminently he is the God of justice. Justice is the central virtue of the Hebrew Bible—those mortals who are just are first among men and women. The Old Testament God is also the God of retribution. When you disobey his commandments he takes revenge, as the Jews learn many times to their sorrow. He drowns the world when it becomes sinful; he destroys the cities on the plain when they sink into depravity. He can be protective and supremely loving. But you must follow his plan, keep the covenant, obey the commandments.

Jesus is occasionally responsive to the image of the retributive God. Kindly as he can be, Jesus sometimes seems to revel in his sense of God's capacity to repay sin with dire punishment. Jesus tells with seeming relish the story of the rich man who was sent to Hell to burn in everlasting torment, while the beggar Lazarus who lived outside his gate was carried away by angels to the bosom of Abraham.

The rich man cries out for a touch of water to cool his tongue. No. He asks to return to earth if only for a moment to warn his sinning brothers there about what awaits them. No, Abraham tells him. You've had your chance and will live in eternal torment (Luke 16.19–31).

Jesus informs his disciples that when they come to a town to preach the word they should seek out the worthy and abide with them. But he also tells them that if anyone denies them welcome, they must take a certain sort of revenge. "If anyone will not welcome you or listen to your words," Jesus says, "shake off the dust from your feet as you leave that house or town. Truly I tell you, it will be more tolerable for the land of Sodom and Gomorrah on the day of judgment than for that town" (Matthew 10.14–15).

Here Jesus echoes Yahweh, both in voice and values.

But at his most original and provocative Jesus tries to change the existing sense of who and what God is. He tells his followers that God is a loving father who will nurture and care for them. He points to the birds in the fields and he tells the people that God loves each one of them. And if God cares so much for a mere sparrow, imagine how much he cares for creatures made in his image. "Are not five sparrows sold for two pennies? Yet not one of them is forgotten in God's sight. But even the hairs of your head are all counted. Do not be afraid; you are of more value than many sparrows" (Luke 12.6–7).

Jesus tells his followers the story of the lost sheep. A shepherd has a hundred sheep in his flock and he loses one. What does the shepherd do? Does he stay where he is protecting the ninety-nine? No, he goes in pursuit of the wandering lamb. "The Lord is my shepherd," the great psalm says—but it is hard to imagine anyone in the Hebrew Bible saying or believing that the Lord God is so full of loving-kindness that he will go far out of his path for just one commonplace being. "Just so, I tell you," Jesus says, "there will be more joy in heaven over one sinner who repents than over ninety-nine righteous persons who need no repentance" (Luke 15.7). When a man wanders from the Hebrew God, there is no assurance that God will take him back into the fold. There are some second chances in the Hebrew Bible (David gets about a half dozen), but the second chance based on forgiveness is not the order of the day.

As Frye, writing in Blake's spirit, puts it, Jesus "said that God was a Father and that we should live the imaginatively unfettered lives of children, growing as spontaneously as the lilies without planning or foresight. The God of his parables is an imaginative God who makes no sense whatever as a Supreme Bookkeeper, rewarding the obedient and punishing the disobedient. Those who labor all day for him get the same reward as those who come in at the last moment. His kingdom is like a pearl of great price which it will bankrupt us to possess. If we want wise and temperate advice on living we shall find it in Caesar sooner than in Christ; there is more of it in Marcus Aurelius than there is in the Gospels" (80). The God that Jesus is describing is a radically new *version* of the established God. He is a deity who loves all equally, who cares dearly for his creations, who is tender and mild—it is, in short, a God the Father who is much like Jesus himself. The Gospels often serve as a brilliant reconfiguration of the Hebrew God on the part of Jesus Christ.

Of course Jesus never tells the people that this is what he is doing. Jesus does not say, The God you have believed in up until this point is not quite the real God. Rather, he begins with part of the standing version of the deity: yes, God is powerful, God is a grand creator, God is eternal. But gradually he shifts the portrait. God is also tender, kindhearted, and merciful. He is much like the father in the story of the prodigal son.

The tale of the prodigal son is a brilliant parable that reveals almost every individual to himself or herself. One does not so much read the parable as one is read by it. A young man tires of his life at home and he goes to his father and asks for his half of the inheritance. His father gives him the money, and the young man goes out into the world, where, in a life of sin, he wastes all he's been given. He's reduced to misery, tending pigs that eat better food than he does. The servants in my father's house live more comfortably than this, he thinks to himself. Why don't I simply return and throw myself on my father's mercy?

He resolves to go back to his former home where he expects to be chastised and at best to live the life of a slave. But his father sees that his son is coming down the road and runs out and meets him. "While he was still far off his father saw him and was filled with compassion; he ran and put his arms around him and kissed him" (Luke 15.20). He puts a robe around his shoulders and a ring on his hand. Kill the fatted calf, he orders. Our son who has been gone is now returned; the one who is lost has been found.

But the wealthy man has another son who is older, and this son is displeased. Why did you welcome my brother back with such joy and ceremony, he wants to know. Why have you never treated me with this kind of respect? Never have you given me a goat to slaughter and enjoy with my friends. His father assures his older son that he loves and honors him, but he also says that he is jubilant at the return of his brother and wants to express his joy.

The brother who has stayed home and lived a life of duty and respect claims *justice*. And he has many sympathizers among readers. They too have been dutiful; they too have done what's been asked of them. And now they get less than the spirited wastrel? They do not like the prodigal son—for they hope to be saved by what is often not much more than dull virtue. But Jesus will not have it so. The father of the prodigal saves people because he is merciful; Jesus preaches to the people, risking his life in the process, and finally losing it, because he himself is merciful. And, the parable suggests,

Yahweh, the father who is the father of all, is far more merciful than his followers previously imagined. If you come to him asking for justice, you may get a sterile reception. But if you come to Yahweh asking for mercy, he will behave much as Jesus would do—he will enfold you in his arms and welcome you back to your heart's true home.

Who is Jesus talking to in the passages where he tries to shift the image of Yahweh? Surely Jesus is talking to his pupils—he is addressing his disciples and the crowds that follow him, seemingly everywhere, to hear his teachings. But is it possible that Jesus has another auditor in mind? Maybe Jesus is actually talking to the Lord God himself. Maybe Jesus is trying to persuade God that it is time to relinquish his identity as a terrible figure of retribution and to adopt another, more generous, milder form. Would it not be wonderful, Jesus implicitly asks Yahweh, if you could be loved more and feared less? God as Jesus finds him generates respect, admiration, awe. But he surely does not always provoke authentic love, even from those who worship him fervently. Yahweh, as Jesus finds him, is emphatically male. He is proud and easily offended. He rarely misses a chance to demonstrate his displeasure when he has been offended.

Jesus offers the world of men and women something new. Maybe the good news is based in the forgiveness of sins, as Blake says, or in a new dispensation where you love your neighbor as yourself. These are marvelous breakthroughs. But to offer God the opportunity to transform himself into another sort of being, one who will have a much different and ultimately more profound relation with his people: what could be more daring—and more promising for humanity? The God that Jesus describes is still potent, still capable of violent action. But he is now also inspired by ever-forgiving affection for what he has created.

But what are we to make of the close of Jesus life? What are we to make of the crucifixion? "This was a great Defeat," says Emerson of the horrible event. "We demand Victory." The remark is enigmatic. What precisely would have qualified as victory for Emerson? What ought Jesus to have done at the point when he stood before Pilate and refused to defend himself?

Whatever the answer, the crucifixion—the willing self-sacrifice of Jesus—can look like a concession to Yahweh at his most brutal. God demanded blood recompense for the crime of Adam, and Jesus offered himself up. This is surely nothing less than a case of human sacrifice. The desert gods with whom Yahweh competed for preeminence early in time were, we believe, inclined to human sacrifice. They were placated by the slaughter of innocents. Perhaps Yahweh is tempted; the supreme tribute that humanity can pay to a god is surely the offering up of the lives of sons and daughters to earn his favor. It seems that Yahweh comes close to demanding the sacrifice of an innocent when he commands Abraham to do away with Isaac, only at the last moment staying his hand.

What if Jesus had refused to become a human sacrifice? What if he told his Father, or the patriarchal spirit, that the murder of innocence has no part in the new dispensation? In the garden of Gethsemane Jesus prays to the Father to spare him. Let this cup pass over me, Jesus says. Do not force me to become a bleeding victim. Yahweh, as Jesus construes him, declines to show mercy, and the crucifixion proceeds on its horrifying course. But what if Jesus had taken it upon himself to escape? Suppose he had simply left the premises and let matters go on without him? Then Jesus would have fully repudiated the faith in guilt, sacrifice, and retribution. He would have fully disowned violence.

But theologically, Jesus is a revisionist, not ultimately a rebel. He does not want to dissociate himself from God out and out. His values may differ radically enough from the values of the Hebrew Bible for him to have founded a new religion, but Jesus strives for as much continuity with the old order as he can reasonably achieve. He does not want a full break.

Why? Why doesn't Jesus become a prophet of humanity, in the mode of Buddha and Confucius, figures who are not terribly attached to transcendental gods? The Buddha never tired of insisting on his mortal identity. What are you, people asked him. I am a man, I will die, just as you will. Perhaps Jesus understands the need for the abiding father figure who grants stability to the turbulent lives of mortals. Maybe he comprehends the need for a loving father (and indeed even a punitive one), as well as for the inspiring brother and teacher that he is. We long for the father, it's been said. Humanely, generously, Jesus grants the satisfaction of this wish. Jesus does all he can to revise Yahweh, to make him less a fearful figment of our childlike imaginations. But beyond that he will not go. His last act, as Blake suggests, was to consent to his own crucifixion—for he could presumably have fled, foreseeing it in the garden as he did; or master dialectician that he was, he could have defended himself against Pilate.

Had Jesus said no to the sacrifice, he would have been saying no to the Lord God. He would have broken off, begun a faith entirely his own. But Jesus would not put too much pressure on mankind. (Human Kind, the poet famously says, cannot bear very much reality.) Jesus did what he could to modify the standing conception of the deity, and he brought into the world his religion of love and forgiveness. He taught the West compassion and opened up another possibility for the life of Soul.

The Soul States of courage and compassion seem quite different, and in some senses they are. The hero fights: he aspires to fight with justice on his side, but his world is the world of war. The saint lives for kindliness and respects all living beings—all that exists is holy, the scriptures of what has come to be called the Axial Age proclaim. Yet both of these states bring on unity of being. They bequeath joy, full presence to life, immediacy. Those who have committed themselves to the ideals are made complete, rather than walking sites of contending elements. The life of the hero and the saint may be short; Jesus dies young, so do many of those who have emulated Achilles, emulated Hector. But while they last, those lives are charged with meaning. Such figures can lead lives of constant allegory, as Keats said of Shakespeare. Everything they do has an archetypal status— they aspire to be living in and sometimes even creating patterns for virtuous human action that will continue on through time. Every achievement of theirs becomes a standard to guide and inspire others.

The hero and the saint are both wanderers in the world. When he is told that his mother and brothers and sisters are outside the temple where he is preaching, Jesus says to the crowd: You are my family. You are my mother and father; you are my brothers and my sisters. "Whoever does the will of God is my brother and sister and mother" (Mark 3.35). To live the life of Soul, it is often necessary to walk away from the pleasures of the home. Achilles is not happy knowing that he will never see his father Peleus again, but he accepts the fact as part of the hero's destiny.

The hero and the saint wander the earth. They go not where they wish to go, but where they are needed. Achilles and his descendants go to war all over the globe; Jesus and his true followers visit the suffering men and women, who need the gospel of compassion, wherever they may be. The heart can become full only when one separates oneself from one's origins and turns in the direction of the ideal.

Neither the hero nor the saint cares much for material wealth. The hero is happy to amass treasure, but the treasure he collects is chiefly a signifier. It tells the world about his achievements. Each piece of treasure he owns has a story attached to it. He knows where he won such and such a sword, who gave him this gold cup for brave deeds. He also delights in distributing what he owns. Achilles, presiding over the funeral games for Patroclus, takes pleasure in the god-like activity of deciding who will compete, who wins and loses, and who gets the prize—which he also delights in presenting. Pieces of treasure are signifiers, tokens of glory.

The hero may in time return to a comfortable home—but the pleasures of home matter little to him. Like Tennyson's Ulysses, he cannot stay still. Ulysses, back from Troy, sees that his son Telemachus is a prudent ruler, who loves the pleasures of the hearth. But Ulysses is no such man—he understands it clearly. So he is off again looking for adventure, looking for trouble, even though he is old. "Though much is taken," he says, "much abides; and though / We are not now that strength which in old days / Moved earth and heaven, that which we are, we are." Soon he will be journeying again, seeking adventure, seeking immortal deeds.

"Render unto Caesar that which is Caesar's," Jesus says, looking at the coin. The true saint has no time for the coin of this world. He does not seek wealth. To him wealth is an impediment. For, as the Savior says, it is easier for a camel to pass through the eye of a needle than for a rich man to enter the kingdom of heaven. The man who pursues wealth pursues many ends. He wants this suit of clothes, that conveyance, such and such a dwelling. But the saint seeks one thing. The saint seeks a life full of meaningful compassion. The acquisition of goods, the piling up of wealth, only serves to draw force from his proper pursuit. The saint lives—or tries to live—beyond desire. The saint lives for hope.

For the individual who lives in the Self, desire is all determining. He wants certain precise and particular objects. His life is determined by wants. He could almost write his autobiography based on his desire for this or that object and his success (or failure) in at-taining it. He wanted a better house, he wanted a swimming pool, a second car was needful—and lo, the event came, and he had what he wished. But the having was as nothing.

Does the saint not also desire? Doesn't he desire sainthood? Not quite. He aspires to ideals, which cannot be possessed in the way that a car, a house, or a lover can be. He wants to embody a set of values and live by them moment to moment. He does not want the happiness that acquisition can bring—if it can. He wants the joy that comes from committing to an ideal. And he recognizes that such joy is dangerous—neither Achilles nor Jesus, nor legions of other warriors and saints, stayed alive very long.

The man or woman committed to ideals doesn't live for desire but for hope. The idealist hopes for joy and presence and unity, not only for himself but for others. A generous impulse lies behind aspiration to the ideal: that much is palpable in Jesus, the Buddha, Confucius, and Hector. Achilles is a more complex case. He does not always seem to care about anyone except himself. But when the dangerous war comes, people look to the descendants of Achilles to carry the fight to the enemy. Achilles is not always beloved, but he is needed, and often desperately, by others. He's especially vital to his fellow warriors. There's an eloquent passage, attributed (wrongly one suspects) to Heraclitus, that crystallizes the value of Achilles and the Achilles-like warrior. "Out of every one hundred men, ten shouldn't be there, eighty are just targets, nine are the real fighters and we are lucky to have them, for they make the battle. Ah, but the one, one is a warrior and he will bring the others back." Hector is a just and admirable man, the sort of person we ourselves might aspire to be. But if one has to pick an archetypal soldier to send into the fray to defend us, there is no doubt as to the choice.

The culture of Self does not know what to do with the lure of compassion. It is baffled by the attraction of collectivity. It does

know what to do with the temptation of the other Soul ideals—
fabricate them and sell them. Culture now largely *is* the counter-
feiting and sale of courage, contemplation, and imagination. The
denizen of the contemporary consumer utopia can buy himself a violent video game or howl with warrior joy when his football team
wins. He can believe that information is wisdom. He can believe that
true insights about the human condition infuse the news reports of
the day. He can imagine that the racket of a garage band or the me-
anderings of a fulminating rapper are art. But compassion is more
difficult to counterfeit.

Churches preach compassion. But many, if not most, are outright
in their worship of Mammon. The fund drive never ceases; the
minister is hot with the belief that the lord shows favor by the dis-
pensing of goods. ("Christianity has completely conquered," says
Kierkegaard, "that is, it is abolished.") The church that still claims
to care for the poor—and sometimes actually does—is ridden into
horrible absurdity by scandal. Jesus may have achieved a great deal
by maintaining the conjunction of the Old Testament and the
New—but he left potentially intact the worship of wealth and power
that the older book sometimes endorses. He did not pull Mammon
all the way down.

But our main defense against the collective is simply to insist on
the individual and nothing but the individual. Greed in our world
is good. Nothing succeeds like success. If you make it, you will be
undyingly happy. Succeed, succeed. Our worship of the individual
who seeks and finds triumph is unending—we have time for little
else. That success attained against others is sterile and lonely—that
fact we contemplate less. The ideal of a brotherhood and sisterhood
among all is now commonly understood to be an absurdity. We are
all in it for ourselves and for no one else. The notion that we can
only be happy when we love—rather than resenting and competing

with—one another is almost out of cultural circulation. Confucius is a curiosity. Buddha and the radical Jesus: they never were.

But this state cannot last forever. People will see that the war of each against all leaves everyone wounded. In time, Soul will reassert itself, and we will again make contact with the feeling of that group on the hill after they had followed Jesus for three days. They were tired and hungry. They were worried about what they would eat, how they would survive. But Jesus and the disciples had a few loaves and a few fishes, and they gave the crowd everything they possessed. The crowd responded in kind, with kindness. And behold, all were fed.

3

The Thinker

When does a human being attain the highest state? At what point is Soul most potently manifest? To these questions, the warrior tradition offers an unequivocal answer. The hero is the ultimate man. He lives for the intensity of being that comes from risking his life honorably in a high cause. He is whole and complete in himself then, for he merges perfectly with an ideal. The observing faculty that makes a human being not one but two dissolves, and the spirit burns with the light of the stars. (The warrior also becomes thoughtless, for the ideal takes the place of significant intellection. He does not ask himself why he acts as he does: the code directs him entirely.) The wholehearted warrior is rounded in his being, one with Nature, and at home in the world—or at least so Homer and the heroic tradition tell us.

The saint at her moments of supreme selflessness also achieves a perfection of being, which is in a sense a non-being. When she annuls Self to become one with the life that is the world's life, the saint arrives at a form of completion. She does not simply understand that there is "one life within us and abroad." Understanding is no longer relevant. She merges with that life and ministers to the being of others as if it were her own. The nun who goes to live among lepers, the monk who feeds the poor, the teacher of love who turns the other cheek, not out of cowardice but out of compassion: these people live a life of fullness, outside of time. Or at least so Jesus and the Buddha tell us.

Perhaps no life that one cannot wish for as a child offers a genuine sense of joy. Virtually no child dreams of being an accountant, an insurance salesman, or even a CEO. Children dream of courage and goodness—and so, in some regions of their spirits, do many adults. The poet Schiller compresses matters: "Hold fast to the dreams of your youth."

How is it possible to talk about both the saint and the warrior as inhabiting States of Soul when the two ideals seem so different? The warrior is a man of violence who lives for victory; the saint lives to heal. On some level, the hero loves war; the saint seeks the blessings of peace. But in this world, there will always be the need for both heroes and saints. Nations and peoples, no matter how just they may aspire to be, will always have enemies, and will always need someone to defend them. Plato, humane thinker that he was, could not imagine a time when there would be no wars. He hoped that a day would come when Greeks no longer fought with Greeks. But between Greeks and non-Greeks, the people he thought of as barbarians, there would inevitably be strife. And of course the world will never outgrow its need for compassion. The poor you have always with you, Jesus said. He might have added that the sick, the old, the grieving, and the mentally distressed will always be part of the world too, and they will forever need the ministrations of loving-kindness.

Perhaps some are made to be warriors, some to be saints—and perhaps there are those who should stay away from all ideals, not having the gifts to pursue them. But no culture can go on long pretending that ideals do not exist and that the world is made for Self and only Self. Without great goals for at least some men and women to aim for, life flattens out and becomes empty. The world goes a blander shade of pale. Without ideals, life lacks significant meaning. The person who lives for desire can experience many satisfactions, but they are temporary. There is the feeling of pleasure when the clothes are purchased, the new home secured, the promotion sealed. But these satisfactions do not last: every satisfied desire is replaced by a half dozen more that are yet to be fulfilled. By committing to ideals, men and women can escape the alternating peaks and low points that the life of desire creates and live in a more continuously engaged and satisfying way—though this way, of course, is not without serious dangers.

The ancient world confronts us with a third ideal, along with courage and compassion, one that, though it burns with a singular intensity, may not be available to all. This is the ideal of the thinker. Plato is its great exponent and exemplar. All philosophy and all images of the philosopher in the West descend from him and from his teacher, Socrates. To think seriously is to Platonize; to Platonize is to think. "Great havoc makes he among our originalities" (633), says Emerson of Plato, and it is so.

Plato teaches not only a grand system of thought; he also teaches us about the life of the thinker. Like the hero, the true thinker is a part of a small community. He is one of the few. But unlike the hero, who is supported by his tribe or his city—as Sarpedon in *The Iliad* insists that he and all warriors are—the thinker's relation to community is filled with tension; sometimes it puts him at risk. The archetypal thinker, as Plato describes him to us and as time corroborates the vision, is beset with privations. He surrenders much of this world in order to realize another. The things most men and women live for—power, pleasure, position—mean nothing to the thinker, except as they arise as impediments along the way. To attain his goal, which is Truth, the thinker often has to contend with poverty, loneliness, the dismaying weight of so-called past wisdom, the misunderstanding of others, and sometimes with persecution. But the potential reward is great: the thinker may actually come to see life as, in itself, it truly is, not only for the present but for the past and future as well; not only for his own culture, or the culture of the West or the East, but for all cultures, all men and women.

The thinker is, first of all, poor: he is poor in youth to be sure, and if middle and old age do not find him in modest circumstances at best, there is reason to believe he has betrayed his calling. He lives simply—Thoreau calls it the life of voluntary poverty—because a commitment to simplicity allows him to take his mind away from what does not matter. All material striving takes place in time—gray grinding Chronos—and the timely, the opportune, and the deadline impede genuine thought. The thinker must rise above time, just as he must rise above conformity and the demands of what Heidegger calls the They-self, if the thinker is going to achieve his goals. So, in his own fashions, he follows the example of Socrates, who wears a simple tunic summer and winter and is rarely seen by his contemporaries wearing shoes.

Like Thoreau, he is inclined to hang on dearly to his old clothes: Thoreau is, among many other things, a philosopher of clothes. He tells us to beware of any enterprise that requires new ones. No man ever stood lower in the estimation of Thoreau—the Socrates of Walden—because he wore a patch on his pants. If you have anything daunting to do, Thoreau says, do it in your old clothes. New clothes are an attempt to create a new self, without the attendant labor that goes into authentic self-remaking. Plato's guardians wear simple tunics; their natures, the philosopher claims, are of gold, but their garments homespun.

Socrates reputedly said that we must eat to live, not live to eat. The thinker avoids complex foods; he generally despises sauces and chefs. Thoreau's preference for corn mash, the beans he sowed and reaped and ate so as, he says, to "know beans," and the woodchuck he eventually shot and consumed (the extreme of dining luxury for him), signify his commitment to simple diet. One of Thoreau's moments of greatest delight in *Walden* comes when a neighboring farmer informs him that no one can be strong and healthy eating only vegetables. In front of the farmer, yoked to his plow, his enormous bullock paws the ground, munching grass.

When Nietzsche lives in Turin, during what was probably the only happy period of his life, he talks about his relish for the dinners at a certain trattoria. He boasts that in the market an old woman who has taken a particular interest in him saves him the plumpest, sweetest purple grapes. Does saying as much sound melancholy, sweetly sad on Nietzsche's part? It is part of his attempt to distance himself from the traditional renunciations of the thinker. He wishes to be a new kind of philosopher. But how much an austere life of material simplicity actually tempts Nietzsche! In *The Genealogy of Morals,* meaning to exorcise the spirit of the arch-ascetic Schopenhauer, Nietzsche begins to parody the philosopher's life of renunciation. He mocks the fastidious older thinker's resistance to certain pleasures. He laughs at Schopenhauer's aversion to frivolous books and to noise and seductive women. But in time the attempted dismissal turns into something close to a panegyric. Imagine a life that fully cleanses the body and the mind for the real work of thinking. Imagine living in such a way that you could know that when you left the world you had done all the work that was in you to do. Nietzsche dreams of "a deliberate obscurity; a side-stepping of fame; a backing away from noise, adulation, accolades, influence; a modest position, a quotidian existence, something which hides more than it reveals; occasional intercourse with harmless and gay birds and beasts, the sight of which refreshes, a mountainside for company, not a blind one but one with lakes for eyes; sometimes even a room at a crowded inn where one is sure of being mistaken for somebody else and may securely speak to anyone: such is our desert, and believe me, it is lonely enough" (244).

Nietzsche broods on his idol Schopenhauer with his massive cup of morning coffee, black as onyx; his four hours of writing; his lunchtime meal with friends at the club; his afternoon spent in the library; his ferocious walks, four miles, five, six; his slight supper, then an evening of opera, light opera if possible, to clear his head for tomorrow's work. This the great thinker does every day, living in an out-of-the-way town, consorting with people of no great interest or understanding, putting all his energy into work that might live for all time. When Schopenhauer learns that his long-ignored writing is being read and debated by the finest minds among the young in, of all places, England, he comes close to tears and says with great relish and even greater relief, "I am read! I am read and I shall be read!"

Nietzsche thinks also of Kant, the celestial virgin of idealist philosophy, walking his customary walk (you could set your clock to his perambulations), his rooms crammed with books, his unmarried state, his perfect devotion to the philosopher's art. In his later years, when his major work was done, Kant allowed himself an indulgence. This was his coffee. "Land," he would cry out, at the appointed time of day as his man brought the steaming pot to him. "I think that I see land." The old thinker had seen the full contents of his mind achieve form and expression. He had discovered and articulated new worlds. He'd done his work. Land, I think that I see land.

Of all the dangers that menace the authentic thinker on his path to the Truth, one of the most formidable is books. (The reckless love of reading is perhaps not quite comparable in strength to the love of fame, which Milton called "the last infirmity of noble mind," but its power is beyond doubt.) One can sense the true thinker almost surely by virtue of his fraught relations with reading. No authentic thinker could write an essay as unambivalently appreciative of books—books as repositories of wisdom, books as physical treasures (especially that)—as Walter Benjamin does in "Unpacking My Library." Benjamin adored his books. When he had ordered and shelved them, he was at home. The true thinker does not ever feel at home, at least on the phenomenal earth. Philosophy is not homesickness, as Novalis says it is. Rather philosophy is homelessness itself, a pained homelessness perhaps, but one replete with the understanding that the un-housed condition (physical, spiritual) is part of what makes genuine thought possible. The wanderer does not carry much. He cannot transport a library on his back, nor should he.

Socrates is he who does not write, nor does he appear to read a great deal. He learns what he does—which is, among other things, that there is no one in Athens wiser than he (though he knows nothing)—through conversation and experience. Famously he and Plato (great writer that he is) mistrust writing. Writing is a poison that dulls the mind, which needs to remember Truth on its own or discover it directly. Writing creates a duality: I and it; the text and me. Whereas unity, becoming identical with the Truth, is what the thinker wants. The true lords of life—the thinker, the saint, the hero, and (perhaps) the poet—are devoted to monism; they want to dissolve the gap between I and it, or between the I and the it that truly matters.

To the thinker, certain books are mere gossip. To be sure, for the thinker after Plato there are books that pay to read and reread, or to ignore with a passion. But thinkers ultimately think their own thoughts, which are the thoughts of humanity, or the thoughts of heaven, and not the thoughts of other individuals. For if you become a thinker, you believe that the work is not yet done. No one has seen the heavens and the earth as, in themselves, they really are.

Reading can take you away from your fundamental task. Thus Schopenhauer's view that most so-called philosophers read too much: they let others think their thoughts for them night and day. They are, in short, "reading themselves stupid." (It is safer to read the newspaper, which is at least self-acknowledged ephemera.) Nietzsche rambled across Europe seeking precisely the right climate, precisely the right diet (those grapes! That soup at the trattoria!). In his trunk he carried his many notebooks, for he wrote all night and into the morning, but few books, few if any. (The horrible parody of the thinker is the fearless dispatch runner Adolf Hitler, navigating the trenches of the First World War with both volumes of Schopenhauer's masterwork in his rucksack, misunderstanding them with a singular fury.) Nietzsche's memory was astounding, and after a certain point he probably did not read much; he wrote and he listened to Wagner—for some time his true inspiration—through the portals of his inner ear.

Emerson read, as he says, "for the lusters." He is not disposed to read consecutively, does not generally "read it through," as Johnson liked to say, unless a book enchants and seduces him, drawing him from his proper task, which is to find what is most original in himself. Thoreau reads and rereads Homer and tries to let Homer gloss Nature at Walden Pond. Hegel reads Kant and is enflamed to world historical objection. Books can be ambrosia to the thinker. Or they can ignite. But books can be delusion too.

Emerson says there is a creative reading as well as a creative writing. How do you read creatively? Often the first step is to throw the book away. Reading a book in the morning at the full pitch of one's energies is a near crime, Nietzsche suggests. Always live like it is morning—live! Then ponder. The inspiring premise of the thinker is that Truth remains unrevealed, so why consult the history of failure too closely?

Yet the thinker is continually drawn to books. How does one read them creatively? "One must be an inventor to read well," Emerson says (59). One must apply one's intelligence and imagination with creative force, dismissing all that is false or ephemeral and grasping onto only that which is true—and true for oneself in particular. "Books are the best of things, well used; abused among the worst. What is the right use? What is the one end, which all means go to effect? They are for nothing but to inspire. I had better never seen a book, than to be warped by its attraction clean out of my own orbit, and made a satellite instead of a system. The one thing in the world, of value, is the active soul" (57). Emerson thinks of meek young men working in libraries awed into silence by the grandeurs of Cicero and Bacon and Locke. What those young men forget is that Cicero, Locke, and Bacon were once nothing more than young men reading and writing in libraries. (Though there was nothing meek about them.)

Another great resource for the thinker, according to Emerson, is Nature. The young scholar starting out is to experiment with the hypothesis that he and Nature have the same essence. He can imagine that the truths of his soul may be mirrored in the truths of Nature. At the moment of the most intense vision, Emerson says, Nature's "beauty is the beauty of his own mind. Its laws are the laws of his own mind" (56). With Wordsworth, and Coleridge in his earliest phase (before he wrote the disillusioned "Dejection, an Ode"), Emerson shares the belief that there is ultimate knowledge to be discovered in the natural world, so that studying it intensely pays back over and over again. In Nature, we can find spiritual inspiration and perhaps moral laws.

We rarely doubt our Darwinian view of the universe. We believe we have the key to the natural world, and that is that. Our cocksure knowledge can make the spiritual aspirations of Emerson, Thoreau, and Wordsworth, all of whom seek ideals in the natural world, seem antiquated and even childish.

But one might stop and wonder. Isn't it a touch suspicious that our reigning account of Nature rhymes so well with our lowest common denominator version of life? In the Darwinian view, Nature is all Self and no Soul. Creatures in the natural world behave with the same competitive verve, the same lack of compassion, the same absence of disinterested courage, that current citizens of the bourgeois world are often inclined to do. If Nature is a realm of Self, no human being can genuinely be blamed for pursuing his own ends and shoving others out of the way in the process. He is acting naturally. He is behaving according to instinct. We need, perhaps, to remind ourselves of Emerson's observation in the late essay, "Fate." Having said all he can for the forces of Nature in its harshest guise, he turns and observes that, "Man is not order of nature, sack and sack, belly and members, link in a chain, nor any ignominious baggage, but a stupendous antagonism, a dragging together of the poles of the Universe" (779). The forces of Self are no doubt great, but in the universe as Emerson sees it, there is more than mere Self.

The Darwinian consensus under which most educated people live has all but closed off Nature as a scene of possible revelation. (Nietzsche, for instance, detested Darwin. He could not believe that the struggle in the natural world was about the war between *species*. Rather, the conflict was about the struggle of certain *individuals* to ascend above the rest. Nietzsche maintained what he thought of as a Homeric theory of the natural world.) To us Nature is rather exclusively about the competitive struggle for survival.

It is as though we have decided as a culture that we know the meanings of all books yet published—they are, let us say, all about power. They are all about the modalities of domination and submission. We need no more interpretation, no more reading. All books have become one book. So Nature is now a closed system, understood (we assume) in its primary form. Nature is about competition. Nature is about survival of the fittest. But, as Emerson suggests, the true thinker will not submit readily to having one of his main sources of inspiration and enlightenment so quickly closed off.

The thinker is often a wanderer. He aspires literally or metaphorically to the un-housed condition. So marriage and family are potential poisons to him. In *The Genealogy of Knowledge* Nietzsche insists on the bachelor status of the true philosophers: Plato, Aristotle, Descartes, Leibnitz, Kant, Schopenhauer. What about Socrates? The one philosopher whose life has become legendary was married to Xanthippe, who was shrewish and prone to temper tantrums. She supposedly flung a dish of urine at Socrates when he displeased her. Socrates married, Nietzsche says, as a sort of existential joke. It was a test of his more than human power to concentrate on what matters despite all the blockages the Self and the world of Selfhood could cast in front of him. "If I can bear Xanthippe," he is reported to have said, "there is nothing that I cannot bear."

Marriage and children take the thinker away from eternal matters and plant him firmly in the dense common soil of the everyday. He must observe the conventions; he must hew to the collective path. (Or pay for it.) Here he risks becoming satisfied, complacent. In *The Symposium* Plato tells us how the thinker converts the energies of his sexual desire into the energies he needs to pursue the understanding of beauty and of Truth. When those energies are absorbed into the (perhaps) real but mundane pleasures of marriage, they have less chance to inspire celestial flowerings. Then there is the constant pressure of domestic distraction: the barking of the family dog, the illnesses of the children, money worries, the Lilliputian triumphs of requiting the mortgage and keeping the taxman away from the door. Schopenhauer actually spent a quotient of his intellectual energies teaching us how to keep these antagonists at bay. He writes grimly practical essays under the rubric of "The Wisdom of Life": he instructs the reader to save money, avoid conflict with fools, and above all stay away from women, stay away from marriage.

Nietzsche, no easy judge of intellectual character, quickly recognizes Emerson's capacities. He does not know how old he is already, Nietzsche says rather enigmatically of the Sage of Concord, or how young he is still going to be. But Emerson never really coalesces as a thinker or a poet (least of all as a poet). His essays provide brilliant provocation, but they can veer wildly, like riderless horses. "O you man without a handle," Henry James, Senior, said. But how could Emerson's thinking become one of a piece? He was an arch-householder, his powerful mind tethered to his wife and his children and his respectability. His friend Thoreau lived alone in the world, without immediate family, with few friends. From what we know he died a virgin. His thinking does not have grand expanse. But it is taut, consistent in itself, and resolved. He died, as Emerson presumably did not, having worked out the terms of his vision.

Though the thinker often has his coterie, his band of brothers (and occasionally sisters), he is fundamentally a solitary. "In severe abstraction, let him hold by himself" (64), Emerson says, and the aspiring thinker is often alone and lonely. He needs time by himself to think matters through, for thinking is a protracted endeavor. Wallace Stevens speaks admiringly of "the man who has had the time to think enough" and of "the impossible possible philosopher's man." Often the thinker spends as much time working his way out of the various falsehoods surrounding him as he does working his way toward the Truth. We are born into a constricted world, where the values and notions that surround us pass themselves off as the only right way to live and to think. The philosopher in the making has to overcome his parochial prejudices to find something better, and this takes time.

But the thinker is often lonely for another reason, too. He discovers that there is no one he can truly talk with. Everyone around him is interested in the things of this world. They want to know how to prosper and succeed. They want to live life, while the thinker wants, first, to understand it. So what he has to say to them sometimes makes little sense, and though he comprehends their utterances well enough, what they say has no application to what truly matters to him. From time to time the authentic thinker will find someone who cares about what he does and who also lives to find the Truth. Then his life is bliss, if only for a while. Thoreau found in Emerson a spiritual friend, just as Plato found one in Socrates. More often, though, philosophic friendships are virtual. Nietzsche only met Schopenhauer in his books, but during the time when Nietzsche was doing his military service he'd often find himself lonely, frustrated with the idiocies of military life, and at wit's end. "Schopenhauer," he'd call out then. "Schopenhauer, help me!"

Plato had no doubt that there were women more likely to become true thinkers than the majority of men. Philosophical ability is not tied to gender. But fewer women have gone down the contemplative road than men. Hannah Arendt, who did, made it a point to be connected to a man who did not want children and who believed that all property was theft: he refused to own the furniture in their apartment. The owning of furniture is for the bourgeoisie, and the bourgeois is by definition not a thinker. He always speaks prose.

One has no doubt that as time unspools and women have more opportunity to choose their paths, more and more will take their places as lovers of wisdom and potential guides to their fellows. Will their wisdom be substantially different from the wisdom of male thinkers? Will they cut new routes toward the center of the major questions? Perhaps they will. But it is more likely that as they approach universal questions, issues of gender will matter less to them (though such issues can never disappear) and issues of humanity writ large will matter more.

If so far the metaphysical tradition has often been homosexual and sometimes misogynistic, which it has, those qualities often rise out of anxiety. Marriage, home, the family: they can bring the states that terrify the thinker—placid contentment on the one hand, or grinding anxiety on the other. Either way the thinker can drop into the State of Selfhood and never leave. This world—the world of immediately apparent phenomenal being—is never the world in which the true thinker can rest.

Even the thinker's own body can be an antagonist. The thinker wants to transform himself into something more pure and universal than he is. The body is a prison to him. He is enchained by his physical being, for the simple reason that a body is a congestion of needs and demands. It is not unlike the thinker's archetypal foe, the home. It is the home within the home, like a second encased Russian doll.

Another encasement is convention, conformity—the way *we* go about doing things around here. The thinker has to burst through the heaped-up circle of convention that would "solidify and hem in the life" (404). He must strain with all his spirit to "expand another orbit on the great deep" (404).

Once, out on military maneuvers, Socrates became absorbed with a question. He left his comrades and stood alone out on a promontory. He was barefoot and thinly clad, and the weather was frigid. Yet he stood all night brooding on his problem, whatever it might have been. In the morning when the army woke, Socrates was still there. He released himself from his reflections, saluted the gods, and rejoined his comrades, none the worse for wear. His fellows seemed to admire his independence and resolve; at least Alcibiades, who tells the story in *The Symposium,* suggests they did. But the echo of the tale is not so certain, for it is the strange and singular nature of Socrates that will eventually put him on trial.

The thinker has much to contend with—the home, marriage, his own body, convention, books, the weight of past reflection, and loneliness. But sometimes he is compelled to contend with something more: not just the indifference or even the mild disdain of the crowd, but its actual hostility. In Western religion the death of Jesus is central; in the heroic tradition, the death of Achilles; in philosophy, much revolves around the judicial murder of Socrates.

Athens kills Socrates for thinking—or at least for clearing the grounds for genuine thought. He is on trial ostensibly for corrupting the young, for teaching them how to make the weaker argument appear the stronger, and for investigating what happens in the heavens and below the earth. But as the trial unfolds, it becomes clear that Socrates is not really hated for his impiety or his sophistry. Those who detest him seem to do so chiefly for another reason. If Socrates' story is true, he has spent his life fulfilling a simple mission. Early on, the Oracle at Delphi says something extraordinary. The god declares that no one in Athens is wiser than Socrates. But how could this be? For Socrates professes to know nothing.

From Socrates' point of view, the god has set him a task: not to fulfill it would be impiety. He has to find out what this wisdom he supposedly possesses really is. So, a bit like a warrior-hero, Socrates goes on a quest. He talks to one fellow citizen after another, paying special attention to those who have a reputation for wisdom, or who take themselves to be wise. He questions them closely. He tries to find out what it is they know. And of course he is badly disappointed. None of the Athenians he talks with can justify their ways of thinking. The poets cannot say anything of value about the meanings of their poems; the men of law have no real sense of where the laws come from and what makes them just or unjust; fathers have no clear idea of their duties to their children; merchants cannot say for certain what qualifies as honesty and what does not.

Of course Socrates cannot answer any of these difficult questions either, or so he indicates. But at least he knows that he cannot do so. Socrates is unsure what justice and Truth and beauty are, but he knows what it is he doesn't know. Unlike Socrates, his fellow citizens believe that they know things that they do not—so they are constantly in a state of error. (As the old American slave adage goes: "It's not that there's so much we don't know; it's that most of what we do know ain't so.") Socrates may be in a condition of ignorance, but he's not ignorant *and* self-deluded.

It's clear that Socrates never quite stops searching for someone who is truly wise. He traverses Athens taking one person after another by the collar and questioning him as to why he lives the way he does. In time, a group of young men begins to follow him, taking delight in his enquiries and examinations. Socrates, it turns out at his trial, thinks of his task quite seriously. He compares himself to a gadfly who lives to sting a lazy thoroughbred horse—the city of Athens. He has always gone about his business with the persistence of a buzzing fly, whether Athens has swatted him aside time after time or not. A stinging fly is nothing if not persistent. If he is judged innocent, Socrates tells the court, he will go back to doing what he has always done. His vocation comes from the gods, and it would be a crime not to follow it.

He goes so far as to compare himself to the man he calls Thetis's son. Achilles was born to be a hero, born to fight, born to distinguish himself at arms. It would be impious for him to leave the battlefield and walk off and live a calm, prosperous life. Just so, it appears to Socrates that he was born to ask questions and to help his fellow citizens reflect on how to live as they should. The comparison to Achilles is startling, for by making it Socrates is claiming that the life he lives—the philosopher's life—is as important as the life of the warrior.

Socrates comparable to Achilles? How outrageous! Socrates was homely and poor. He had no noble lineage; his mother was nothing like Thetis, the sea goddess. Socrates' mother was Phaenarete, a midwife. His father was a stonecutter. Achilles' father was Peleus, the king, formidable with a spear. Socrates was married to Xanthippe, a shrew formidable with a plate of urine. But Socrates says it directly: he is like Achilles in that he has a duty to himself and to the gods. And, Socrates suggests, his way of life is no less important than the way of the warrior. The quest for wisdom matters, and it matters as much to the world as the quest to become a hero. "When a man has once taken up his stand, either because it seems best to him or in the obedience to his orders, there I believe he is bound to remain and face the danger, taking no account of death or anything else before dishonor" (Plato, 54). This is the traditional language of heroism: now, with Socrates, it is also the language of the philosopher.

But of course the majority of Socrates' fellow citizens cannot concur with his high sense of his vocation: they judge him guilty, and eventually he is put to death. What has he done wrong? By the end of the trial it's clear that the overt charges against Socrates don't amount to much. No one is seriously worried about his not believing in the gods or making the weaker argument appear the stronger. What raises his contemporaries to the pitch of murder is that he has made fools of them. He has asked them the simplest questions about who they are and why they live as they do, and they have found they cannot answer them, either to Socrates' satisfaction or (presumably) to their own. They can't employ reason, the gift that Nature has given them and that separates them from animals, to understand themselves or the world as they truly are. They can calculate; they can measure and weigh and discern their material advantage in this exchange or that, but they cannot give an account of what a just life or a good life might be. This might cause them to pause and think hard about themselves, but such thinking would be painful and it might result in their having to reorder their lives. It is more convenient to kill the person who is asking them the noisome questions.

To philosophize, it has often been said, is to learn how to die, and in his encounter with death Socrates is entirely admirable—for he is richly consistent with the central premise of his thought. All through his life as a thinker, Socrates has prefaced his annoying inquiries with a simple disclaimer: I do not know the answers to the major questions about life, but it appears that you yourself do. Tell me what you think. What is a good life? What is a bad one? What makes an existence worth sustaining?

Faced with death, Socrates shows what makes him different from other men—and also suggests that his professions of ignorance were something more than a game. Most men, he says, presume to know something about death: they know that it is bad. Death almost always involves suffering, and of course it is horrible to have to leave the earth. But from this view Socrates dissents. He does not really know what death is or what the afterlife entails—though he is willing to guess in a more or less playful way. (Maybe death is an eternal sleep; maybe death takes you to a world where you meet the good and great who have lived before you.) What he does know about death is that, really, he knows nothing at about it. Death might be a very bad thing, but it might be quite a pleasant matter. No one really knows. No one knows but all have their ideas. Socrates does not know, and that is all there is to it. He will keep open to death—he will sustain his ignorance about the matter despite the temptations that arise. He will die, in other words, as he has lived: not claiming to know what in truth he does not know. Socrates' mode of ignorance sustains him serenely and potently at the threshold of death. The so-called knowledge of his contemporaries would probably not serve them half so well.

Socrates' death dramatizes the most daunting of all the thinker's challenges. He is forced to contend with poverty, loneliness, and the derision of the crowd. But sometimes the crowd's derision can turn murderous. It happened to Socrates as it has happened to other intellectual and spiritual rebels through time, from Giordano Bruno to Martin Luther King. People, especially people who live aggressively in the State of Self, do not like being reminded that there are other ways to conduct life. They don't like having to feel that they are behaving like beasts and that there are those, however few, who see what they are doing and do not approve. When Socrates compares himself to Achilles, he may even be suggesting that the authentic thinker exposes himself to death much in the way the heroic warrior does. Schopenhauer, brooding on the life of the philosopher, considers the young man who spends his time in isolation, writing and thinking until he seems to himself to have achieved a breakthrough. He steps out into the world and begins to spread his ideas. Maybe he expects some measure of fame. He expects at least a dram of gratitude. He is badly mistaken, Schopenhauer muses, for in fact the young man is lucky if he escapes with his skin.

Emerson declares that though the thinker may suffer on his way to enlightenment, the culmination of his labors is often joyous. When the true American scholar proclaims his findings, Emerson says, "the people delight in it; the better part of every man feels, This is my music; this is myself" (64–65). Emerson had his hopes for America, which he felt might cultivate a fresh kind of appreciation for thinkers. How well those hopes have been realized one may discern for oneself.

Poverty, isolation, loneliness, popular contempt, and even (perhaps) danger: these can be the wages of the thinker. What could possibly compensate for such sorrows? What does the existence of the thinker deliver that makes the many obstacles worth facing?

This is the question that Plato, Socrates' pupil, sets out to answer. For Socrates has done only half the work of philosophy. He has cleared the ground. He has shown the enormous flaws in the understanding of life that most men and women sustain. But he has done little to replace error with Truth, doxa with enlightenment. Socrates has demonstrated how deep the human need is for positive enlightenment, but he has not provided the teachings. And it is this that Plato and all who have followed him have tried to do. But Socrates begins it all. He shows us time and again—and dies to prove it—that common understanding is not enough. The way that most people live and think is inadequate, and something better must be found. For a time agile doubt will have to do. But eventually the Soul must present to the world a way of life that contends with, and can conceivably overthrow, the life of the Self.

Does Socrates ever leave Plato's cave? In the cave parable—the most famous in philosophy—there are represented three stages of being. The first is the life of the Self. It is the life that most men and women live most of the time, and Plato renders it harshly. The majority of human beings sit on a bench, chained by the leg but also by the neck. They cannot move from where they sit, and they cannot look anywhere but straight ahead. They stare at a screen, and on that screen they see images cast forward by a fire burning behind them. They do not know that they're imprisoned. They think that this is the natural state of human life. But it is only a matter of their educations: they have been accustomed since youth to taking illusions as realities, and as life goes on they continue to do so, with ever-growing conviction.

Virtually all human beings live in a prison, under confinement; what they think is freedom is bitter enclosure. But they have grown used to this state, and they cannot conceive any other. They cannot explain why they are here, or why they behave as they do; they take their confinement to be natural.

But suppose, Plato says, one of them is suddenly set free and begins to make his way around the cave, exploring. Quickly he understands that what he thought was real isn't. The images he saw in front of him are mere shadows cast by objects passing before the fire at the back of the cave. This life is all illusion, all a show. He understands that what most people live their lives for amounts to nothing: they do not possess the Truth; their two is not the real two; their three not the real three. He is able to look at all the prisoners locked into their seats and see how they suffer. It is to this point that Socrates arrived. He broke away from the chains that bound him, and by his questioning he understood the nature of the illusions that enchanted his fellows. And for this, naturally, they hated him.

But other than pointing to their illusions with his incessant questioning and declaring that the images on the screen were nothing more than that, images, there was not a great deal that Socrates was able to do. (At least Socrates as he is depicted in the early dialogues, when Plato renders him as he presumably was.) His irony and ignorance served him brilliantly at the moment of death, but he never really created a doctrine as to how to live. At the end, he was still in the cave, though he was by far the freest individual living there. Only Socrates could move at his ease among the benches, only Socrates could get back and look over the machinery of illusion that created the fantasia that mesmerized his fellow Athenians.

Socrates saw that all his fellow citizens could apprehend were individual items, single objects that they regarded according to how much use they might be. They were ruled by their desires. Someone who only cares about what he can do with this or that object does not care what it has in common with all other objects of its sort. All he cares about is whether he can profit from the item or not. Objects are only real to him if they can satisfy a desire. The objects passing in the cave are a parade of discrete items—rather than elements in a drama, say—because most people look at life as a sequence of things that they can or cannot use. Socrates sees this and sees how stifling it is to be limited to looking at the world as a mere theater of desire.

He wanders the cave much as he wanders Athens, exposing the limits of confined life again and again. But what he does not do—and what his pupil Plato does, though in his name—is attempt to leave the limited reality of Athens and the cave and rise to another level, the level of true and unconditioned reality. The student of Socrates will surely spend some time in the cave, exploring the sorrows of conventional life, but then, if he is like Plato, he will seek something better. He will make his way up into the bright world that lies outside. He'll stop thinking about Athens and his own immediate life and begin thinking about what is true for all men and women at all times.

In the beginning it hurts to enter the sunlight. The young person who is genuinely becoming a thinker can't look directly up at the sky, where Truth resides. He can only look at the reflections of the moon and stars and, in time, the sun in streams and pools of water. But gradually he becomes accustomed to the light. He starts to expand his mind to the point where he does not take it as sufficient to brood on what is good and true for himself or his family or even his nation or race. He wants now to think about what is good for everyone. This expansion of mind is painful. We are far more comfortable in the cave, where we can think about what we want for ourselves. We're at ease reflecting on what we hope to achieve in our lives and what pleasures we might enjoy. Outside in the sun, we feel the demand that we forget ourselves and live for more consequential matters. But this demand is difficult and painful to contemplate. How will we live now? Who will take care of us? Plato's fable is the story of the passage from the State of the Self to the State of Soul. The passage hurts. It maybe even run against the grain of our biological natures. It is the passage from I to we, and from now to all-times; it is a great enlargement and, like every such achievement, it can be strenuous and disturbing.

But the more time we spend trying to focus on the light of the sun, the richer life grows. We begin to achieve release from slavery to our own wants. We stop being so ambitious and vain. We cease reflecting on what will make us happy—what will give us pleasure. In the light we become free from the dark and tedious Self that abides underground. This Self, a little like Freud's unconscious, seeks only its own satisfactions. We now look for more out of existence.

In the light, the thinker begins to change. Socrates lived a virtuous life, yes. But as his mind's light expands, Plato asks what it would mean for everyone to live a virtuous life. He begins to wonder how he can give humanity a blueprint for creating a just world. For he understands that Socrates' kind of good life is not for everybody; in fact, it may only be for the few, the philosophers. What about the rest of mankind—all those who are left down in the cave, wasting their lives like prisoners? What kind of life might they at their best have? To philosophize in the highest form is to think on behalf of everyone and then to offer them—as a gift, not as a form of coercion—a vision of how life can be truer to humanity's best promise. The fruit of Plato's encounter with a life outside the cave is *The Republic.*

It is impossible to encompass the achievement of this, Plato's greatest work. Since at least Aristotle, thinkers have been pondering it; virtually all of what qualifies as philosophy has been a reaction to *The Republic,* and yet its resources are far from exhausted. Here there is everything to delight and enhance the mind and to strengthen character.

The book is almost spectacularly bold, yet it revolves around a simple premise. The best kind of human life is the most serene. Calm, balance, detachment, humanity: these are the states that Plato most treasures. He clearly believes that as we read him and look back on our past experience, we will see that he is right. As turbulent as our lives may have been, we will still have experienced moments of calm. We will be able to recall times when our minds and hearts were balanced in harmony and the world outside seemed serene. We will recall those states and we will want to reproduce them for ourselves and to offer them to others. A clear mind and a steady heart are the best gifts life can offer. How are we to acquire them?

The great book is, among other things, a transvaluation of values. Plato is writing in the midst of a culture shaped by Homer. His contemporaries, fed on the two epics, admire nothing as much as martial courage. Those who live in the age of Athens aspire to make it a heroic age.

It is common to believe that the thinker and the warrior are archenemies. On this matter, Plato's genius shines through, though it has not been apparent to all his readers. Most of the world believes that Plato and Homer are pure antagonists. After all, in Book X of *The Republic* Plato banishes the poets—Homer preeminent among them—from his ideal state. But in fact Plato deeply respects the warrior mentality. Plato insists that those who will be the rulers of his Republic have a strong element of spiritedness in their constitutions. They must be brave. To Plato spiritedness is a crucial element in all human beings. We're all more or less brave. (Freud, who also deploys a tripartite model of the psyche, often said to be beholden to Plato's, does not include courage as an integral element of being—the reasons for this are perhaps becoming evident.) The quality that Homer celebrates is greatly prized by Plato. However.

It is prized in its place. In the best of men and women—the philosophers—courage is *subordinated* to reason. The philosopher is not intemperate. He does not unthinkingly exchange blow for blow. When pushed by the likes of an envious and greedy Agamemnon, he doesn't leap back ferociously. The thinker is brave, but he puts intelligence before violent action. What is courage? Plato asks. The answer is brilliantly apt. In Homer the brave man is the one who fears nothing. In martial culture the archetype of the hero is Achilles, who is always ready for death. True courage to Plato is not being without fear: true courage is based in knowledge. It is *knowing* what to fear and what not to fear.

In *The Republic,* the heroes—who are akin to Homer's heroes—have a place of honor. The thinkers are made of gold. The warriors are men and women (in Plato there are women warriors, too) whose spirits are composed of silver. Plato understands the importance of the warriors to the state and understands something too about their inner lives. They are (like the guardians) a class apart; they are (as all the male citizens of Sparta below a certain age were) professional soldiers. They spend their lives in training and in combat. For this their fellow citizens look upon them with reverent gratitude. The warrior class in Plato is a class of heroes.

And Plato comprehends them well. What they want most is not wealth or possessions; gold coins mean about as much to the warriors as they do to true philosophers. Both have evolved beyond the Self's hunger for lucre. Warriors live for esteem. They exist to incite awe and inspire praise in others; this is clear all through Homer, and it is not lost on Plato. So the fellow citizens of the warriors deck them with garlands and give them kisses in recognition of their brave deeds. When the warriors go into battle, their children watch from surrounding hillsides to applaud their bravery and urge them on to noble achievements.

Plato understands that there is something theatrical in the warrior's makeup, and he wants to give it opportunity for expression. (Recall Achilles' need to have all the Greeks and Trojans watching when he duels with Hector.) Plato's warriors live within an epic context. They are characters in dramas, mortal dramas, seen by all. They are duly celebrated and held in something approaching reverence.

But they do not rule. Ruling is for philosophers, who are akin to fighters in their spiritedness (and so understand them), but in whom reason is sovereign. Plato does not detest Homer, as the world has come to think. He holds Homeric values in high esteem, but not the highest. No society that denigrates its warriors, Plato suggests, will ever be just and thriving. We need to be defended from our enemies, and this has to be done by people for whom honor comes first. To slight such people, as Agamemnon slights Achilles, can unbalance them, even drive them mad. And when mad they are dangerous: the warrior driven off his true, honorable path becomes a brute. He falls in love with death—his enemy's and sometimes even his own. ("Long live death," the fascist warriors chanted in Spain.) The heroic ideal is easy to pervert, Plato knows, and that is why he takes such care to understand it.

In Homer, a man is defined by the quotient of thymos he possesses. How spirited is he? What will he dare do to gain glory? In Plato, courage matters, but reason matters more. Plato cannot believe that the often brief, turbulent life of the hero is the best kind. For him the best life by far is the life of calm, directed by reason. Plato does not want to banish Homer's heroic tradition so much as he wants to subordinate it. He wants to replace the rule of thymos with the rule of reason. Where warriors were, there philosophers shall be.

One of Plato's most daring strokes is to speculate that the state and the spirit are mirror images of each other. In a soul where thymos reigns there will be turbulence; from the Platonic point of view, the warrior often enters a state of protracted agitation, attempting to enhance his reputation. He is always on the lookout for the next opportunity to win glory. A state that is guided by the warrior ethos will be similarly turbulent. It will always be at war or preparing for war; one ruler will displace another based not on probity but on power. There will be no peace, no contentment.

Every state of the soul, according to Plato, has its corresponding state of public life. The soul of the democratic man is inconsistent,

anxious, unmoored. The government that reflects this inner state
is similarly chaotic. Democratic man cannot decide what he wants
to do with his life: one day he wants to be a fighter, the next a thinker,
the next he simply wants to lay about and enjoy his possessions. The
democratic state vacillates in a similar way: no one knows who
should follow, no one knows who should lead. One day we are all
for war; the next day we are a people of peace. In democracy there
is no sense of what matters now and for the future. There is no sense
of continuity. Democracy is a ship that everyone takes turns cap-
taining, just as the soul of democratic man continually rearranges
itself, with one then another faculty lording it over the others.

Plato's major work is a testament to harmony: thus the central
importance of music for him. Nietzsche, who aspired to be Plato's
great antagonist (he sometimes aspired to be everyone's antagonist),
was greedy for the rousing sounds of Wagner, who fired the passions
in his soul. Plato seeks balance in the private sphere and the public
world, and so he is an advocate of music that is harmonious, well
structured, and that helps create in the individual that unity of being
that is conducive to happiness. In time, the young person will study
geometry, another activity that brings balance to the spirit. (The
phrase over the door of Plato's academy: "Let no one enter who is
ignorant of geometry.") But the central substance of early education
for Plato is musical.

Plato sees the life of harmony and contentment as the best of
human lives, and he wants to offer it as broadly as he can. But to do
so persuasively, he finds he must accomplish a great deal. There is
the critical labor of displacing the heroic ideal—not destroying it,
or even trying to, but putting it in what he perceives as its proper
place. But then so much of a positive or constructive nature remains
to be done. To imagine his ideal city and his ideal life, Plato must
reflect on every conceivable subject. He broods on music and government, to be sure, but also on literature, on art, on crafts, on child

rearing, on the relations between the sexes, on the right kind of diet and the best modes of exercise. He comments on the way to good health. He'll tell you almost as readily how to plant crops as how the soul is composed. By the time his book is over he has thought about the nature of the good and the true, the relation of immediate experience to the forms that live on high, and what happens to us after we die.

To be sure, there have been few who would willingly go off and live in Plato's state. There are no longer many who value precisely what he values. True Platonists are rarely found in the current world, and yet his influence is everywhere.

Plato's achievement is to consider every significant area of human life, and do so wisely. There is not a consequential subject that he does not talk about in his inimitable way—that is to say, both brilliantly and sensibly. He considers all the great matters, and every time we do as much, we are following Plato's path. What achievement could be grander?

Just one—the achievement of being right. For Plato did not want his work to be merely provocative or intellectually distinguished or superbly eloquent. Of course it is all of these. But Plato wanted to disclose the Truth. He believed that he had ascended to the highest level that the thinker can aspire to reach: the level where he receives and reveals what is enduringly so. Plato believed he had achieved contact with ultimate and absolute Truth. He did not think that his findings were good for himself and his circle only, or for Athenians, or for Greeks, or even for all men and women living when he did. He sought Truth that would last forever.

For Socrates it was enough not to lie. He sets forth an example of a certain sort of thinker, one who always describes life precisely as he sees it. When his fellow citizens seem to be deluding themselves, he tells them so. When he is mystified by some explanation they give, he admits it. He is candid about his confusion. He never tries to make himself look good by making claims he cannot support. Socrates is the one who does not lie.

During his trial, the question of what he might do if he were set free arises. It would surely be in Socrates' interest to tell the jury that he will retire from the public square, stop annoying people, and lead a quiet, normal life. Saying so would save him. But Socrates cannot do it, and he will not. He tells his accusers that if they free him, then the next day he will be back doing what he always does, inquiring into the lives of his fellow Athenians. Not to do so would be to outrage his own nature, and that he refuses to do. Socrates: he who does not lie.

Nor will Socrates deceive. When he is awaiting death in prison, his friends come to him with a plan. They will bribe the guards, hire a ship, and spirit Socrates away at the darkest point of the night. He'll sail off to another state, where he'll be free. Nonsense, says Socrates. I stood trial, I defended myself, I was convicted: Why should I deceive the state that nursed me from the time I was young?

Socrates' candor can sometimes upset others—he will say anything to people that he thinks to be so, no matter what the cost in discomfort, embarrassment, or anger. But he is candid and upright, too, in the way that he deals with himself. Socrates: the man who does not lie, does not deceive.

This commitment to candor that Socrates nurtures may not seem much at first glance, but consider the matter more closely. How much deception does the average individual practice in a day or a week? People say what they can to avoid conflict, to please their superiors, to advance their interests. When they do not lie directly, they lie by omission. They fail to speak up when their principles are under attack. They offer instead what Emerson calls their "mortifying social smiles." They hide within the contours of convention, even when convention seems to them empty or unjust. They go along to get along. Socrates will not do so: he is always ready to offer his perceptions, no matter how unpleasant or unpopular they may be. He never trims his truth and never backs down. Socrates: the man (is he maybe the only man?) who doesn't lie.

But Plato does more. Plato seeks the Truth in its absolute form, and when he feels he has found it, he declares it to the world. *The Republic* is the culmination of a rich life's hard and joyful intellectual work, and it declares its ambitions openly. This is how it is! If you would know what justice and virtue and beauty genuinely are, then read these pages. And who is to say that Plato is not right? Twenty-five hundred years have passed, and we still cannot get him out of our minds—he has, in fact, done much to create our minds. To think is to Platonize, to Platonize is to think.

But others will come along (one hopes) and attempt to do better, or to do for themselves, what Plato did. Their road will be difficult, as the thinker's always is. More than likely they will begin in poverty and isolation; as time passes they'll be shouldered aside by the ambitious and the guileful. They'll be mocked by those who live only in the Self and only for the things of this world. The powerful and the adept will laugh at them. But even early on, as they enter the first phase of their lives as thinkers, they'll have one of the greatest satisfactions a human being can have: they won't lie. They'll follow Socrates, and they'll look out at the world, and with whatever mix of irony and sweetness and exasperation, they will describe it as it is to them. When others trim and sidestep, they will have the satisfaction of voicing honest perceptions. For what do they have to lose? They are already poor. They have no wish to ascend in the world. We all should go about speaking our truth with the confidence of boys who are sure of a dinner, Emerson says. But how few of us do—even when our dinners are assured for the rest of our days. Not lying, telling the truth, creates a sense of inner well-being that is like nothing else. Candor is to the spirit what a hard physical regimen is to the body: both are demanding, both produce salutary results.

The young person starting out as a thinker soon develops a sense of proportion: it's clear to him that, as Emerson says, a popgun is just a popgun, even if the ancient and venerable say it is the crack of doom. He has studied the past, and so he knows that what shakes the crowd this way or that on a given day is usually nothing more than a light breeze; the real perturbations go unfelt. In time he learns to smile at the pretensions of the wealthy, the successful, those who claim they have made themselves happy. For he knows that, even now in this first stage of thought, he is putting his mind to use nobly. He's engaging in the ancient and honorable project of clearing away error. He is attacking, in himself and outside (but mostly in himself), the reigning forms of deception.

The Self and the culture of the Self have other uses for the powers of the mind. Self takes the beautiful and perhaps near-infinite force of reason and puts it to work on the mundane. It curses the mind with twelve cumbersomely "profitable" labors, and when those are done concocts twelve more. The mind of the Self is pragmatic. It holds a thought to be true if it helps the Self get closer to fulfilling its desires. The Self uses the mind as a slave and sends it on errands: it puts the mind to work sweating over an account book; it uses it to get one up on the competitor, or the friend. Of what value is reason to the Self? It helps the Self gain more of what it desires. The practical mind schemes and strategizes and thinks only for and about the individual. It also feeds the Self the necessary justification for all its acts, however base. The practical mind helps the Self create arguments that will let it go on living in the manner it has been. Truth, the pragmatist says, is that which gets you what you want. You: the individual. The pragmatic mindset has little to do with anything more than you—there is no necessary concern with *us*, with *we*, with *humanity*. The pragmatist, enemy of idealism and idealists, makes respectable the self-advancing tactics of the marketplace.

The advent of academic philosophies such as neo-pragmatism and deconstruction seemed to be of a piece with various movements of liberation that arose a little more than halfway through the last century in Europe, Latin America, and North America. The theorists had the aura of subversion about them. They seemed in accord with aspirations to human equality and humane pleasure—and they seemed to shake the walls of the academy, making the ivy tremble. They were, needless to say, anti-Platonic: the large-scale Platonic thinker was understood to be an ally of the oppressors in government and society, who also had large-scale truths they wanted to impose. It is worthwhile to consider how readily the most prestigious institutions absorbed and digested these ostensibly rebellious intellectual movements: deconstruction, pragmatism, new historicism, Foucault's critique of power. Why did the most established universities not rise in revolt against the new intellectual apostasy?

Maybe what inspired the debunkers was not hope for liberation or equality but contempt for ideals. Gifted-deconstructionists taught that Plato's texts were so variable and inconsistent that they were not readily readable. Figurative language distorted aspirations to cogent and clear sense at every turn. And if one could not read Plato and emerge with a more or less unified sense of his work, how could one base a way of life on his thought? So let us put Plato and Plato's ideals aside.

The bourgeoisie, the culture of Self, does not find ideals readily tolerable, either. Ideals impede the one truly necessary project, the fulfilling of Self-interests. The objectives of debunking theoretical education rhyme well with certain bourgeois aims. For theoretical education is all too often the dismantling of ideals and thus the opening up of the Self's right to proceed as it wishes, and with a good conscience. What appeared to be a rebellion of the professors was in fact conformity, conformity with the middle-class ethos of de-idealization. Deconstruction's true polemic is not against metaphysics per se, as Derrida claims in his early work. (In the later work, he will become something of a conventional moralist.) It is rather against aspirations to any way of thinking and being that sets up ever-demanding standards for the conduct of life. Deconstruction delivers the young Self-seeker from the burdens of the ideal.

Most contemporary intellectual life is designed to lead the young thinker, who has perhaps begun to experience the light of the ideal, back down into the cave. The passage can be difficult. The mind has started to expand, but now it is time to close it down, darken what was bright. In time the descent back into Plato's cave can feel like a relief—de-idealization often does, at least at the start. A burden has been lifted. It is no longer necessary to strive to transcend the Self. Now one can relapse into the Natural Man (as Blake called him), who is defined by his wants. No doubt the life of the true thinker, or of anyone who dedicates herself to Soul, is arduous. The current academy can rescue one from such burdens and make life less weighty, less demanding—at the same time sapping existence of consequential meaning.

The true thinker must struggle for a long time. She's bound to be poor; she's bound to be ignored; opportunists will push past her; she'll feel constant doubt. And her labor is hard. She's got to study; she's got to read; she's got to reflect. But in time, her satisfactions begin to mount. At a certain point she'll achieve something like what Socrates did. She'll be able to hold the forms of her own culture at arm's length. Without prejudice, she'll be able to look at what passes for truth and knowledge and see how local, how time-bound, how geared to mere expediency they are. She'll rise above her circumstances. Lonely and poor as she may be, she'll be able to walk through the world, speaking her truth and not being taken in by the appearances. She'll be a free woman—she'll have the run of the cave, the run of the world.

But for the true thinker, that Socratic freedom will probably not be enough. She will want more than Socrates' joyous skepticism— she'll want to pass beyond the pleasure of knowing that nothing is all that she knows. Then she will begin the thinker's exalted task, to develop her own version of the truth: day by day and piece by piece. Plato was not born with *The Republic* on his lips. It takes time and effort and no little faith and love to make such a book. But when the thinker begins to build her mansion of Truth, life—no matter how difficult externally—can become joyful. Every day she adds something to her store of perceptions about what the true and good and beautiful are, and how men and women might live rightly in the world. She tears the masks off common life, but she does more than that. She works herself gradually to the point where she can say with Plato—You, whoever you are: there is a way you can live happily. You can step out beyond the great majority of your woes—for they are Self-inflicted—and by a simple discipline you can have the best that your spirit and your mental powers have to offer.

Not everyone will listen to you, the thinker; most will not. But those who do will be grateful to you until the ends of their lives, and the best members of future generations will give thanks as well. You will have opened up a door in the grimy prison wall that is conventional life and allowed the most sensitive and strong to walk out into something better. Having freed yourself, you will make others free. The young person growing up amid fear and worry feels calmer and somehow assured of escape. We all live, at least for some measure of our lives, in the cave; the great thinker forces a gap in the wall and lets us breathe—then the hole expands and out we pass.

The true thinker, Emerson says, must "feel all confidence in himself and . . . defer never to the popular cry. He and he only knows

the world. The world of any moment is the merest appearance. . . .
In silence, in steadiness, in severe abstraction, let him hold by himself; add observation to observation, patient of neglect, patient of reproach; and bide his own time—happy enough, if he can satisfy himself alone, that this day he has seen something truly" (64). In time he learns that in descending to the secrets of his own mind he has unlocked the secret of all minds. When he offers his vision to the world he risks the greatest disaster. How many have sought to strike through the pasteboard mask and see the ultimate forms that lie on the other side, discerning Truth from what merely appears to be the case? How many have come anywhere close to plausible success?

For what the true thinker hopes for is rather outrageous. Naturally, he dreams of understanding the present and the past. But he wants something more. If the thinker has fulfilled his dream he is also someone who can predict the future—in the only authentic sense there is. He can tell you not only what men and women are like now, and what the world is, but how those things will be for all time. Plato knows—or believes he knows—the possible shapes, both of happiness and sorrow, that the spirit can take, not just for the Athenian present but for all time. He knows—because he knows Nature—what kinds of government will succeed and fail, who the gods are and how to worship them, what a child is and how to give it the fullest chance for growth. And these matters will—if Plato is right—never change. Seeing humanity as it is, he knows humanity as it ever will be. Knowing what is Good now, he knows the Good for all time. A man or woman who has reached such a level of apprehension may be truly said to have touched the immortal, for then all of time is present here and now. In every instant of pure thought, the true thinker lives amidst eternal life.

II

Ideals in the Modern World

4

Shakespeare and the
Early Modern Self

Shakespeare, we are told, invents the human. This is a statement full of consequential truth, though not quite the truth that its originator conceives. Harold Bloom says that "the human" as we know it comes into being when the playwright's characters display a certain interior life. Shakespeare's characters are distinct not only because their speech reveals their minds and hearts so brilliantly. They are also distinct because they can reflect on their own utterances, and through their reflections change their sense of who they are. Shakespeare's characters read and interpret themselves. "I think, therefore I am," Descartes asserts. Shakespeare's characters, according to Bloom, think about their own thought, and so represent a level of being that makes them different not in degree but in kind from previous representations of human beings.

One of Shakespeare's most ferocious villains, Edmund, about to die, cries out "Yet Edmund was beloved." He surprises himself by what he says—up until this point Edmund has thought he was incapable of love and completely unlovable. He overhears himself and he has to reconceive himself. He is not quite the being he thought he was: he's more capable of affection and generous feelings than he had imagined. He calls out to the guards to try to save Cordelia

and Lear, whom he has sentenced to death; his final breath is, surprisingly to himself and everyone else, a generous one.

Perhaps what Bloom says about self-overhearing and change
is so. Maybe Shakespeare's characters are, to use Bloom's idiom,
"strong mis-readers" of themselves. But the most significant truth
about Shakespeare's "invention of the human" is both simpler and
more complex. Shakespeare does not quite invent the human as we
know it. Rather he makes way for the flourishing of a new human
type, a type that he does not especially endorse, or perhaps even
like terribly much. Shakespeare helps create the grounds for the presiding form of modern subjectivity through his acts of demolition
as well as through his acts of representation. He clears the way for
the triumph of the Self. His work helps open a space in which it can
unfold and triumph. In Shakespeare's world only Self lives on and
thrives—though this fact is no cause for celebration to him and
surely it shouldn't be to us. Shakespeare is the first great secularist;
the first authentic renderer of the marketplace philosophy, pragmatism, and the primary artist of life lived exclusively in the sublunary
sphere. Seen from Shakespeare's vantage, the pragmatic life is
not especially enticing or glorious, but it is all we genuinely have.
Shakespeare is the ultimate poet of worldliness.

What is perhaps the best-known sentence of literary criticism is
devoted, not surprisingly, to Shakespeare—and it is extremely
misleading. The sentence comes from John Keats and deals with a
quality he believes Shakespeare to have possessed more fully than
any other author and, presumably, more than any other man or
woman, negative capability. That is, Keats says, when an individual
is capable of being "in uncertainties, mysteries, doubts without any
irritable reaching after fact and reason." Keats's line, which comes
from a letter to his brothers Tom and George, has been glossed in
numberless ways. But the most common interpretation is that
Shakespeare, poetic genius that he is, actually holds no perceptible

views. Read the plays as closely as you like, Keats suggests (and virtually all critics have concurred), and you still will never know what he thinks about any consequential subject: about religion, monarchy, marriage, love, honor, what have you. Shakespeare preserves sublime neutrality. He stands above his creatures, aloof as a god, staring down into the universe that he's made.

But suppose that matters are actually rather different. Suppose Shakespeare does have a worldview and a strong one. Suppose that his work, subtle as it is, brilliant as it is, is replete with *values*. Imagine that Shakespeare has designs upon us. But. But suppose that we cannot readily perceive those values because they are so much our own. We've become enclosed within them. We have, without quite knowing it, adopted most of Shakespeare's vision of experience. (This is a very real sense in which Shakespeare has created the human.) What he fears and dismisses, we too fear and wish to dismiss. The world he renders is the world we live in—and he admits the reality of no other world. As bad as that world may be, it brings a sort of comfort to believe that it is the only possible world and that to ask for something more or something different out of life would be vain. Shakespeare *seems* to believe nothing because most of us, on some level below articulation, believe rather precisely what he did. Shakespeare's beliefs, we might even say, have become our assumptions. He has created the most powerful literary mythology that the Western world has ever seen.

How does Shakespeare gather his amazing energy? Close to forty plays, then long poems, sonnets, collaborations, a career as an actor and a businessman: where does the vitality come from? It is not possible to say with certainty. But one might speculate that beyond his unparalleled inborn powers, the poet taps a broad collective force. He writes so much and so well in part because he writes with the concentrated energy of a world- transforming movement. He expresses—in a sense he *is*—the power of a rising middle class, a class tired of the arrogance of nobility but still fascinated by what is (or what might be) noble. This is a class that disdains high heroic honor but delights to see it rendered—and undone. Shakespeare also writes for and *as* a figure within a class that has little use for deep religion, the religion of compassion. His audience is Christian, but does not seem especially drawn to what Thomas à Kempis called "the imitation of Christ." And he writes for a class with no real use for high thought—though Shakespeare is from time to time tempted by the ideal of contemplation.

Bloom says that Christopher Marlowe is Shakespeare's primary precursor and that Shakespeare overcomes him easily. Not quite. Shakespeare's primary precursor is not the fledgling genius Kit Marlowe, who dies young, murdered (as the legend goes) over "a great reckoning in a little room." Shakespeare's major influence is the most accomplished prior writer in the Western tradition, Homer. The war between the two is not primarily a war over originality. It is a war over vision. A significant proportion of Shakespeare's work is an assault on Homer, *The Iliad,* and on what we have called Homeric values. At the same time, Shakespeare derives no little profit from the allure of the ultimate Homeric theme, the theme of honor. Repeatedly Shakespeare kills the Homeric hero (or his descendant) on the stage. Then he revives that hero again (so great is our fascination with him) for one sacrifice more in another brilliant play.

Shakespeare, as Jonson said, had "small Latin and less Greek." He had not been to the university; he was no classical scholar. But Shakespeare did have access to George Chapman's translation of Homer, which began appearing in 1598. He would have seen the opening books, and would have known a great deal about Homer's depiction of Achilles. So too would Shakespeare have had access to other legendary sources about the Trojan War, including Chaucer's *Troilus and Criseyde,* on which he bases his most unrelentingly polemical play. No one who has read Shakespeare's *Troilus* with any care can readily believe in Shakespearean negative capability.

Almost all lovers of Shakespeare's art are united in one wish, the wish that Shakespeare did not write *Titus Andronicus*. Yet the play is his first tragedy, and it has a central part in his development. As the critic Katharine Maus says: "he returns to the Machiavellian villain in *Richard III*, to the urgency of revenge in *Hamlet*, to the old man unwisely relinquishing power in *Lear*, to questions of race and intermarriage in *Othello* and *The Tempest*, to important moments in Roman history in *The Rape of Lucrece*, *Julius Caesar*, *Coriolanus* and *Anthony and Cleopatra*" (Greenblatt, *Norton Shakespeare*, 371). All this is true, but *Titus* matters for our understanding of Shakespeare in a cruder and more central way. In this play Shakespeare begins his strife with heroic values. The image of Titus and the torments that Shakespeare visits upon him never seem to leave his mind. The degradation, torture, and disgrace of this, his first tragic protagonist, is a great Shakespearean resource, and the playwright will draw upon it again and again.

What is tragedy in its essence? A question with many answers, no doubt. In *The Birth of Tragedy* Nietzsche speculates that tragedy is the drama of the rise, apotheosis, then the torture, dismemberment, and death of the deity. For the deity, substitute the hero—the vividly Homeric hero—and you will begin to approach the inner form of Shakespeare's martial tragedies. And no Shakespearean hero is as brutally tortured and sacrificed onstage as Titus.

Titus has been daring or foolish enough to embrace the Roman code of honor as it has been passed down through Homer and his heroes. He has fought and fought well for Rome, much as Shakespeare will depict Coriolanus and Caesar and Antony as having done. When the play begins, he has lost twenty-one of his twenty-five sons to the wars. As Maus observes, "Titus . . . in his austere patriotism, his intolerance of dissent, his acute sense of personal and family honor, his traditional piety, and his ferocious commitment to patriarchal hierarchy . . . is a recurrent Roman personality type" (Greenblatt, *Norton Shakespeare*, 372). Titus is an exemplar of the peculiarly Roman version of the warrior ideal:

> Rome, I have been thy soldier forty years,
> And led my country's strength successfully.
> And buried one and twenty valiant sons,
> Knighted in field, slain manfully in arms,
> In right and service of their noble country.
> (I.i.193–197)

Titus is at the end of his life and feels justified in proclaiming that he has fulfilled a high ideal. Titus is not Achillean: he does not seek glory for himself. He is—or wishes to be—a descendant of Hector.

Titus demands that the eldest son of Tamora, queen of the defeated Goths, be sacrificed to the memory of his own slain sons. The sacrifice, Titus claims, has the status of religious rite. It is intended to appease the suffering shadows of the departed, his sons killed in the wars, and so it must take place. Not long afterward, Titus kills one of his remaining sons for opposing him when he declares that Lavinia, his daughter, will marry the newly proclaimed emperor, Saturninus. Titus has—honorably, nobly—ceded his right to the imperial seat to Saturninus and intends to give him absolute loyalty, whatever the cost. When Titus' son, Mutius, tries to block the marriage, Titus draws his sword and kills him. In Roman life, it was often considered an act of nobility to put the state or one's conception of honor before family. Maus mentions Horatius, who killed his own sister for lamenting the death of her husband, whom Horatius killed in battle; Titus Manlius Torquatus, a general who had his own son executed for too eagerly anticipating an order to close on the enemy; and Appius Claudius, who murdered his daughter when her honor was undermined (Greenblatt, *Norton Shakespeare*, 372). Perhaps the best-known example of such action, though, is Lucius Junius Brutus, who killed his sons for siding with Tarquin. (Lucius turns up in Book VI of *The Aeneid,* where Virgil calls him "infelix.") When Titus kills his son for defying the emperor's wish, he is following in a long line of distinguished Romans, following their version of the code of honor.

After the first scenes, the play consists in the humiliation, the debasement, and finally the destruction of Titus. By the close of the tragedy, the once valiant, noble Roman is as depraved as the human fiends who torment him. His daughter is raped. She has her tongue cut out. Her hands are sawed off. The corrupt emperor arrests Titus' oldest remaining son. Aaron the Moor, an enemy of Titus with connections at court, informs Titus that if he will cut off his own hand and send it to the emperor, the emperor might spare his son. Titus severs the hand and sends it as a gift. The emperor laughs and kills his son anyway. By the end of the play, Titus is a mad, disfigured animal. He kills the two men who have raped and mutilated his daughter and bakes them in a pie and invites their mother to eat it. She does. Then Titus kills Lavinia to spare her further shame, or so he says. Titus dies a self-justified but ruined man, his body maimed, his spirit destroyed.

Titus' loyalty to the emperor and to the values of republican Rome doesn't elevate him, not in the least. It debases him. In his own terms, Titus does virtually nothing wrong. But the play shows us time after time that *everything* Titus does, from murdering his own son to taking bloody revenge on Tamora to sawing his hand off in hopes of saving his son is completely, almost insanely, wrong. When the heroic code collides with the harsh exigencies of life, the result is more absurd than it is tragic. Titus dies not only debased, but also ridiculous. It is Titus' commitment to the old Roman martial values that causes his destruction. His honor is his undoing.

Titus is Shakespeare's tragic beginning, and he never travels as far away from its spirit as one might wish. In time, he will become a more sophisticated assassin of the heroic ideal. But the modus operandi will remain: the glorious must be debased. Then, in future plays, it will be brought back to life again to be debased once more.

That Shakespeare's Othello is a figure with epic stature is beyond doubt. Those around Othello recognize him as a hero: when trouble arises, he is the one the citizens depend on to save Venice. But we also know that Othello is a hero because he tells us so. Homer sings the song of Achilles and Hector; Othello sings the song of himself. Early in the play he tells the story of how he wooed and won Desdemona by rendering the tale of his own life. He wrote a compressed epic poem about himself: his battles and triumphs, his privations, and his wanderings.

Like Odysseus, Othello describes the wonders he has seen and the amazing events that have befallen him. Othello is a heroic figure in a literary production of his own devising. So to Brabantio and then to his daughter Desdemona, Othello tells the tale

> of most disastrous chances:
> Of moving accidents by flood and field,
> Of hair-breadth scapes i'th' imminent deadly breach,
> Of being taken by the insolent foe
> And sold to slavery, of my redemption thence
> And portance in my [travel's] history;
>
> (I.iii.134–139)

Othello finishes his story with a flourish, speaking of "the Cannibals that each [other] eat, / The Anthropophagi, and men whose heads / [Do grow] beneath their shoulders" (I.iii.143–145). At the end of Othello's grandiloquent recitation, Desdemona expresses the wish that "heaven had made her such a man" (I.iii.163).

For Othello there is one central truth in life. It is the epic truth of Othello, the victor who has come through struggles, who is the safeguard of the city of Venice and the lover and husband of the beautiful Desdemona. He has no desire to inquire into the validity of his terms for self-rendering. The Othello we meet at the beginning of the play clearly believes that there is one truth (his) and a set of words that perfectly expresses that truth (his as well). He has no awareness of (or no use for) ambiguity, complexity, or irony. Not for him what Nietzsche calls a "perspectival" seeing, in which there is no central truth about a person or event, only multiple interpretations. Othello is immune to the idea that every human occurrence is charged and changed by virtue of being seen from a different angle. He is incapable of entertaining the idea that there is no disinterested, determining vantage. The notion that perspectives compete with each other and that one perspective ascends to something called truth because of the authority of the perceiver, or the force of institutional power that underwrites him, is not available to Othello.

Othello is a truth-teller. When he is accused of bewitching Desdemona, Othello confronts the elders of Venice with his reputation and his faith in his power to tell absolute truth. "My parts, my title, and my perfect soul / Shall manifest me rightly" (I.ii.31–32). But the world is changing, and truth is no longer so simple a matter.

Othello, the heroic literalist, almost seems to call up the demon Iago from the depths. For Iago is Othello's dark inverse. "I am not what I am," says Iago. In what tone of voice does he speak these words? Is it wonder? Is he shocked and rather delighted at the unresolvable complexity of feelings and thoughts that he sees when he examines his inner life? Perhaps he speaks in horror. He cannot find his fundamental self, so he does not know what he will say or do next. He does not know what in the world might make him happy, or bring him to grieve. One thing is likely though. To be able to say "I am not what I am" can be a great asset for certain ways of life. To have a shifting, mobile sense of self (or no sense of self at all) can be an advantage for someone who aspires to be an actor—or even a playwright.

What enrages Iago so much about Othello? Surely he is wounded when Othello passes him over and appoints Michael Cassio as his second in command. Iago may even believe, as he claims, that the Moor has cuckolded him—done his office between the sheets. (But then Iago is free with such inferences—he also claims to suspect Cassio with his nightcap.) One might speculate that what galls Iago is not only being passed over for the lieutenancy in favor of the lightweight Michael Cassio or a hunch that the Moor has been to bed with Emilia. It is also something both deeper and more elusive. Perhaps Iago is enraged by Othello's confidence of being, by his grace, his assurance, his lack of uncertainty. Othello epitomizes a manner of being that is aristocratically certain and at home in the world. To be in proximity to such a singularly composed personage could only be an insult to the man who has no fixed sense of identity—"I am not what I am"—and who is, perhaps, alternately elated and distressed by the fact.

The noble individual, Nietzsche suggests in *The Genealogy of Morals,* lives in a paradise of univocal meaning. He knows only one manner of apprehending the world: with himself and his sort at the center. He knows only one set of values, heroic values, and he does not doubt them. But then he meets the man of resentment. The resentful man knows he cannot overthrow the noble man in battle, yet the resentful one still wants supremacy. How does he get it? By using his wits. He deploys his intelligence and imagination to spin out other interpretations of life in which the hero is anything but preeminent. He says that it is better to be learned than to be brave, or that it is better to be a man or woman of compassion, a saint. He claims that Nature does not endorse heroic values, but that Nature is simply a blind, unknowable force to which all human life is alien. "The Moor," says Iago, "is of a constant, loving, noble nature" (II.i.289). And for this Iago hates him: nobility is anathema to him, love an illusion, and the apparent constancy of Othello's being is, in Iago's world of ever-shifting perceptions and values, a rank imposture. It is an illusion that calls to be undone.

Iago lives in the world of no meaning. Or one might say he lives in a world in which meanings proliferate without end—which is much the same. Nothing truly anchors Iago to his life. Seeing that he cannot be a part of the artificial coherence of the established institutional sphere—becoming Othello's lieutenant would have given him a fiction of identity—he takes arms against all that appears to be solid. And nothing appears to be more sound and stable than Othello. Iago's perspectivism is not a stylized condition. Nietzsche, the son and grandson of ministers, can conceive the vertiginous world of jostling interpretations with a smile. But Iago often seems as disturbed as he is disturbing. He lives in the confusion of competing visions, competing interpretations, without center, without unity, without predictable form.

Iago is the force that multiplies perspectives, seeds the mental ground with doubt, and creates complexity where ostensible simplicity existed. The process at times brings him satanic delight, but at other times his plotting seems to bring him nearly as much pain as it does Othello. On some level Iago appears to love Othello, but for reasons that seem larger than himself, Iago must turn against the Moor.

Iago can play the part of friend, ally, confidante, rogue, beast, man of sensibility. He embodies all these figures, creates all these fictions, much as the playwright does. Iago broods often on the techniques of self-extemporization: "Virtue? A fig! 'tis in ourselves that we are thus or thus. Our bodies are our gardens, to the which our wills are gardeners; so that if we will plant nettle, set hyssop and weed up [tine], supply it with one gender of herbs or distract it with many, either to have it sterile with idleness or manur'd with industry—why, the power and corrigible authority of this lies in our wills" (I.iii.319–326). Then too we can presumably pull up the garden when we like and start anew.

In order to undermine Othello, Iago becomes him. He pretends to value what Othello values—he tells Othello in the most eloquent terms that there is nothing in life worth more than name and reputation. "Who steals my purse steals trash; 'tis something, nothing" (III.iii.157), he informs Othello, echoing the archetypal noble man's contempt for money. (In fact, Iago's stealing from Roderigo suggests that he has real affection for cash—a substance as protean in its possibilities as himself.) "But," Iago goes on, "he that filches from me my good name / Robs me of that which not enriches him, / And makes me poor indeed" (III.iii.159–161). The noble man cares for reputation—true reputation—more than almost anything, and for the moment Iago is the noble man. Or at least the one who can act the part, for he also tells Cassio (II.iii.266ff.) that reputation is of no value whatever. (Prince Hal also plays the role of the man of honor, though not to such horrible effect.) When Othello says that Iago must unfold his suspicions about Desdemona to him, Iago—like a hero—asserts that he will face torture rather than disclose his thoughts against his will. "By heaven," says Othello in an emblematic moment, "thou echo'st me" (III.iii.106).

Othello cannot bear doubt. Up until the play begins he has been a creature of assurances, committed to demonstrable truths, and this has surely served him well. The military commander needs to take in all he can, make up his mind about the situation at hand, and then act—unequivocally and finally. But the mental virtues that have served Othello so well in his heroic role as soldier are of no use in the erotic inferno that Iago creates. They are positively detrimental to him. Othello's major fear is not death, as it is for most men. Othello the hero seems ever ready to die. What frightens him is the chaos of not knowing. When he thinks about what it would mean for the worst possible to happen—for him to stop loving Desdemona—he says it would be "Chaos . . . come again" (III.iii.92). One might say that Othello takes an epic mind into the provinces of the erotic and is doomed for it. A. C. Bradley has said that if you put Hamlet into Othello's play, the prince would quickly make Iago for what he is and laugh him to scorn. In Hamlet's place, Othello would draw his sword and slice Claudius nave to chops in the first act. In either case: no play. But in the world that Iago creates, Othello is helpless as a child.

For Othello does not know the fundamental fact that most of Shakespeare's characters assume. Few characters in the plays use language as a transparent medium to represent the world as it is, or as they deeply believe it to be. (Those who do often pay a high price: think of Cordelia, Desdemona, Kent, and Hermione.) Characters in Shakespeare use language as an instrument to help them get what they want. They are pragmatists, as the critic and scholar Lars Engle suggests in his fine study of the playwright, and they talk for victory. They try to bring themselves closer to fulfilling their desires by what they say. Iago is the extreme example of this phenomenon, but it is pervasive. Othello uses language to disclose the Truth as he sees it, and also to continue to add layers to his self-portrait as a heroic individualist. Othello woos Desdemona with his tales, yes; but one has no doubt that he believes what he says to her word for word and in the most literal sense. Part of what wins her is his sincerity: he makes her weep by telling his story. Others in the plays use words the way chess players use their pawns and rooks, knights and bishops—to get them closer to victory. Schopenhauer observes that in Shakespeare's work "we see how the characters, with one or two exceptions that are not too glaring, are set in motion generally by motives of self-interest or wickedness. For he wishes to show in the mirror of poetry *men*, not moral caricatures; and so everyone recognizes them in the mirror and his works live today and for all time" (67).

Othello cries out for "ocular proof" of Desdemona's betrayal. He must know. He cannot be content with half knowledge—he cannot reside in uncertainties and mysteries and doubts in the way that Iago (and purportedly Shakespeare) can do. He reaches the point where the stability of his vision of the world—his heroic vision— becomes more important to him than his wife's virtue. (Othello, we might say, is an unsophisticated proponent of what Derrida would call the metaphysics of presence, the idea that Truth must be clear, present, and beyond interpretation. Iago: the first deconstructionist.) And no wonder: Othello's heroic epistemology—the idea that words are transparent to things and that seeing is believing—is what keeps him sane and allows him to maintain his dignified sense of himself. "I had been happy," he says, "if the general camp, / Pioners and all, had tasted her sweet body, / So I had nothing known" (III.iii.345–347). Othello had rather his wife had been a whore and he had known nothing about it than be in the state of uncertainty that so torments him—and that is Iago's element. Othello can live with ignorance and he can live with absolute Truth, but not with the states in between.

Othello is in uncertainties, and he senses that he will never have true resolution. He readily sees how deadly the consequences of this state are for him: "Farewell the tranquil mind! farewell content! / Farewell the plumed troops and the big wars / That makes ambition virtue" (III.iii.348–350). Othello knows that he has fallen. His worldview based on transparency and assurance is now lost, and without his epic senses of fullness—the one that Achilles possessed and lost and found again—Othello cannot be the man he was. Unlike Achilles, Othello has no way to repossess his stability of mind.

From the point where Othello says farewell to his spirit's tranquility, Iago has won. He has won the battle of mind, and all that is left is to claim the joys of victory, witnessing the complete humiliation and near madness of the heroic individual.

Who is Iago? He is Shakespeare's character (and anti-character) to be sure. He is a brilliant invention of the playwright. But there come points in the play where we see another dimension. We encounter moments when playwright and character seem to merge, and Iago's voice might almost as well be Shakespeare's. As Stephen Greenblatt and Stanley Edgar Hyman have seen, there is something theatrical in Iago's temperament. "In *Othello*," Greenblatt says, "Shakespeare seems to acknowledge, represent and explore his affinity to the malicious improviser" (*Renaissance Self-Fashioning*, 252).

At moments, Iago broods on the plot against Othello in terms that the playwright could easily use brooding on the plot of his play—at the heart of which is the plot against Othello. Iago can sometimes sound like the playwright in mid-draft, full of doubts and aspirations. All through the play, we hear Iago plotting aloud, and frequently he is not quite sure how he is going to bait and place his traps. He'll go free-form, he tells us, extemporize, take what circumstances give him:

> Cassio's a proper man. Let's see now:
> To get his place and to plume up my will
> In double knavery—How? how?—Let's see—
> After some time to abuse Othello's [ear]
> That he is too familiar with his wife.
> (I.iii.391–395)

"'Tis here," Iago says, later on, after he's been considering the course of his plot (and Shakespeare's), "but yet confus'd / Knavery's plain face is never seen till us'd" (II.i.311–312).

Later, Iago will take another step forward in laying out the plot—and again sound rather like the playwright talking to himself about his next move. "So will I turn her virtue into pitch, / And out of her own goodness make the net / That shall enmesh them all" (II.iii.360–362). With some foresight, but not too much (not enough to inhibit his capacity for improvisation), Iago is weaving the tragic net that will catch Desdemona and Othello, and while he does so, Iago and his author almost seem to plot in tandem.

Is Shakespeare Iago? Both delight in impersonation, in play-making, in creating scenes. Both are versatile, both protean, both accomplished actors. Both are capable of being in uncertainties, mysteries, and doubts without any irritable reaching after fact and reason, to think back to Keats's memorable lines. But Shakespeare's objective, one suspects, is not the destruction of an individual figure, like Othello. Shakespeare's objective is the destruction of an ideal. His is the force of mobility that attacks too-solid, monolithic Othello. Shakespeare's, at least in this play, is the energy that undoes heroic perfection.

At the end of the play, after Othello has killed Desdemona and destroyed his reputation, as well as scorching the reputation of the hero proper, Othello reaches his most horrible moment. He tries again to be the poet of his own life and to write himself an epic epitaph. Before he dies in the noble Roman fashion—thrusting a dagger into his chest—Othello seeks to have the last word: he aspires again to be both heroic actor and heroic poet. "Speak of me as I am," he says, "nothing extenuate." But immediately he offers a litany of extenuations. "Then must you speak," he says, "of one that lov'd not wisely but too well; / Of one not easily jealous, but being wrought, / Perplexed in the extreme" (V.ii.343–346). Not easily jealous! Loved *too well?* Othello still but slenderly knows himself—or rather he cannot understand the force that he has met with in Iago.

In the last moment of his self-elegy, Othello speaks of how in Aleppo once he accosted a Turk who had beaten a Venetian citizen and threatened the state. "I took by th' throat the circumcised dog, / And smote him—thus" (V.ii.355–356). Then he drives his dagger into his own heart. Othello wants to conflate his suicide with a heroic act from his past, making of the suicide an admirable deed. The knife thrust recapitulates his brave former gesture and is, by association, a comparably intrepid act. Thus Othello dies by his own hand and in a state of self-delusion, thinking he is still a hero. In the world that Shakespeare is helping create, there may be no more martial heroes, no more men who can believe that the fire that burns in their souls is identical to the fire that burns in the stars.

For his part, Iago goes silent. Torture him as the state will, he affirms that "from this time forth I never will speak word" (V.ii.304). He and his view of life have triumphed, though in some part of himself Iago is probably horrified by his victory.

How could an upwardly aspiring merchant's son from the provinces not sustain a measure of resentment for aristocrats and their pretensions? Or, more to the point, how could the middle class of London—rising, prospering—not take delight in watching one or another of their antagonists being undone?

Though, to be sure, the political and economic climate in which Shakespeare writes is not uncomplicated. Arnold Hauser tells us that "all the fears entertained by the middle classes about the increase in the powers of the sovereign were silenced by the support they had in the monarchy in waging the class war. Elizabeth promoted the capitalist economy in every way. . . . The acquisitive economy rose uninterruptedly and the spirit of profit-making connected with it embraced the whole nation" (2.137). In the forefront of the urge for profit was the new middle class and those members of the nobility who were inclined to behave like them—to invest and invest again. Still, the court formed the center of public life, and the crown sometimes favored the old established nobility, though generally only when it could do so without harming the material interests of the new acquisitive classes. A social leveling was taking place, in part as the children of the middle class married their ways into the aristocracy, in part as the younger sons of the nobility entered bourgeois professions. "In England," Hauser continues, "what takes place is essentially the leveling down of the nobility to the middle class" (2.138). The old nobility still exists, and it still has a measure of power and prestige, but the new classes are in contention with it, much as they are in contention with the poor and the working orders. On the one side, threatening the acquisitive classes, is the entrenched nobility; on the other side the urban and rural poor, who always represent to Shakespeare (as they must have to many of his contemporaries) a threat of rebellion, perhaps chaos. The fear of anarchy threads through the plays, much as the fear of nobles in their traditional ideal (and perhaps idealized) form does.

But the culture's collective feeling about nobility and honor will inevitably be ambivalent. Merchants have their own measure of spiritedness. They too have felt—or imagined feeling—a jolt of courage pass through them. They cannot help but be fascinated by a character who embodies the heroic ideal to self-destructive perfection. They love what they loathe, and wish to see destroyed that which they might also worship. This is the ambivalence of Shakespeare's tragedy, its richness and its soul. Aristotle says that tragedy must be about the undoing of someone who is *greater* than we are. For us to live in good conscience, Othello and his ilk must be brought to what appears to be self-made ruin.

The Soul can create a sense of bad conscience in the Self. It is not enough for the Self to dominate the material world. Victory is never complete. Somewhere, someone always feels the lure of ideals. One may even feel it oneself.

Did Othello try to reach above the gods? Is he a victim of hubris? Oh no. He simply tried to reach above the members of the all-conquering middle class, and for that there is a harsh verdict and sentencing without appeal. For Self suffers from self-doubt. In some quadrant of its being, Self understands its limits: in its essence it is teeming, ravenous, grasping life. It is the will of the world, the energy in all that lives. But at the same time it is *merely* a force of life and appetite—a force common to men and to animals and in some measure to plants. The Self is what life is all about, for the Self is a concentration of vitality. In most people the intellect is merely a servant of the Self. It aids self-seeking and does nothing more. The Self is striving will. But a person does not feel he is fully human when he lives only to survive. It is not enough when he lives to eat, lives to prosper, lives to procreate. He feels there is more to life, but that *more* frightens him. So he has a double task. He must find ways to denigrate intellect and compassion and (at Shakespeare's moment in particular) courage. He must be able to laugh with Cervantes at the spindle-shanked, delusional knight, who sets his lance at windmills.

But he must also find a way to invest meaning in Self. He must create a philosophy of life that circulates around what he eats and what he wears and what he buys. He must create for himself a life-style. His story about middle-class existence has somehow to compete with Homer's story about martial glory, or Plato's about the heights of contemplation. He hoards and sleeps—"he hops and blinks" as Nietzsche says—and he listens to the songs of happiness (he must be sung to day and night), and he feels almost justified.

Shakespeare reinvents woman. Or rather, he gives the world female characters who are unprecedented. Shelley compares an adored woman in his life to "one of Shakespeare's women"—"a wonder of this earth." And Shakespeare often does seem to prefer women to

men: consider Juliet, Beatrice, Desdemona, Cordelia, Marina, and
Rosalind, all of whom have found warm favor with audiences and
readers. Women are more likeable, maybe more lovable, than men
in Shakespeare, granted. But as women rise—as in the bourgeois
world of Self they will do—must men inevitably fall? Consider Lady
Macbeth and what she does to (and perhaps proves about) her valorous husband.

Macbeth is strong on the battlefield. The opening scenes of the
play take pains to affirm his martial prowess. The language
that describes Macbeth's exploits is stirring, almost Homeric,
though it lacks Homer's supreme detachment. Here in the play's
first act is the Sergeant recounting Macbeth's contention with
Macdonwald:

> Brave Macbeth (well he deserves that name),
> Disdaining Fortune, with his brandished steel,
> Which smok'd with bloody execution,
> (Like Valor's minion) carv'd out his passage
> Till he faced the slave;
> Which nev'r shook hands, nor bade farewell to him,
> Till he unseam'd him from the nave to th' chops,
> And fix'd his head upon our battlements.
>
> (I.i.16–22)

Macbeth the warrior is elevated prior to his fall. But before he does
fall, he's pinned in place, almost Prufrock-like, for diagnosis.

What is the source of Macbeth's amazing courage? How does he
manage to be fearless? Macbeth doesn't celebrate his own powers.
He isn't a singer of himself, like Othello, though he will become a
graphic chronicler of his own terrors. But Macbeth is an instance
of the ultimate warrior. He has the power to step to the forefront of

the battle line, deal death, and risk it. Macbeth is not a strategist pondering a map in his tent, surrounded by subordinates. He's far from Shakespeare's Caesar Augustus. He goes where the fighting is hottest, from the beginning of the play to the end. "We'll die with harness on our back" (V.v.51), he says on his day of doom, and he does. But what is the key to his courage?

Macbeth is pushed on to do daring, murderous deeds by his wife. Lady Macbeth, who may or may not know herself, knows her husband well. The key to Macbeth's motives is at her disposal. She wishes him to kill Duncan, his anointed king, his kinsman, and, symbolically perhaps, his father. All she needs to express, with due subtlety and craft, is that unless Macbeth does the deed he is not a man. Fears about masculinity, critics have rightly told us, are at the center of Macbeth's character. On some level, his heart is tender. "Pity," he says memorably, is "like a naked new-born babe, / Striding the blast" (I.vii.21–22). A man who can compound such a phrase is on some level a sensitive one. To force him on to inhumane deeds is no easy endeavor.

Macbeth has no children. After his men kill Macduff's wife and all his brood, Macduff says as much. But Lady Macbeth apparently has had children. She has nursed a child, she tells us. But if she had sworn to do so, she continues, she would have torn the child from her breast and smashed its skull on the flagstones:

> I have given suck, and know
> How tender 'tis to love the babe that milks me;
> I would, while it was smiling in my face,
> Have pluck'd my nipple from his boneless gums,
> And dash'd the brains out, had I so sworn as you
> Have done to this.
>
> (I.vii.54–59)

Murder is Lady Macbeth's element, though the closing scenes of the play when she tries to wash invisible blood from her hands indicate that even she is not entirely immune to guilt.

Macbeth, it seems, cannot do for her what her first husband or paramour could do: give her children, males if possible. Macbeth's admonition to her to "bring forth men-children only" (I.vii.73) is also probably an admonition to himself to plant them with her and, one might speculate, expresses his hope that if he behaves as a man he may be able to do so. Has Macbeth been impotent? Infertile? The suggestion is surely present.

The play is fixated on children, and sons in particular. Sons revenge their fathers; sons continue a royal line. Sons give meaning to the harsh life of the thanes. The promise of a son's succession makes one's own achievement of the second place, rather than the first, more bearable. You will not be a king, Banquo learns, but you will be the begetter of kings, and discovering this gives him a measure of contentment. Yet Macbeth has no children. He has no sons, in particular. He's not man enough to produce them. So he is valorous, then more valorous still, until he passes from valor to brutality and becomes a beast.

Macbeth struggles against his wife's attacks on his manhood. She rates him hard, insisting that he go ahead with his plans and do away with the mild Duncan. "Art thou afeared," she asks, "To be the same in thine own act and valor / As thou art in desire?" (I.vii.39–41). Overtly the lines are about committing the murder. But they also suggest that there have been other times when Macbeth has not been able to translate desire into an act. Macbeth appears to know where she is going—they have presumably traveled this ground before: "I dare do all that may become a man," he says. "Who dares do more is none" (I.vii.46–47). But Lady Macbeth is ready for him. "When you durst do it," she says, "then you were a man" (I.vii.49). "Screw your courage to the sticking place," Lady Macbeth tells her husband, "and we'll not fail" (I.vii.60–61). Screw your courage to the sticking place: the language is suggestively sexual, merging thoughts about erotic success and the success of their plot. Potency becomes synonymous with murder, murder with potency. And Macbeth—his fixation on the masculine enhanced—offers his wife his song of subordination: "Bring forth men-children only!" (I.vii.73).

"Is this a dagger which I see before me?" Macbeth asks in his first soliloquy (II.i.33–61). The Freudian reader tells us—but perhaps we do not need the Freudian reader to see—that Macbeth's weapon of choice, the weapon he can readily possess and wield, is rather a close approximation of the implement that he seems unable to command. Much of what Macbeth has to say about the hallucinatory dagger in front of him does resonate well enough with the urge for an organ that he can employ as he will. It is an ideal of potency he wants to grasp, yet it eludes him. The objective is perhaps to use the dagger to acquire phallic power. "I have thee not, and yet I see thee still." "Art thou but a dagger of the mind?" "Thou marshals't me the way that I was going / And such an instrument I was to use." He cries: "I see thee still." The idea that the sword and the dagger—symbols of martial bravery—are often seen as signs of phallic anxiety is a blow against the heroic ideal. Here the playwright makes way for the analyst. The theory of the phallic symbol is one of Freud's minor weapons in his arsenal of soul-assaulting devices.

Macbeth's anxiety about potency and engendering is continually evident. When he becomes king, he tells us, he will hold nothing but "a barren sceptre" (III.i.61) because no son of his will succeed him. The "barren scepter" suggests both kingly and sexual inadequacy. Macbeth is everywhere beset by his creator with symbols of his impotence, symbols of which he is sadly unaware. For the hero does not know that the world can exist in a double and triple sense—he knows only one meaning for things, their right and natural meaning.

Part of the play's genius lies in the way it traces Macbeth's afflic-tion with the disease of sexual anxiety. Himself infected by Lady Macbeth, he infects others. He passes the malady on. When he is suborning men to murder Banquo, he begins by telling them all that Banquo has done to them and asks, implicitly, if they will bear it. "We are men, my liege" (III.i.90), one says, and by saying so shows signs that he may be possessed by a version of Macbeth's erotic anx-iety. (Perhaps all men are, the play ultimately suggests—or at least all men with a capacity for violence.) Macbeth sees the possibilities and answers: "Ay, in the catalogue ye go for men, / As hounds and greyhounds, mongrels, spaniels, curs, / Shoughs, water-rugs, and demi-wolves are clipt / All by the name of dogs" (III.i.91–94). You're biologically men, certainly, but manhood is more than simply a state of being. It is a capacity for doing.

Macbeth presents himself to the murderers as someone who knows what manhood is and who can confer its status on others. He plays the role for the murderers that Lady Macbeth plays for him. (In fact, Macbeth is still pining to be anointed as a true man himself.) Dealing with the murderers, he sees what a powerful magic manhood anxiety is. "Now, if you have a station in the file, / Not i' th' worst rank of manhood, say't" (III.i.101–102), he com-mands the potential killers. Having suborned the murderers, Macbeth can answer his wife when she asks, "Are you not a man?" "Ay and a bold one, that dare look on that which might appall the devil" (III.iv.58–59). He has achieved the temporary relief that passing one's malaise on to others can supply. For if he can be an arbiter of manhood, then surely Macbeth must be a man himself.

"What man dare, I dare," Macbeth says as Banquo's ghost ap-proaches; if he runs afraid, he says, "protest me the baby of a girl"

(III.v.98, 104–105). Struggle as Macbeth might, he still cannot possess full manhood. When he faces the ghost he feels like a baby girl (or perhaps a girl's doll)—not a man, not a warrior, not a fully sound and whole being.

Only a man who is not of woman born can harm Macbeth (IV.i.80–81). Macbeth hears this prophecy from the witches, and it deludes him into thinking that no mortal being can kill him in battle. But of course there are human beings who are not of woman born. Macduff, who does away with the tyrant, was "from his mother's womb / Untimely ripp'd" (V.viii.15–16), delivered by Caesarian section. Like Oedipus, Macbeth is faced with a riddle, but Macbeth cannot answer his. The whole process of conception and birth is presumably a mystery to Macbeth. It is something he knows all too little about. When he approaches these subjects he becomes anxious and confused. Told that no man born of woman can harm him, he does not have the mental flexibility he needs to see that the prophecy is not airtight testimony to his being indestructible in battle. He can only take it in its literal sense. Oedipus, the orphan, has clearly thought a good deal about human origins and ends, and can answer quite well when he is asked who goes on four legs in the morning, two in the afternoon, and three in the evening. Faced with a riddle involving children and birth, Macbeth is helpless.

There is a normative version of the warrior in *Macbeth*. When Macduff receives word that Macbeth's henchmen have murdered his family, including all his "pretty chickens" (IV.iii.218), his children, he is staggered with grief. "Dispute it like a man," says Duncan's son Malcolm. "I shall do so," Macduff returns, "But I must also feel it as a man" (IV.iii.220–221). And so he does—if Macduff's lament is brief it is also eloquent. "I cannot but remember such things were, / That were most precious to me" (IV.iii.222–223). But then he turns from lament to resolve:

> Front to front
> Bring thou this fiend of Scotland and myself;
> Within my sword's length set him; if he scape,
> Heaven forgive him too!
>
> (IV.iii.232–235)

But naturally Macbeth will not escape. Macduff harks back to an old and honorable image of the warrior not commonly seen in Shakespeare. (Alcibiades in *Timon of Athens*, Talbot in *Henry VI*, and Pericles are also of this ilk.) By and large, Shakespeare's relation to the culture of honor is that of self-designated assassin. Overall one hears his voice in Falstaff's great denunciation of the code of heroes in *Henry IV, Part I*:

> What is honor? A word. What is in that word honor? What is that honor? Air! A trim reckoning! Who hath it? He that died a' Wednesday. Doth he feel it? No. Doth he hear it? No. 'Tis insensible then? Yea, to the dead. But will['t] not live with the living? No. Why? Detraction will not suffer it. Therefore I'll none of it, honor is a mere scutcheon. And so ends my catechism.
>
> (V.i.132–141)

Honor is a mere scutcheon, a heraldic device, or what critics would now call an empty signifier. Honor is a concept, an ideal—and thus to the man who lives to eat and drink and dull the pain of being alive in any way he can, honor is an empty puff of air. Honor can get you killed, put you out of life, and so is to be detested by the man who wants to live as long as possible, the sort of man that Falstaff both affirms and mocks.

Macbeth too says a farewell to the code of honor, though the farewell is far harsher than Falstaff's high-hearted aria. At the end of his play, having been duped by the witches and abandoned by his troops, Macbeth knows he's doomed. Then he hears the news of his wife's death, and it shakes his worldview to its base:

> Tomorrow, and tomorrow, and tomorrow,
> Creeps in this petty pace from day to day,
> To the last syllable of recorded time;
> And all our yesterdays have lighted fools
> The way to dusty death. Out, out brief candle!
> Life's but a walking shadow, a poor player,
> That struts and frets his hour upon the stage,
> And then is heard no more. It is a tale
> Told by an idiot, full of sound and fury,
> Signifying nothing.
>
> (V.v.18–28)

Macbeth's speech is a hymn to nihilism. Nothing matters; nothing is of value. Life is a matter of "walking shadow," human beings who traverse the world like the ghosts who populate the infernal regions in Homer or dwell in Plato's cave. The world that Macbeth describes is one where no human action counts; everything is an empty play, and all the tumult and expenditure of force mean nothing. It is a world, in other words, that is nearly the inverse of the heroic, epic world. In that world human excellence matters. There glory counts. The world that Macbeth describes is a world of sterile drama, full of players, who perform shadowy, transient plays, not the substantial, glowing men and women who populate the world of the epic. Excellence in that world matters to the gods and to men and women of discernment. No one in *The Iliad*, except for vile Thersites, could entertain sentiments like Macbeth's. At the end of the play, Macbeth is entirely unlike Othello, who can still delude himself into thinking that he can construct his own reputation and that the construction will matter. Macbeth suffers the horrid disillusionment of seeing that whatever aspirations he may have had to kingship and glory, nothing in this world really counts. It is all empty, all void.

By the end, the major thrust of the play is clear—even Macbeth may understand it. What looks like daring on Macbeth's part is merely a form of compensation. What appears to be courage is no more than the disguising of an inadequacy. It is compensation that takes Macbeth into crime. But the suggestion remains that it is compensating for sexual inadequacy that makes him valorous to begin with. He is, we are led to think, "Bellona's bridegroom" (I.ii.54), the husband of the goddess of war. And this may be because he cannot be the proper bridegroom of any living—which is to say desiring—woman. (Bellona was a virgin goddess, a fact Shakespeare makes clear he knows in *I Henry IV* [IV.i.114].) However long he has been married to Lady Macbeth, he has produced no heirs, no children. There was, evidently, another man who could. It is not her problem. Instead of producing children, Macbeth has produced victories. Instead of being sexually potent, he has been what the old aristocratic culture would have called brave.

Shakespeare, an admirer of women but no feminist himself, has offered terms that, in the centuries to come, will be applied by feminists to the oppressor, the hypermasculine man of prowess. He is brave because he is frightened. He is manly because he is weak. His martial potency is a sign of a more intimate impotence. Macbeth is not a representative figure in the way Othello is. He is too irrational, too emotional, too bloodthirsty. His imagination ignites too readily—it is too much his own. But the play allows one to ask, in a fashion that Freud among others will go on to do, whether or not this aristocratic aspiration, this ideal called courage, may actually be a pathology. How often is courage a quality we need to diagnose rather than praise? How often does the aspiring hero require treatment rather than an education at arms? If the hero is a sick man, then the man who lives the life of Self can rest more content, for he is healthy. There is good reason for his not venturing into the bloody wars. He is not a coward. Put no white feather in his hand. The man of Self is sane; the hero is . . . the hero is not mad: there is something glorious in certain sorts of madness. Rather, the hero is simply ill.

One of the main functions of Shakespeare's great inheritor, Freud, is to redescribe the ideals of compassion and courage and the exercise of imagination as pathologies and forms of delusion. (He will also help redefine thought as that which demystifies, rather than that which inspires and exalts.) Freud makes the middle-class people who live by half measures feel much better, allowing them to understand that the virtues that intimidated them are forms of sickness and that normality—clear-eyed and stable—is the true achievement. What a reversal! What a transvaluation of values. What victory for those who wish to live as long and securely as possible.

Ancient honor, legendary or historical, is not something Shakespeare abides easily. His major source for classical lore, Plutarch, has an entirely different vision of this subject than Shakespeare does.

Plutarch's Caesar is a hero out and out. The historian (if that is genuinely what Plutarch is) delights in telling stories about Caesar that border on legend. In Plutarch's life of Caesar we learn how pirates captured him when he was young. Caesar spends his time in captivity with the pirates telling them stories, drinking, and joining in their games while he waits for his ransom money to arrive. He also makes threats, laughingly. He tells the pirates that after he's ransomed he is going to raise an army and come back to the region, defeat them in battle, then capture and crucify the ones who haven't been killed. They laugh uproariously at him. But of course that is precisely what Caesar does.

Plutarch's Caesar aspires to renown. Crossing the Alps, Caesar and his retinue pass through a tiny out-of-the-way village where the people are miserable—hungry and soiled. His men joke about whether there is a great deal of competition for high office there, or whether there are major feuds among the most formidable men. Says Caesar, "For my part I would rather be the first man among these fellows than the second man in Rome." At another point, Caesar is found brooding on Alexander (who attempted to model his life on the life of Achilles) and his massive achievements as warrior and general. Caesar is in tears. "Do you think," he says to his friends, "that I have not just cause to weep, when I consider that Alexander at my age had conquered so many nations, and I have all this time done nothing that is memorable?" (206).

When Caesar becomes a general in the Gallic wars, he achieves almost astonishing victories. He comes up with brilliant strategies for battling far more numerous enemies. But his powers do not end there. He is also a warrior, and like Alexander he fights at the head of his troops. He takes all the risks his men do and shares their lives in camp. Says Plutarch, "There was no danger to which he did not willingly expose himself, no labor from which he pleaded an exemption" (210). Though he was not born with a strong constitution, Caesar's will is fierce. He used war, Plutarch says, as a physic against his maladies. "By indefatigable journeys, coarse diet, frequent lodging in the field, and continual laborious exercise, he struggled with his diseases and fortified his body against all attacks" (210). Caesar the warrior is stunningly successful. As Plutarch puts it: "He had not pursued the wars in Gaul full ten years when he had taken by storm above eight hundred towns, subdued three hundred states, and of the three millions of men, who made up the gross sum of those with whom at several times he engaged, he had killed one million and taken captive a second" (209).

Plutarch's Caesar demands to be first at all times, and he usually is. But when Shakespeare depicts Caesar, he is a timid, superstitious, uxorious man, vain and befuddled. He is gaudily boastful and refers to himself frequently in third-person. Brooding on the threat Cassius poses to him, he informs Antony:

> I . . . tell thee what is to be fear'd
> Than what I fear; for always I am Caesar.
> (I.ii.211–212)

Immediately, Shakespeare undercuts the great man's boast, in which, if Plutarch and many other historians are to be believed, there is more than a little truth. "Come on my right hand," he tells Antony, "for this ear is deaf" (I.ii.213). The figure Shakespeare gives us could never have conquered the Western territories or come in ruthless glory across the Rubicon. He is a tottering beast, fit for sacrifice. Shakespeare's Caesar is confused, vulnerable, vain, and easy to eliminate.

And Coriolanus, whom Plutarch gives to us as large, bold, proud, and desirous always of the first place? *Coriolanus* is one of Shakespeare's most interesting works, featuring as it does the two forces that seem to give the playwright the most uneasiness, the aristocracy and the mob. The play's major opposition is between the crowd and Coriolanus. Shakespeare disliked and feared the crowd, though he can feel some measure of sympathy for it, too. Coriolanus is, emotionally, a large child. But he's also a potent warrior, who spends the time when he's not engrossed in fighting insulting the members of the lower orders. They insult him back. The play lets Shakespeare show both elements, aristocrats and plebeians, in their worst light, and he takes constant advantage of the opportunity.

In Plutarch's account of Coriolanus, he is beloved by his mother and loving. But Shakespeare takes this matter further, making Volumnia a major figure in the play. She controls her son—dominates and oppresses him in ways that Plutarch does not even hint at. Almost as much as Macbeth is dominated by his wife, Coriolanus is dominated by his mother. Again there arises the question: Is courage a noble virtue? Or is courage a form of compensation for defects? Macbeth's defect may well be impotence. In the case of Coriolanus, the defect is that of never having grown up—of being a boy, and sometimes a "boy of tears." Is courage at bottom merely a way to win a wife or a mother's love?

Shakespeare almost always tends to bring identity back to the family. We get to know the intimate lives of almost all his protagonists, and we see that they are defined by what they experienced at home. As Schopenhauer says, the apple doesn't usually fall far from the tree in the plays. Identity is familial, the plays often insist. Recall how much the life of the Soul is at variance with the life of the family. The individual in the State of Soul—thinker, saint, or warrior—is prone to leave the family and strike out on his own. He will not let his identity be determined by the circumstances of birth and upbringing. Freud's insistence that we are who our families make us—that radical self-reinvention is largely impossible—is in many ways affirmed by Shakespeare. Coriolanus is his mother's son; Laertes the true child of Polonius; Hal the emanation of Bolingbroke; the list could continue on and on. Though there are, to be sure, exceptions: large-hearted Juliet bears almost no resemblance to her vulgar, feuding family.

In *The Iliad,* Thersites, the misshapen soldier who rails at Agamemnon and the other heroes, has twenty-five lines. In Shakespeare's most Homeric play, *Troilus and Cressida,* Thersites has about ten times that number. Here, with the assistance of Thersites,

Shakespeare becomes something less than a god, paring his nails above his creation. Here he displays his prejudices—which are in many ways those of the contemporary human, those of the Self.

The quality of the play is almost spectacularly high. It contains one of Shakespeare's most famous set pieces, Ulysses' speech on order and degree, which was once taken to illustrate something called the Elizabethan World Picture. If there was an Elizabethan World Picture, with due commitment to the Great Chain of Being and the rest, then Shakespeare is a writer out to smash it. Chains and hierarchies set by God are the last standards that Shakespeare affirms, and the speech figures in the play as a piece of irony. Ulysses is an arch double-dealer and hypocrite in a play teeming with double-dealers and hypocrites. After he hits high oratory on the matter of order and degree, he goes to work hatching a new plot.

It is in *Troilus and Cressida* that the poet of negative capability makes his view of the world most positively present. There are twin protagonists in *Romeo and Juliet,* the two lovers, but Troilus and Cressida do not dominate the play that takes their names. Quickly they drop to the background of the piece. The play develops into a Brechtian mélange of characters for a while, until one emerges at the center. But what happens to that mélange is well worth contemplating. Achilles is a besotted fool; Patroclus a figure both narcissistic and stupid; Hector a fraud; Ulysses a hustler; Ajax a lout; Paris a ninny. Helen is a whore and Cressida (in time) is too.

One knows these facts because one follows the characters and their actions, but one knows, too, because Thersites proclaims them, over and over again. Homer gives Thersites his few lines close to the opening of the great poem. Shakespeare allows his Thersites gradually but inexorably to take over his play. Thersites is the rancid, resentful, poxed chorus who reduces everything he encounters to a level even below his own, impossible as that may sound. He is the walking embodiment of the reductive fallacy, the view that the worst that one can half-plausibly say about a given individual is the most central truth.

As the play proceeds, Thersites' presence increases and the temperature of his invective goes up. He progresses from bitter to rancid to rank to rotten. And it is difficult not to feel that he is registering Shakespeare's growing contempt for his characters as he continues—through the act of writing them and inhabiting them in the intimate way a playwright does—to spend his hours in their company.

An exchange among Thersites, Achilles, and Patroclus at the end of the play shows how far matters descend. Thersites enters and Achilles greets him:

> How now thou [core] of envy?
> Thou crusty batch of nature, what's
> the news?

Thersites: Why, thou picture of what thou seemest, and idol of idiot worshippers, here's a letter for thee.

Achilles: From whence fragment?

Thersites: Why, thy full dish of fool, from Troy.

Patroclus: Who keeps the tent now?

Thersites: The surgeon's box, or the patient's wound.

Patroclus: Well said adversity! and what needs [these] tricks?

Thersites: Prithee be silent [boy], I profit not by thy talk. Thou art said to be Achilles' male varlot?

Patroclus: Male varlot, you rogue! What's that?

Thersites: Why, his masculine whore.

    (V.i.4–18)

Without much effort, Thersites has brought the noblest of the Greek heroes down to the base level. In fact, one might say that Thersites is superior to Achilles in the contention that matters most here in this play—the exchange of vile wit.

Achilles and Patroclus depart and on come Agamemnon and Menelaus. "Here's Agamemnon," Thersites informs the crowd, with whom the playwright seems to believe he's formed a confederation, "an honest fellow enough and one that loves quails; but he has not so much brain as earwax" (V.i.51–53). As to Menelaus, Thersites says, "I care not to be the louse of a lazar" a parasite on a leper, he says, "so I were not Menelaus" (V.i.65–66).

By the middle of the last act, the play's spirit is fully the spirit of Thersites; he has come to dominate matters entirely. "Lechery, lechery," he chants, "still wars and lechery! Nothing else holds fashion. A burning devil take them" (V.ii.194–196). But it is not merely that there is one infected character at the center of events. It's also that the spirit of Thersites seems to be at the heart of the *composition* of the play. When it is time for Hector to die, Achilles does not face him alone on the field as he does in Homer. Instead he allows his Myrmidons to surround the Trojan hero and slaughter him; the mob pounces on him all at once. It is outright murder, not a duel between matched warriors. "When I have the bloody Hector found," Achilles tells his men, "empale him with your weapons round about" (V.vii.4–5). And they do. One understands that in a recent production, Achilles draws an anachronistic revolver and shoots Hector without warning, which is a fair enough interpretation of Shakespeare's designs.

In *Troilus and Cressida* Shakespeare attempts to pull the cover off Homer. He reveals his heroes to be not warriors with ideals, but Selves of the lowest order. What makes them so bad is that, having basic animal natures like all other men, they pretend otherwise. They do not know their own capacity for corruption, so besotted are they with their ideals and their images. They are without internal checks, without the sense that they are really no different from other men and women.

No one who reads *Troilus and Cressida* with even half-open eyes can leave it believing that Shakespeare had no convictions, or at least no negative convictions. Clearly there are forces in his inherited culture and in his contemporary world that he despises. For though it may be difficult to see what Shakespeare valued—difficult, but perhaps not impossible—it is palpable what he condemns: chivalry, honor, nobility, the heroic code. Titus, Hotspur, Othello, Macbeth, Timon, Coriolanus, Caesar, Lear, Achilles, Hector, Ulysses, and the entire sorry cast of *Troilus and Cressida* leave this beyond doubt.

So why is this palpable fact not common knowledge?

One reason is literary. Shakespeare writes in what can only be called a high, even a noble, style. His diction is almost always elevated. His servants are inclined to speak like counts, his counts like demigods. The diction is refined, yes, but the content is generally debunking. It is harder to see how the polemical thrust of the plays goes, since it is so out of keeping with their richly royal verbal texture.

But another more pertinent reason for this lack of recognition may be that Shakespeare finds his most adept audience among the educated middle class. His convictions about nobility are not, to them, *convictions*. They are not mere beliefs. Rather they have the authority of facts. And Shakespeare's text is now in the hands of a certain professional cadre—the professors. Professors are equipped to understand and sympathize with many sorts of figures, but they are usually worlds away from admiring heroic prowess. How many English professors now in the Anglo-Saxon world have served in battle? What fraction of literature professors can approve of war, any war, or revere warriors? The strong polemic against martial heroism in the plays looks to them simply like a set of natural facts. Those who aspire to heroism *do* tend to be braggarts and bullies. They may have sexual issues like Macbeth's; they may be compensating for being dominated by their mothers the way Coriolanus appears to be. They may be as un-self-knowing as Othello or Hotspur or Lear. Professors will be the last people in the world to tell you that virtue, true to the Latin root *virtu*, means strength, as the Romans believed. On the first page of his life of Coriolanus, Plutarch tells us the Romans believed that virtue equaled martial prowess and that was that. What Shakespeare despises, those who are currently intelligent enough or refined enough to comprehend his work will likely despise too.

Shakespeare is by far the most quoted author in the English-speaking world. But I would dare to say it is often a mistake to do so. This is because almost every Shakespeare passage comes from the mouth of a character speaking to achieve his or her desires. They speak from desires for and of the Self—they articulate, directly or indirectly, self-interested aspirations. "There is a tide in the affairs of men," we say, "which taken at the flood leads on to fortune." But Brutus, the character we quote, has just conspired in an assassination and is now endorsing a strategy, engaging Antony and Caesar Augustus at Philippi, that will fail utterly. "Neither a borrower nor a lender be," we say, "for loan oft loses both itself and friend and borrowing dulls the edge of husbandry." But in saying so we forget we are quoting, and thus summoning as our corroborator, a foolish counselor who spies on his own son and daughter and who lives for court intrigues. One says, "the lunatic, the lover and the poet / Are of imagination all compact," and feels he has wittily slandered the aspirations of poets and poetry. But one is likely to forget that the speaker is the rather unimaginative Duke Theseus, who understands almost nothing of the world of *Midsummer Night's Dream*. One says, "The devil can cite scripture for his purpose," and forgets that the devil in question is Shylock and that the line is inflected with Antonio's bitter anti-Semitism. "I never knew so young a body with so old a head" is a line one has heard as a birthday toast. But it's said of Portia, who will soon initiate the scapegoating of Shylock.

In Shakespeare, characters generally speak because they are trying to get something. They want to enhance their images, improve their lots, speed their designs. Most are pragmatists to the tips of their fingers. To quote them is to join with them in their plans and strategies, the plans and strategies of their Selfhoods—there is little creditable Soul in Shakespeare—whether one likes it or not. When we quote them, we import their desires into our speech.

Shakespeare's plays are ripe with subtext. You can almost always translate an utterance into an unspoken but highly pressing desire. The characters speak to get what they want. When you quote them, you become party to their desire. They speak strategically—join them and their plan fuses itself with yours. The harsh joke is that the speakers sound wise. Because of Shakespeare's brilliantly authoritative style, they sound like they speak of the universe as it is. But really they are doing no more than what Boswell accused Johnson of doing, talking for victory, talking to get their ways.

To this rule there is a salient exception. In Hamlet—the poet's greatest creation—one often encounters the free play of intellect. At times he thinks pragmatically. He thinks in stratagems and (as Rosencrantz and Guildenstern, among others, discover) he can be adept. But he can also think in quest of the Truth. He ponders matters—suicide, heaven, love, revenge—in the soliloquies, not just for the sake of his own plans and not just to find out what is good in the way of belief *for him*. He ponders these matters to explore what might be true for others, true perhaps for all men at all times.

Hamlet's speech on suicide in the third act is one of the greatest meditations on that subject the world will ever hear. And its content can apply to all women and men, not merely to the speaker:

> For who would bear the whips and scorns of time,
> The o'pressor's wrong, the proud man's contumely,
> The pangs of despis'd love, the law's delay,
> The insolence of office, and the spurns
> That patient merit of th' unworthy takes,
> When he himself might his quietus make
> With a bare bodkin?
>
> (III.i.64–70)

Here Hamlet touches a set of thoughts that might actually be universal, so superbly does he evoke the reasons to terminate this sad life. And it is not the only time that Hamlet approaches what Johnson called "just representations of general nature."

What is in it for me? That is the central question that most Shakespeare characters (and most of us) ask most of the time, if not all of it. Hamlet sometimes asks what is in it for us all, now and forever. On occasion, other Shakespeare characters burst into untrammeled thought. "We are such stuff as dreams are made of and our little lives are rounded by a sleep." W. H. Auden says that, in the middle period of Shakespeare's work, utterances of various characters can stand alone. "The soliloquies in *Hamlet* as well as other plays of this period are *detachable* both from the character and the plays. In earlier as well as later works they are more integrated. The 'to be or not to be' soliloquy in *Hamlet* is a clear example of a speech that can be separated from both the character and the play, as are the speeches of Ulysses on time in *Troilus and Cressida,* the King on honor in *All's Well That Ends Well* and the Duke on death in *Measure for Measure*" (Auden, 159–160). Auden seems entirely right, though Ulysses' reflections are the victim of some dramatic irony, since he moves from them to some very un-disinterested plotting. Shakespeare's commitment to something like pure contemplation comes and it goes, but most of the time, it is well in abeyance.

Shakespeare clearly detests chivalry and condemns it almost outright. For the Platonic ideal, the quest for Truth, he has some use, though not much. He never dramatizes the quest for ultimate Truth and never investigates it, even negatively, as Marlowe does in *Doctor Faustus.* Shakespeare, who creates models for almost every type of literary endeavor after him, creates no prototype for the *Faust* of Goethe, who admired him greatly, or for the *Doctor Faustus* of Thomas Mann. At the beginning of *The Tempest* we expect that Shakespeare will anatomize the character of the wise man—or the quester after wisdom—in Prospero, but Prospero is not wise, only sour and angry and old.

About religion and the life of the saint, Shakespeare seems to care almost not at all. The person in his work whose life is most clearly defined by religion is Isabella the pseudo-saint in *Measure for Measure,* a prig who will not trade her virtue for her brother's life. Isabella's rather unusual psychosexual constitution is manifest in a short speech wherein she declares that she would greatly prefer death to sexual dishonor:

> Were I under the terms of death,
> Th' impression of keen whips I'ld wear as rubies,
> And strip myself to death as to a bed
> That longing have been sick for, ere I'ld yield
> My body up to shame.
> (II.iv.100–104)

To Isabella, probably the most overtly religious of Shakespeare's characters, death is the only lover that she can imagine stirring her. She can readily conceive having erotic relations with death—as Emily Dickinson does more decorously in "Because I could not stop for death." And those relations are of a rather flamboyantly sadomasochistic sort.

Shakespeare's Joan of Arc often comes off as a half-mad witch. The clergymen who try her and eventually have her executed are by and large sadistic demons. The prelates we encounter at the start of *Henry V* goad the new king to war to augment their own fortunes. Scrope the Archbishop appears in only one scene in Shakespeare, where he is brought forth, accused as a traitor and sent to execution. The Doctor of Divinity in *Hamlet* churlishly refuses Ophelia full burial honors. Shakespeare's friars tend to be corrupt or readily corrupted, as Friar Laurence is in *Romeo and Juliet*. (An exception is Friar Francis, in *Much Ado about Nothing,* one of the saner individuals in the play. He concocts the useful scheme that gets the lovers back together.) Granted, when Shakespeare wants to get rid of a character in a more or less creditable way, he is inclined to send him off to a monastery, as he does the Duke at the close of *As You Like It.*

The overall point isn't that Shakespeare is anticlerical, though he does seem a bit more skeptical about the virtues of priests and bishops than he is about the virtues of the laity. (Shakespeare tends to be skeptical about everyone's claim to virtue.) It's rather that his anointed religious figures enjoy no particular prominence *as religious figures.* He treats them the way he treats everyone else, though he does seem to like them a bit less.

Overall, religion gets the silent treatment in the poet we imagine takes the whole of human life as his field of inquiry. How can a playwright be considered universal and have no consequential interest in what is arguably the most important of human commitments, religion?

Leo Tolstoy's essay on Shakespeare may be the most reviled piece of critical writing committed by a major author. Yet at the heart of the novelist's indictment is a simple observation. Shakespeare is not a Christian. Nor, one might add, is he anything else. Religious values have no significant place in his work. None of his characters possess true faith. But, Tolstoy accurately says, no religious vision irradiates the plays, either. Shakespeare, says Tolstoy, is a man who "in his own soul had not formed religious convictions corresponding to his period, and who had even no convictions at all" (263). There is no figure in Shakespeare who tries in any serious way to imitate Jesus Christ. There is no one who is truly inspired by the words of the Gospel. From Shakespeare, Tolstoy says, arises the aesthetic theory "according to which a definite religious view of life is not at all necessary for the creation of works of art in general or for the drama in particular; that for the inner content of a play it is quite enough to depict passions and human characters; that not only is no religious illumination of the matter presented required, but that art ought to be objective, that is to say, it should depict occurrences quite independent of any valuation of what is good and bad" (262).

What Tolstoy sees is not only that Shakespeare's characters are devoid of authentic religion. Tolstoy also understands that Shakespeare himself, at least as an artist, has no interest in faith. He is a poet of worldliness, who contributes to the comprehensive disenchantment of experience that Marx and many others have seen as central to the rise of the bourgeois world order. Though— to repeat—Shakespeare does not endorse that world order. He does not celebrate the life in which Self is triumphant. When he depicts the life in, say, *Merchant of Venice,* it seems to repulse him. What he does do is to contribute to a massive demolition, assisting in the process whereby all the ideals that have been perceived as solid begin to melt into air.

Was Shakespeare a Catholic? Some scholars have suggested he was. We might like him to be, but at least in his work he is neither Catholic nor Protestant nor Jew. Religion does not matter all that much—and sainthood even less—to the true man of the middle class. George Santayana corroborates Tolstoy's sense of Shakespeare's feel for religion. Santayana admits that if we were compelled to send to another planet or some faraway people a literary work to let them know who and what we are, we would probably choose Shakespeare. Yet, he says, reading the playwright, "they would hardly understand that man has a religion" (91). Santayana, displaying what seems a nearly encyclopedic knowledge of Shakespeare, points to three moments when he believes that something close to authentic religious sentiment penetrates the work: the passage in *Richard II* that commemorates the death of the Duke of Norfolk; Hal's hymn of thanks to God after Agincourt; and the beautiful sonnet that begins "Poor soul, the centre of my sinful earth." But he finds only three, out of all the poet's vast work. Says Santayana: "Shakespeare's world . . . is only the world of human society. The cosmos eludes him; he does not seem to feel the need of framing that idea. He depicts human life in all its richness and variety, but leaves that life without a setting, and consequently without a meaning" (95).

Shakespeare is cutting himself and his audience loose from their trammels—compassion, courage, and (for the most part) contemplation—and setting them free. Setting them free to do what, exactly? To be themselves, to be sane and circumspect and to pursue their own advantages: to eat and to fatten and to live a long time. To enjoy. The injunction to love one's neighbor as oneself—the idea that there is only one life and we must honor it—such an ideal interferes with the odyssey of Self.

Granted, Shakespeare does not always seem delighted with the results of his poetry of disenchantment. The youthful characters in *Merchant of Venice* are radically post-Christian. But that does not seem to grant them enviable freedom. Merely it makes them free to rob Shylock and pursue their dreams of wealth in the manner that they wish. They are selfish, wasteful, insensitive, and cruel. Though some of them are also glamorous and brilliant. (It is easy to be brilliant, Goethe said, when you do not believe in anything.) They are harbingers of the world from which ideals have departed.

Hamlet is the great exception. He is often a true thinker, brooding in terms that would have impressed Plato with aspirations to touch the absolute. He is a warrior also, though a rather conflicted one. He takes seriously the commandment of his father to avenge him and do it quickly, but he cannot quite bring himself to the deed. Hamlet is not always religious in the senses that Jesus commends when he tells us to love our neighbor as ourselves. But Hamlet does express respect bordering on awe for the figure he calls "the Everlasting" and takes quite seriously the Christian injunction against suicide. When Polonius says he will use the visiting players after their deserts, Hamlet rebels. "Use every man after his deserts," he says "and who shall scape whipping?" Mercy, not justice: though the context is casual, Hamlet's view is clear. It's a sentiment the Gospels would endorse. Hamlet, I think, exemplifies all three of the great ideals, at least to a certain degree (though he exemplifies the religious ideal least), and the tragedy of his suffering and death is in part the tragedy of the destruction of hope for humanity to live for principles larger than a given individual. Hamlet the idealist is a *sympathetically drawn* exemplar of that which Shakespeare the playwright works to destroy, and no little of the play's pathos comes from precisely this fact.

After glory, what? After Othello and Hotspur and Hector, who inherits the world? Shakespeare shadows forth an answer to that question, beginning at least with the *Merchant of Venice,* though the answer may well disturb him.

Late in *Antony and Cleopatra,* the old warrior Antony finds himself cornered by Caesar Augustus and his troops. Antony's forces are in disarray; the god Mars has left him; his friend Enobarbus has gone over to Caesar. What is there for Antony to do? He challenges the mighty Caesar to a hand-to-hand fight, single combat, as any angry old honor-bound warrior must do. And of course young

Caesar laughs at him. Caesar has no interest in personal courage or personal honor, though he seeks to put on the appearance of both.

In this late play, Shakespeare seems to see the death of the heroic ideal—a death he worked to help bring about—and almost to mourn for it. The order that Antony represents is clearly passing away. He and Cleopatra live for excess, pleasure, glory, fame. Caesar lives coldly and cautiously. He is intrigued by Cleopatra not as a potential lover, as Pompey, Antony, and Augustus' uncle Julius Caesar have been. He wants to use her as a prop in the theater of his greatness, bringing her to Rome in his triumphal procession. Later her image can appear onstage where a youthful actor will, as the queen says, "boy" her greatness to the multitudes.

Yet Caesar Augusts will rule well. He will inaugurate the Pax Romana, the three-hundred-year period of relative peace that is perhaps connected in Shakespeare's mind to the peace that the equally evasive and resourceful Elizabeth provided Britain. Though her motto is *semper idem,* always the same, she is as much a shape-shifter as nearly any character in the plays.

But more even than to Augustus—who is to be respected but never can be loved—the future seems to belong to Prince Hal. He is one of those uncommon personages who can stimulate both love *and* respect in the many he enchants. (Augustus stimulates only respect.) The character of Hal is the concentration of all Shakespeare knows about rulership, after meditating on the unfortunate Richard and on the icy Bolingbroke, Hal's father, who becomes Henry IV. Hal is the simulator par excellence. (He is, one might say, Iago in a more benign form.) At our first encounter with him, he tells us exactly who and what he is. He is an actor, who will pretend to be a member of Falstaff's tavern world, learning all he can from it and biding his time as he prepares to rule. He'll transgress, he says, but only so that his reformation will shine more brightly than if had always played by the rules. "I'll so offend, to make offense a skill,"

Hal tells us from the tavern at Eastcheape, "redeeming time when men think least I will" (I.ii.216–217). Hal is an actor, yes, but as Stephen Greenblatt argues, he is also a playwright, and he has already written and mentally rehearsed the play that will be his life. Hal is not a wild improviser like Iago, but one who has already outlined the drama in which he will play the leading part.

Men and women still thrill to the heroic ideal. (They always will.) Very well, Hal can play the part of the hero. He can kill Hotspur and take his honors, as if they were a sum of money in a bank account. So one may defeat, close out, bankrupt, and appropriate the possessions of a rival business. "Percy is but my factor," Hal tells his father the king, "To engross up glorious deeds on my behalf; / And I will call him to so strict account / That he shall render every glory up, / Yea, even the slightest worship of his time" (III. ii.147–151). Hal refuses to accept honor as it has been understood—as a State of being. He prefers to think of it as a state of having. It is analogous to bourgeois ownership, which in his world, where the audience conceives of achievement as entwined with possession, it must be. Hal's duel with Hotspur is a hostile takeover bid.

Surely defeating Hotspur in battle is no easy matter. And Hal does take him on face-to-face. But the play shows that there has been a stratagem involved. Many warriors in Hal's faction have dressed themselves up to counterfeit the king. Hotspur, it seems, has chased them up and down the battlefield seeking glory. By the time he meets Hal, he is presumably weary—far easier to kill then he would have been if Hal had taken him on in single combat early in the battle. What looks like the apogee of heroic honor in Hal is in certain ways a matter of cunning and deception.

Hal will feign being a robber and actually steal the crown. He will feign friendship for Falstaff—the Socrates of Eastcheape, as Harold Bloom calls him—and then repudiate him. The repudiation comes, perhaps, because Falstaff's nihilism is the prince's own. Falstaff's speech in contempt of honor could come from the prince's heart, but for obvious reasons it can never come from his lips. The prince holds all values light. But to have Falstaff on hand is a danger because his uninhibited rancor at values and ideals is too close a clue to the contents of the prince's own mind.

The prince can play at statesman—as when, as Henry the Fifth, he, with the aid of the opportunistic prelates, fabricates reasons to invade France. He can play at lover when he charms the French princess. He can play at being a friend and at being a son. Finally he will become a player king and foment a real war. It is as if Hal has been schooled into being who he is by watching Shakespeare's dramas. He has learned that honor is a sham, faith in religion a diversion, and the quest for Truth largely irrelevant. Yet he knows that the ideals will always command fascination, even from those (especially from those) to whom they present themselves as a threat. Few can be as enchanted with honor as the man who has had to thrust it aside in order to get where he is going in the world. Hal is a tactical shape-shifter. He is Shakespeare's primary man—and he is, perhaps, the future.

And Hal is not without brothers. He is the best result of the kind of provisional, positional pragmatism—the extemporization of Self—that Shakespeare presents as the alternative, the victorious alternative, to the old ways. Hal is of the brotherhood of Edmund and Iago and Caesar Augustus, and the Antony of *Julius Caesar*—modern men, men of the present and future. Gods, as Edmund says, stand up for bastards!

Where does the force of genius come from? Surely there are many sources. But it is not wrong to see some measure of *social energy* at the core of Shakespeare's magnificent work. He writes for his class, his uprising class. He opens a space for its members. In not too long, the force of his strong descendant, Charles Dickens, will be augmented by the need for the middle class, having stepped into the space opened out by Shakespeare and Cervantes and their own ferocious energies, to answer the question: Who exactly are we?

By the time the demolition is close to over, Shakespeare can even afford a tear for Antony, who is not only noble and wild but also an instance of the greatest of dramatic figures, the man of honor. Even Augustus at one point seems to be half in love with him, comparing Antony to a potent stag browsing the bark from trees "when snow the pasture sheets" (I.iv.65). But that transient admiration is as nothing compared with the force of destiny, and destiny is not with Antony, as Hercules, the god who leaves Antony when his fortunes turn, and Enobarbus (Shakespeare's gruff Reality Principle) both show. Now the world has changed, and even the dice obey Caesar.

5

The Poet

Say that what we call the early modern period, with the ascent of capitalism, initiates a relative triumph for worldliness and a victory for the spirit of Self. But Self cannot triumph forever. People, and young people especially, do not always live easily with the evasions of middle-class life. They can't always tolerate the exaltation of Self and the denial of Soul. They will not always abide the view that what is palpably the world of Self has all the beauty, grandeur, and meaning of the world that Soul can create. Middle-class culture can fabricate Soul, but there will always be those who see through the fabrication. Late in the eighteenth century an attempt arises not so much to reassert the traditional ideals of the Soul as to disclose another one. This new ideal is the ideal of imaginative creation—the ideal of the imagination fired by erotic love and thus empowered to change the world, or at least some part of it.

Nietzsche once sneered at Romanticism, calling it the spiritualization of sensuality. The wager of the great Romantics is more worthy of consideration and respect, if not yet quite of reverence. More sympathetic than Nietzsche to Romanticism, Harold Bloom remarks that, for many in the West, our erotic lives have become our spiritual lives. Eros in some form has become what we perceive to be the source of meaning, which to past women and men arose from thought and bravery and faith. But Eros can be many different things, from Shelley's intense and overtly sexual desire to Wordsworth's quietly dispersed love, not for any individual woman or man, but for Nature. The wager that love, taken up by the imagination in the interest of human freedom, can provide fullness and dangerous joy: that is the Romantic wager. For the Romantic, love is a means to break through the Selfhood into another mode of being, one that can contribute to the redemption of the world.

A great deal of art and literature since the late eighteenth century has defined itself in relation to the question of erotic love. Some writers celebrate its power to give life depth and fullness: Blake and Shelley, Whitman and Hart Crane and Ginsberg, and more. Others have rebelled potently against what they see as the overvaluation of imaginative desire. Schopenhauer, Freud, and T. S. Eliot are among the most prominent of these deniers of the erotic imagination. And yet they exist within the Romantic horizon, as Jesus and Homer do not, in that they see the question of love as a, and perhaps even the, central question in human life. Freud may call love the overestimation of the erotic object, but he understands the centrality of love to his patients and readers. Many of them are, in their ways, Romantics. They have placed their hopes in Eros, attempting to make their erotic lives their spiritual lives. Freud is determined to cure them of their delusion. But Freud does not doubt the centrality of Romantic love to modern life. He simply doubts—in the most comprehensive terms—what can be made of an erotically charged imaginative existence.

The Romantic faith in Eros is inspired at least in part by Shakespeare. Shakespeare's renderings of love tend to be bittersweet, but he clearly feels a sympathy for individuals in love, and particularly for women in love. Juliet, Rosalind, and even Cleopatra are rendered with brio and affection. In Shakespeare the Romantics found a mag nificent poet who affirmed nothing except, in a most guarded way, Eros. And thus they found an inspiration.

Shakespeare also manifests himself to them as a poet with the sort of imaginative power that might change the world. Infinitely fertile, original, and daring, Shakespeare offered an image for poetic potential. Inspired as they were by Shakespeare's (qualified) affirmation of love and his grandeur as a creative force, the Romantic idealists seem to have missed the aggressively anti-idealist energies of the playwright's work.

The question of Soul and Eros remains unresolved. The detractors of Romanticism continue to fight against the idea that Eros, taken up into the imagination, can change the world or some fraction of it—and they have, in general, won at least a temporary victory. We no longer look to poets, and particularly not to Romantic poets, past or present, as sources of existential wisdom. But this may change.

Perhaps the most passionate of the High Romantics was the first. William Blake came to his faith in Eros and the imagination in relative solitude. He was not well-to-do, not formally educated; he had not been to Oxford or to Cambridge. Blake was virtually a lifelong Londoner and made his living, often precariously, as a printer and engraver. He was married—his wife's name was Catherine—and despite what seem to have been episodes of jealousy (probably on her part) he was devoted to her. Blake was not only a poet, but also a visual artist; almost all his work was illustrated with engravings. Blake believed he had perceptions of the greatest moment to offer his contemporaries. He modeled himself on the Hebrew prophets— Isaiah, and Ezekiel, and Jeremiah—but his greatest inspiration was Jesus Christ.

Yet Blake was largely ignored. Wordsworth read some of his work and feared he might be mad, though Wordsworth's friend Coleridge admired what he encountered in the *Songs of Innocence and of*

Experience. But Blake could simply not garner significant attention. He tried to sell his illuminated books; he tried to find buyers for his grand illustrations. He was often poor—he and his wife had to scrape. At one point finances became so strained that Blake went off to the country under the protection of a prosperous, kindly mediocrity named William Hayley. But Blake loved London, and loved his independence more. In time he broke with Hayley, returned to the city, and continued his struggles. By the end of his life, Blake had gathered a small group of young admirers around him, but he never lived to see the recognition that his original and profound work deserved. Yet Blake did not die unhappy—far from it.

One poem of Blake's, above all others, compresses his diagnosis of the world he lives in and its need for transformation. The world has become the province of the Self: Soul has been driven out. To use Blake's parlance, Satan has triumphed completely, though it is not the conventional Satan, but Satan in a new guise. The poem is "London" from *Songs of Innocence and of Experience.* "London" is spoken by a poet-prophet wandering through the imperial city stunned by what he sees and feels. Human misery is everywhere around him: "I . . . mark in every face I meet / Marks of weakness, marks of woe" (26). There are multiple sources for this misery, but perhaps the main one—or at least the one Blake cites first—is the locking down of human consciousness. The people Blake sees are miserable because their minds are radically restricted. They are victims of "mind-forg'd manacles" (27). They are imprisoned by their own mental limits and by the limits imposed on them by the culture. To Blake, many of the most esteemed among his contemporaries and near-contemporaries have created shackles for the mind: Pope and Dryden, Locke and Hobbes, Samuel Johnson and Joshua Reynolds are all enemies of imagination and allies of smothering conformity.

What does it mean, from Blake's perspective, to be mentally imprisoned? It means first that you see the world from your private perspective. You look out for your own advantage. You pursue your own success. You hog and you hoard. You've entered the State of Selfhood: individualistic, reductive, and isolating. You think that affirming Selfhood will get you what you want in the world—the Self is a radical pragmatist. But affirming the State of Selfhood simply cuts you off from the possibility of better life. The ascendancy of Selfhood separates you from other humans. Selfhood destroys the drive for community and solidarity. It makes you lonely, frustrated, and angry—onto your face come "marks of weakness, marks of woe" (26).

Through the eyes of the poet-prophet, we see how the spirit of Selfhood dominates in three consequential regions of experience. The prophet tells us, first, "How the Chimney-sweepers cry / Every blackning Church appalls" (27). The chimney sweepers of Blake's London were children who had been sold into something close to slavery. Frequently they came from rural families too poor to feed them. For a price, their parents turned the children over to owners of chimney-sweeping companies. The alternative might well have been seeing their children starve. It was necessary that children clean the London chimneys: you had to be small and lithe to scramble up and down the flues. Still, there were accidents; children fell from roofs and down flues and ended up radically disabled. But the need for the sweeps was strong. Chimney fires could beget larger blazes that destroyed blocks and blocks of London's wooden dwellings.

The chimney sweeps cry out, in Blake's dream vision, and their cry turns material and darkens the walls of the church. Why the church? Presumably because Christians—clergymen in particular—ought to be standing up for the children and making sure they're not misused. Jesus said that it is better to put a millstone around your neck and fling yourself into the abyss than to harm a child. The church, as Blake sees it, prefers the abyss to the vision of Christ centered upon compassion. As we have seen, Jesus brings into the Western world the doctrine of compassionate love already potently influential in the East through the teachings of Confucius, Buddha, and the Hindu sages. Committing oneself to compassion means to Blake what it means to Jesus: every man and woman is of value, no one is intrinsically better than anyone else. We owe each other loving-kindness.

Blake suggests that if you want to understand the moral state of a country, you need to look at how it deals with its children. Does it treat them with compassion, or does it exploit them? Does it look down on them from the perspective of the greedy and frightened Selfhood, or regard them with the generosity of the enlightened Soul? Blake's verdict on his own nation is not hard to discern.

As the children suffer, the rich plunder the nation, taking all they can get and then diving for more. The Selfhood is so scared of the future, so isolated and loveless, that it's constantly grasping for security. Its fear makes it almost entirely without conscience. The Selfhood might surrender its aggressive individualism and seek solidarity with others through compassion—but this possibility the Self cannot and will not understand. The Self believes that if it could only get to the next rung of wealth, the next tier of society, the next level of recognition and success, then all would be well. So the Selfhood pushes on in its impossible task, creating sorrow for others and more anxious fear for itself.

Next the prophet looks out into the political world where, he says, "the hapless Soldiers sigh / Runs in blood down Palace walls" (27). The hapless soldier, we can presume, is the fighting man compelled to enter the service because of his poverty or brought in through outright coercion. He's been sent half a world away to defend the empire, so that the burghers at home can continue to enrich themselves.

Blake may be thinking of the redcoats sent across the world to America to try to put down the revolution, which Blake saw as a genuine movement for human liberation. (He writes a brief celebratory epic about the rebellion of 1776, *America, a Prophecy*.) Blake doesn't blame the soldier—he's "hapless." His cry of distress runs in blood down the palace walls and no one inside hears it or sees it. The soldier is shedding blood—his blood—for people who care nothing about him.

Blake has an instinct for the significant spot—the place where he can see into the condition of the nation's spirit. In the ancient world, courage is of course the preeminent virtue: it is the virtue of Rome and Athens. Just so, compassion is the virtue of Jerusalem and of the dusty Indian roads the Buddha walked and the out-of-the-way villages in China where Confucius laughed and drank a bit of wine and taught his disciples. To truly exercise courage, a soldier has to believe he's fighting in a just war—as Blake thought the American revolutionaries were. The soldier must also sense the support of the nation. The soldiers who went to fight for Britain in America didn't feel unity back home; the formidable Edmund Burke sympathized with the American cause, and many others concurred.

Where is renovation to come from? Blake, the High Romantic, believes in the power of imagination, and he believes in the redemptive force of a certain kind of erotic love. Blake's sense of the possibilities of erotic love is not unlike Aristophanes' in Plato's *Symposium*. Aristophanes' myth is both grotesque and lovely. Once upon a time, he tells us, there were creatures with two heads, four arms, and four legs; at times they traveled by cartwheeling from place to place. But one day the gods, in a fit of anger, split these creatures down the middle. Sorrow and woe! From then on the poor beings, cut in the middle, roamed the earth in quest for their lost part, their other half. The fable ends by affirming that all who

seek love seek our other half, the individual who can complete us—
make us whole, rather than partial. A High Romantic, one might
say, is someone who believes passionately in the idea that by joining,
sexually and spiritually, with the beloved, one can be transformed
into a higher, better version of oneself and help transform the beloved
as well. And from there one can do something—and perhaps more
than a little—for the world at large. Blake believed this literally: he
tried to make his marriage to Catherine a conjunction of Soulmates.
He also commits himself to a more complex version of Aristophanes'
ideal in his poems; there, the poet figure is in constant search for the
Emanation, the female being who can give him erotic and creative
energy.

What is the condition of the erotic life that Blake sees around him
in London? It has gone over to prostitution—the whore and the john
are the representative figures. For Blake, sex should be a sacred
matter; it's at the heart of the holy fusion between one human spirit
and another. To make of sex something that is bought and sold is
to give over to the Self sacred terrain that rightfully belongs to the
Soul. For Blake this is an enormous surrender, for a purified Eros
actually can help throw off the Selfhood. Prostitution gives away to
the enemy one of the spirit's best means for rebirth. The fruit of
prostitution is disease, both physical and spiritual. The "youthful
Harlots curse / Blasts the new-born Infants tear / And blights with
plagues the Marriage hearse" (27). The infant inherits syphilis from
his prostitute mother; the bride acquires it from her husband, who
has been consorting with the harlot. And along with this physical
decay comes spiritual sickness.

Love for sale! To the High Romantic this is the greatest oxy-
moron. Love is never for sale, but sex always has been and will be.
Blake requires spiritual connection and sexual passion from love.
Anything less will not give you the force and fire necessary for
renovation.

Compassion, courage, and erotic life have all fallen to disease in Blake's world. So too has intellection: men and women are not elevated by the culture's supposed thinkers. According to Blake, men like Hobbes and Locke are enemies of true thought; they create the "mind-forg'd manacles." The three great ideals of the ancient world are dead in Blake's London. But though the tone of Blake's poem is angry and impatient, its spirit is hopeful. Blake shows us where to look—those children, those soldiers, the prostitute on the street— to visit clarifying judgment on ourselves. But he also shows us the way to renewal: that way is through love and through the exercise of a poetic imagination that never gives up on itself or on the responsive powers of other men and women, who on some level always want to be freed from the prison of Self.

But what, precisely, are the dynamics of that liberation? How does an individual—or a society—that desires to throw off Selfhood proceed? How does the Romantic imagination, or at least Blake's Romantic imagination, move from the State of Selfhood to the State of Soul? The Romantic quest for the Soul, at least in Blake, is the process by which the imagination discloses the forms of current-day error, then burns through them to a version of liberation or paradise.

In "London" and the other salient poems in *Songs of Innocence and of Experience* Blake focuses on disclosing the reigning forms of error, which are, perhaps, much like our own.

In "The Chimney Sweep," perhaps the most piercing of the *Songs* after "London," Blake unfolds the complexly devious terms of the Selfhood's domination. The poem dramatizes what one might call the compassion of the Self. The narrator of the poem is a young chimney sweep sold into the sweepers' slavery when he was very young: "while yet my tongue, / Could scarcely cry weep weep weep weep," he says. "So your chimney I sweep & in soot I sleep" (10). The narrator, Camille Paglia and others have observed, is trying to call out to potential customers: "Sweep! Sweep!" But his actual words, "weep, weep," evoke both his extreme youth (he can't yet pronounce the word "sweep") and his sad heart. The narrator, we sense, has been a chimney sweep for some time and has grown accustomed to his lot. Onto the scene comes a new sweep, younger and less experienced: little Tom Dacre, who cries when his head "that curl'd like a lambs back" is shaved (10). There are practical reasons for shaving Tom's head; he needs to keep the soot from befouling it. But compulsory head shaving is also the fate of convicts and soldiers and students at certain kinds of academies. It's a practice that submerges what is individual about the person—heads shaved, we all look more alike. The personality is rubbed down. The individual becomes more anonymous, more a part of a collective and less himself. It is, it seems, easier to mistreat a person whose head has been shaved. He does not seem fully human. Our narrator comes to comfort Tom—telling him that when his hair is gone there's no way that soot can stain it.

One feels that there is sweetness still latent in the narrator. He acts from a certain sort of misguided compassion. (Volumes could be written on the misuse of the Ideals.) He tries to cheer up little Tom, ineptly enough, simply because crying will not do Tom any good. If Tom continues to cry about his shaved head and lost hair, he may give himself over completely to grief, fall into despair, and die. The narrator wants to save Tom from the worst possible misery. The best response may be to harden up, detach oneself, let the needs and desires of the Self take over. If the Soul exposes itself in such a world as this one, it will probably be crushed.

But Tom's sensitivity goes beyond upset about his lost hair. He's also something of a visionary. He is a poet and a dreamer, more tender than the fierce prophet who chants the words to "London" but comparably alight with imagination. The night Tom arrives among the chimney sweeps, he falls asleep and has a blissful dream.

There are thousands of sweepers—"Dick, Joe, Ned, & Jack"—and all of them are locked up in black coffins. They are experiencing Death in Life. The coffins are the chimneys they sweep, where they are confined for hours a day; and the coffins are the emblem of their closed-off conditions, locked away from joy and pleasure and the hopes that go with being young.

But in Tom's dream, a powerful angel comes along and, with a bright key, opens all the coffins and sets the chimney sweepers free. Liberated, they experience a rebirth. "Down a green plain leaping laughing they run / And wash in a river and shine in the Sun" (10). Now the once-imprisoned sweeps are full of joy. "Naked & white, all their bags left behind, / They rise upon clouds, and sport in the wind" (10). The scene is of innocent, mildly erotic play, in which the sweeps are released from slavery and free to be what they are, children.

Who is this angel and what liberation does he bring? What is the bright key he uses to release the children? The angel, one might say, is the spirit of Christianity, but in a rather complex sense. At the heart of the poem is the beautiful vision of the once-enslaved children free and romping in Nature. And such a vision is at the heart of Jesus' teaching. "Let the little children come unto me," the Savior says. He tells people that if they are going to be saved, they need to make themselves openhearted as children. Jesus himself has a childlike side. He's often innocent and spontaneous, a free spirit. The message that Jesus would have for the chimney sweeps is simple and direct. No one has a right to do this to you. Nobody can make you a slave, exploit you, cripple you, lead you into early sickness and death. You have a right to get together and to rebel. At the very least, you have a right to collect yourselves and *run*.

The angel delivers Christ's vision, yes, but he delivers something else as well. He interprets the dream in which he participates. In the dream, he tells Tom that "if he'd be a good boy, / He'd have God for his father & never want joy" (10). "Be a good boy": that is, do your duty, obey your master, clean the chimney, and submit. Do that for your entire miserable life and you'll have joy in heaven. Blake's Jesus is not much interested in a transcendent heaven. He wants freedom now. But the church and the other temporal powers are very taken with the idea of future reward for which one has to sacrifice and behave well in the present life. Be humble, accept your lot, and do as you're told—then you will taste all the joys in another world.

The narrator of the poem, the experienced chimney sweep, pretty much concurs with the angel about the vision's meaning. What the dream proves to him is that "If all do their duty, they need not fear harm" (10). Presumably he shares this angelic sentiment with Tom, much as he shared his thoughts about Tom's hair being shaved. Now that your hair's gone, it can't be soiled, you don't need to worry about that. So too, if your dream is all about the future, you (and I) don't have to worry much about the present. We don't have to plan an escape; we don't have to pull all the other chimney sweeps together, unite, and figure out our next move. We can simply do our duty and wait for our heavenly reward.

Perhaps the narrator senses the insurrectionary energy in Tom's dream and sees Tom for the newly fledged poet that he is. But he wants to save Tom from the existential burden of having to act on what the dream brought to him. In doing so, he may think he is doing Tom a favor. He is, of course, doing himself a sort of favor, in that he does not want to brood any more on his sorrowful lot. So the narrator goes along with the angel and perverts the beautiful dream.

The teachings of Jesus are to Blake an ongoing beautiful dream. But they are constantly being perverted by the greedy and the timid. Few things make Blake more distressed than the established church—"the Chimney sweepers cry / Every blackning Church appalls" (27). But Blake also believes that within the old coffin of religious dogma lies the prospect of resurrection—not resurrection after death, but rebirth, here and now. Much of Blake's poetry seeks to contribute to that resurrection. Religion in Blake (and in Tom's dream) is potent: it contains delusions, but it contains motives for liberation, too.

In his early work, Blake is an anatomist of oppression. He finds the places where society reveals itself for the corrupt operation it is. He looks at the way children are raised, how and why soldiers fight, and at the state of erotic love. He's also interested in patterns of social indoctrination. "The Chimney Sweeper" is an allegory about how conventional interpreters hide what is most liberating about the Gospels and substitute oppressive dogmas. In "The Lamb" Blake shows how a child is indoctrinated with a vapid, dangerously innocent view of who Jesus was and what he did. In "The Tyger," Blake impersonates a hysterical (and gifted) poet who uses his prodigious imagination to scare himself and make himself timidly ineffectual, rather than a smasher of mental chains. In "The Little Black Boy," Blake shows how a child becomes the object of subtle self-disgust for the crime of being born dark-skinned.

But for Blake it is not enough to describe and evoke the mind-forged manacles. One must also break through them and liberate oneself into something akin to the world that little Tom Dacre glimpsed. How does one do so? When you know who your adversary is, and where he is strong, what you need to do next is rally your forces, which is what Blake does in his best-known poem, "The Marriage of Heaven and Hell."

"The Marriage" is an extremist poem. It is the work of an individual who feels completely beleaguered: everywhere he looks there is opposition to what he knows is right. The men society calls poets are in love with the status quo, as are the priests and, unsurprisingly, the politicians. So where is one to find allies? Blake's answer is provoking. One finds an ally in the devil. In an age of timid conformity, you can turn toward Satan—and in particular Satan as John Milton imagines him—to find energy, independence, passion, and freedom. Blake's contemporaries already spend a great deal of time contemplating heaven, albeit naively enough; it is time to greet them with the wisdom of hell.

In the wisdom of hell, "Energy is Eternal Delight" (34). Men and women need to cast their passivity away and embrace the will to life that is inside them. Too much has been given over to culture—it is time for Nature to reassert itself. Nature reasserts itself in Blake's willingness to speak provocatively about desire and its liberating power: and so he presents the proverbs of hell and the wisdom of hell. "The road of excess" Blake (or the devil within him) tells us, "leads to the palace of wisdom" (35). "Drive your cart and your plow over the bones of the dead!" (35). And "He who desires but acts not, breeds pestilence!" (35). And "Prisons are built with the stones of Law, Brothels with bricks of Religion!" (36).

That a proverb of hell is true in some absolute sense does not matter very much to Blake. What does matter is that hell's wisdom wakes us up to all the concessions we have made to the conforming and the coy. Are these lines true? There is truth in them—and the truth is larger to the extent that the vision of the devil, which is often the vision of Nature inflamed, has been suppressed. The devil becomes plausible insofar as the angels have too fully had their way.

At the center of the gospel of hell is an erotic wisdom. One feels that Blake comes close to speaking in his own person when he announces ideas about the rejuvenation of heaven and earth. Blake says that when the cherub who guards the tree of life—that is, the tree of desire, will, passion—leaves his post, matters will change. All of creation will appear as it is, "infinite and holy," whereas now it "appears finite & corrupt" (39). How will this change take place? It "will come to pass," Blake says, "by an improvement of sensual enjoyment" (39).

Blake is a prophet of the redemptive power of heterosexual love. Men and women coming together, matching their strengths, in equal and loving and heated conjunction, can remake the world, or at least their own corner of it. We are equal, we men and women, equal in our desires and in our erotic aspirations. "What is it men in women do require?" Blake knows the answer to the question with certainty: "The lineaments of Gratified Desire" (474). But what does a woman want? Freud indicates that he spent years pursuing this question. Women are a mystery to him. They are, he says, the "dark continent." But to Blake it is not so hard. He strikes to the center of the issue: "What is it women do in men require?" The reflection is perfect: "The lineaments of Gratified Desire" (475).

An improvement of sensual enjoyment, the lineaments of gratified desire—one touches here on what makes Blake one among the High Romantics. Sensual enjoyment is for Blake a part of the centrally redeeming human experience, which is love. A High Romantic is someone who seeks through love and the imagination to burst through the bounds of Self. As Blake's poetry becomes more expansive and more complex, he ramifies his sense of love. He affirms it as a spiritual pursuit, not simply one that relies on sensual enjoyment—though such enjoyment must never be sacrificed. He comes to the conclusion that love can save us; through love, we can be reborn into joy.

This belief is at the core of the Romantic faith. One encounters it not only in Blake, but also in Shelley and Keats, Coleridge, and (very indirectly) in Wordsworth. It is there in Walt Whitman (though not in Thoreau or Emerson). It's readily found in Yeats and in D. H. Lawrence and strongly present in Hart Crane and Allen Ginsberg, where the love desired is homosexual love. Closer to the present, the Romantic faith in rebirth through interfusion of love and imagination is vital for Bob Dylan and Joni Mitchell and Neil Young and every rocker who sings about the way love can open the door to the expansion of consciousness and make us wiser and kinder and sadder and stronger. The faith in the Romantic ideal is not only alive in artists. Everyday people risk (every day) their fortunes and futures on the proposition (dubious as it might be to some) that by falling in love with the right person they can be reborn.

The Romantics are not of course the inventors of love. Before them come Donne and his beloved, Heloise and Abelard, Antony and Cleopatra, and even (dare one say it) Adam and Eve. But what distinguishes the High Romantics is the conviction that love is at the root of self-transformation—and social and cultural transformation too. When Soulmates meet and join, both can move to a higher state of being. Love opens the door to a shift in identity; one is no longer what one was.

But for the High Romantics love is about more than transforming the self. For Romantic love puts one in the position to do one's work in the world. "Do your work and I shall know you," says Emerson, prophet of self-reliance, who has little if any time for the intensities of erotic life. High Romanticism is not about self-reliance, but the reliance of one highly sensitive and imaginative person on another—or, in the case of Whitman, upon many others. When the Romantic lover joins with the beloved, he garners an energy that can result in new perceptions and new possibilities in life—which can lead to productive change for others as well.

The Romantic quest is akin to the philosophic quest, in that it seeks knowledge. But it seeks knowledge not purchased by the loss of erotic power. In *The Symposium,* Socrates' teacher Diotima, expressing the Platonic view, insists that sexual love must in time by sublimated into love for the Beautiful and for the Good. Erotic love is where the philosophic quest begins, but it should not end there. Rather, the energies that once infused sexual desire have to be redirected (and subdued) in the quest for Truth. The Romantic will not accept sublimation. He demands the intensities of deep erotic attraction at all times, and when those intensities wane, it is time to move on. The idea of passing beyond desire into tranquil wisdom—what Wordsworth calls "the philosophic mind"—is anathema to the High Romantic.

The dangers of such a quest should be clear—and they are clear to the most sophisticated Romantics. All too often erotic desire takes place within the State of Self and never leaves it. The Romantics would usurp Eros for the needs of Soul. But how easily then can one be fooled! How readily might a questing lover mistake an object of carnal desire pure and simple for a Soulmate? How disposed might he be to ignore a potentially inspiring lover who does not come with the right overt characteristics? The Romantic hopes to enact a raid on the domains of the Self—the realm of desire—bringing back energy and passion for the uses of Soul. But how often will he or she be fooled? Can the Romantic ever capture the fullness of being that the saint and the thinker and the warrior claim?

In Blake's terms, the crucial human quest is to use love and the power of imagination to burn away the Self. Blake's Self—Blake's Satan in the later works—is not the fiery figure who haunts the orthodox mind. As we have seen, Blake is not entirely ill-disposed to that figure. But in Blake's compressed epic, *Milton,* Satan (also known as the Selfhood) is a highly sensitive, genuinely well-intentioned man of letters and leisure. He's bland, kind, and helpful, not unlike the boy-narrator of "The Chimney Sweep," who tries to seal Tom off from the radical side of his vision. But Satan's so-called friendship will eventually do away with what is best in one's character—which is to say the willingness to live in the world with the independence and compassion that Blake's hero Jesus embodied. "Corporeal Friends are Spiritual Enemies," (98) says Blake, thinking of his overbearing patron William Hayley, but thinking also of all the time-conscious, supreme administrators who dominate the cultural-political world of Blake's time and (Blake is a prophet, or aspires to be) of our own.

The way to throw Satan off—the way to defeat the Selfhood—is to recognize him not only in the outer world, where he is priest and preceptor and more, but also in oneself. In *Milton* Blake finds everything in himself that is opposed to vision and that would rather be safe than be true to his imaginative spirit. And layer by layer, moment by moment, he purges the haunting creature away. Everything in Blake that is timid and conformist, jealous and repressive, must be identified, isolated, and burned away.

Critical in the metamorphoses of Blake and Blake's hero Milton from men who are only a part of what they might be to fully redeemed individuals, is the embrace of what Blake calls the Emanation. Blake's Emanation is a female figure—part muse, part image of Blake's devoted wife, Catherine, part trope for the emotional fullness that Blake feels he too often lacks. Joining with the Emanation in a way that's both carnal and spiritual propels Blake toward secular salvation.

At the climax of Blake's brief, densely packed epic, Milton (who is in certain ways a stand-in for Blake) manages to come together with his Emanation, a figure Blake calls Ololon. Ololon embodies the spirits of the six women in Milton's life—she's called occasionally a "six-fold Emanation." Milton was married three times and he had three daughters and he treated both wives and daughters shabbily. But more than that, he aggressively built himself (as Blake feared he was himself prone to do) into a man without much compassion, without mercy, without humane mildness. Blake believes that the women in Milton's life probably had these qualities—and he also believes that Milton's work is deeply flawed for lacking them. Milton's God is a legalistic crank; his Christ is not a forgiver of sins, but a warrior who sends his enemies tumbling into the fiery abyss. The only sweet-natured figure in the poem is Eve, whom Milton draws with genuine tenderness. But then, quite unfairly, he makes her almost entirely responsible for Adam's fall and for the fall of humanity.

To marry Ololon, which Milton has to do if he's to be saved, is in a sense to merge with Jesus as Blake took him to be. Embracing Ololon means leaving behind Urizen and Nobadaddy, Blake's harsh versions of Yahweh, and affirming the Gospels, where forgiveness and understanding are preeminent. As the critic Laura Quinney says of Ololon, "She is in part the Divine Voice he had forgotten, and in part a feminine 'mildness' he had exiled from his personality" (148). The conjunction of Milton and Ololon is the conjunction of love and wisdom, the two qualities that Blake's Jesus so amply possesses.

Having burned through his Selfhood, serving his own active time in purgatory, Blake can stand forth as the man who has thrown off the rotten rags of memory and the past and lives in pure inspiration. He's passed over the fear of being mad, or considered mad. He's thrown out the Idiot Questioner—the skeptic within who cannot commit himself to the faith that Blake has in the Savior. He's cleared away Locke and Newton with their appalling reductions—he's flown free. He's bathed, he says, "in Self-annihilation & the grandeur of Inspiration" (142). And he has embraced his beloved—without whom none of these marvelous changes could come to pass. He is free—or so he believes.

Is Blake's drama of self-remaking in *Milton* akin to the transformation of self that psychoanalysis offers? Freudian therapy is akin to Blake's self-anatomizing in that its objective is to purge the individual's disabling illusions. The patient is often someone who is prey to idealizations: he invests more hope and energy in love or religion or god or country than those allegiances can repay. The therapeutic process is in large measure the attempt to pry the individual away from his errors about who he is and what truly can give him satisfaction in life. Yet even at its most successful, psychoanalysis will change the patient by only a few degrees. Freud thinks that the past is so potent in us that even a modest shift in identity must come gradually and be painfully won.

Blake too believes that spiritual gains are arduously achieved, that is for certain. Images of strife proliferate throughout *Milton*. In the most memorable, Milton, acting as a stand-in for Blake, wrestles with Urizen, one of Blake's images for the Selfhood. Urizen is the Self as reductive reasoner: he wants to enclose experience in his empirical grip and, by doing so, control it. As the two struggle together, Urizen pours ice water onto the head of Milton (and Blake), trying to baptize him in the name of cold reductionism. At the same time Milton, emulating the creator Yahweh, slaps red clay onto Urizen's frigid bones, trying to help him return to his mortal state:

> But Milton took of the red clay of Succoth, moulding it with care
> Between his palms; and filling up the furrows of many years
> Beginning at the feet of Urizen, and on his bones
> Creating new flesh on the Demon cold, and building him,
> As with new clay a Human form in the Valley of Beth Peor.
> (112)

Blake is struggling to deliver himself from what is coldest and harshest in his own makeup by becoming conscious of it and creating an image—the wrestling match—that imaginatively dramatizes the contention within. If you can imagine an internal victory, the poem suggests, and render it with honesty and conviction, then you might actually achieve that victory. This is self-transformation through the work of imagination.

As the layers of the Selfhood peel away in Blake's self-analysis, more possibilities open up for him. He comes to understand what is happening in the cultural world at large. Satan has taken the harrow away from Palambron: the bureaucrat has displaced the artist. Blake knows who his enemy is and must be. He sees that he's in a real fight, that his side is losing culture (and culture is everything to Blake), and that he had best join battle. But as the poem deepens, Blake sees that it is not simply himself against the world. The world has also colonized William Blake: witness his friendship with Hayley. Blake now sees that he is his own foe, as well as his own champion. That perception brings strength. Every time Blake cracks through an illusion in this poem, he grows more potent. He is able to see further, to love, and to experience joy. The victory of insight does away with homosexual investment in Hayley and makes the generative love for his wife and his Emanation more potent. Peel away illusion: become stronger. Become stronger: be able to embrace more pleasure, beauty, and joy. Exorcize paranoia and be happier and more responsive to being.

What Blake depicts as Urizen, Freud might think of as a coldly oppressive superego. Freud might see the struggle against that agent of oppression as a critical part of therapy. But Freud believed that only the smallest change in the superego could take place—and that it might require years to happen. ("Where super-ego was, there ego shall be," might be a fitting slogan for Freud's late career approach to therapy. In other words, where unconscious, cruel judgment was, reasonable self-evaluation will be.) Freud could never believe that in that process of change love could play an authentic part. Freud often speaks disparagingly of the "cure through love," which is something very different from his own cure through self-knowledge. Freud believed that patients often try to evade the rigors of therapy by falling in love and achieving temporary happiness—a happiness they take to be a cure. Blake wants to free himself totally from what oppresses him. He wants complete liberation—and he thinks that through the imagination and through love he can achieve exactly that.

For Freud, Romantic love is always an illusion. It is narcissistic, or it is regressive, or it is a way of installing a temporary (and mild) superego created in the image of the beloved. Love, to Freud, arises when the ego is so full of energy (which he calls libido) that it must either send some out into the world or grow ill with anxiety. Or love is the inevitably failed attempt to embrace the parent of the opposite sex. Freud has no end of ways to denigrate love; never mind that they are not always consistent with one another. Love to Freud is not part of the solution but part of the problem. In fact, it often *is* the problem. It seems sometimes that he comes on to rid the world of Romantics, people who think that love and imagination can change them from what they have been into something better.

We live, Northrop Frye says, in two worlds: the world we experience day to day and the world we aspire to live in. The Romantic poet uses his powers of imagination to disclose the truth about the world that we actually inhabit. For what is in front of us is not always understood for what it is. We are too busy, too preoccupied, too concerned with the desires of Self. "The world is too much with us," says Wordsworth at the outset of a sonnet that in many ways crystalizes his Romantic faith. "Late and soon, getting and spending, we lay waste our powers." We've given too much to commerce and hustle. And—the word "spending" suggests—we may even have turned erotic life into a matter of business. We're in a mess. Blake registers a similar sense of dislocation in "London" and all through the *Songs of Innocence and of Experience*. Shelley registers the feeling that we have fallen low—and by our own devices—at the outset of his greatest poem, *Prometheus Unbound*. Jupiter, Shelley's equivalent of Blake's Urizen, rules the world, exacting brutal tribute from men and women. Keats is shadowed by what he calls "the Identity," a version of Selfhood that bottles up an individual within himself and prevents his going out to merge with the being of others. The Identity is what makes Keats's negative capability, the capacity to annul Self and imagine the other, impossible. Ginsberg calls his power of negation Moloch—eater of children, devourer of the best minds and hearts of his generation—and strives against it in *Howl*. In doing so, he calls on the inspiring powers of his beloved, Carl Solomon.

The Romantic poet is compelled to anatomize the opposition. He finds the spirit of Urizen where it dwells in the world, to be sure. But he also needs to seek and disclose it in himself. Yet still there is more to do. The Romantic poet needs to teach us, and himself, how to break through the merely given life to make contact with Frye's second world, the world we aspire to live in. The poet tries to make himself and the world around him new. And to do so, he relies on the dangerous powers of love—dangerous because love is a source of energy and joy, but also of illusion.

To defeat Jupiter, Shelley's Prometheus has to forswear his own spirit of revenge—he must repudiate that which is most Jupiter-like in him. Just so Blake tries to repudiate his own Urizenic side. But Prometheus has also got to join himself to his beloved, Asia, who completes him and makes him a full creator once more. Together they can live in the world of art and science that once was and, through defeat of the tyrant, is now going to be regained and renewed.

Yet there is a danger here. By forswearing violence and revenge, the individual makes himself someone who is, perhaps, far too vulnerable for life in this world. He is too open, too easily wounded, and also too ready a prey to disillusion. Shelley's poetry is both a hymn to the blessed self re-creation available through love and a series of dirges about its frequent failure and about the failure of the world to sustain the hopes that love can ignite.

Keats, in his beautiful "Ode to Psyche," creates a vision of an inner life—his own we must imagine—that is ready for creation and ready for love. "A rosy sanctuary will I dress / With the wreathed trellis of a working brain . . . / With all the gardener Fancy e'er could feign." And then he promises infinite receptivity, both to the beloved and, implicitly, to the life of poetry and imagination they will create together. "And there shall be for thee all soft delight / That shadowy thought can win, / A bright torch, and a casement ope at night / To let the warm Love in."

A Romantic is in love with love, what more is there to say? A great deal, it turns out, in that the Romantic poet, or at least the Romantic worth reading and studying, is also more alert to the possible delusions that arise from love than men or women who follow the Romantic path without thinking much about it. Wordsworth loves Nature with an intensity that borders on the erotic—for he has been disappointed in love of the conventional kind. Yet he never stops asking if Nature will betray the heart that loves her. "We Poets in our youth begin in gladness," he writes "but thereof come in the end despondency and madness." Keats writes the "Ode to Psyche," the hymn of praise to Eros and its potential to inspire creation, but he is also the author of "La Belle Dame sans Merci" and "Lamia," two studies of erotic disillusionment. The knight of "La Belle Dame" is sure he has found erotic bliss when he encounters a lady that seems kindred of his soul. But it is all an illusion—he was tricked, it seems, by the desires of the Self. He's left on a cold hill's side, not in the Eden he had hopes to create with his beloved. "And this is why I sojourn here" he says, recounting his sorrows, "Alone and palely loitering, / Though the sedge has withered from the lake, / And no birds sing."

The true Romantic calls into question his faith in love and imagination much more intensely than the saint questions compassion or the hero martial valor. Much of the poetry we call Romantic is a harsh interrogation of the faith of love by those who nonetheless want to embrace it. Hart Crane writes: "The bells, I say, the bells break down their tower." The bells, one might imagine, are the poet's lyric power—which he acquires when he succeeds in marrying love and imagination. But even at its best—even when the bells ring most beautifully—there is a cost. The intensity the poet seeks can weary the body and taint (and sometimes even overthrow) the rational mind. "We poets in our youth begin in gladness." Some of Coleridge's best poems are farewells to his powers to love and imagine. Though he finds the fusion of love and the shaping power for a moment in his early "Aeolian Harp," he quickly loses it and descends into an abyss, unable to love, unable to create what he might have. In time, he comes to see that he has no force of imagination to send out into Nature. "O Lady, we receive but what we give and in our life alone does nature live," he chants in the mordant *Dejection, An Ode*. We receive but what we give and Coleridge, alas, has nothing to give. He has failed in love. His own marriage is a shambles and the woman he adores, Sara Hutchinson, the sister of Wordsworth's wife, will not have him.

For the High Romantic—as against the common man or woman who is mesmerized by romantic hope—it is not enough simply to fall in love and to live happily in private bliss. This is the indolent mode of being that Blake associates with Beulah, the false paradise where all contraries are true. Blake believes that creation arises from strife. Remaining too long in Beulah restores the Self rather than nurturing the Soul. The true poet knows love is authentic because it makes him stronger—more inventive, more humane, and better able to keep on contending with the spirit of Jupiter, who, though he may be defeated from time to time, will never die. Love inspires creation for the Romantic, and it is creation that produces good for other men and women. Shelley asserts as much when Asia, Prometheus' Soulmate, looks back at the achievement that she and Prometheus enjoyed together:

He told the hidden power of herbs and springs,
And Disease drank and slept. Death grew like sleep.
He taught the implicated orbits woven
Of the wide wandering stars; and how the sun
Changes his lair, and by what secret spell
The pale moon is transformed, when her broad eye
Gazes not on the interlunar sea:
He taught to rule, as life directs the limbs,
The tempest-wingèd chariots of the Ocean,
And the Celt knew the Indian. Cities then
Were built, and through their snow-like columns flowed
The warm winds, and the azure ether shone,
And the blue sea and shadowy hills were seen.

(238)

To Shelley and to Blake the proof of erotic life lies in the creative
force that it releases. It ought not to make one passive and complacent. True love does not make us happy—if we equate happiness
with contentment. It is a goad to further creation—an inducement
to what Blake would call "mental fight."

Love is a way through the Self the poets show us, but in time it
can become a refuge of the Self. Love has to be the door to creating
Frye's second world, or it is not true Romantic love. In the "Crystal
Cabinet" Blake brilliantly anatomizes what happens when a young
poet falls in passive self-delighting love—love that does not lead
toward creation, but easy pleasure:

The Maiden caught me in the Wild
Where I was dancing merrily
She put me into her Cabinet
And Lock'd me up with a golden Key

> The Cabinet is formd of Gold
> And Pearl & Crystal shining bright
> And within it opens into a World
> And a little lovely Moony Night
>
> Another England there I saw
> Another London with its Tower
> Another Thames & other Hills
> And another pleasant Surrey Bower
>
> Another Maiden like herself
> Translucent lovely shining clear.
>
> (488)

The young poet enters the Crystal Cabinet, which is the bejeweled world of luxury and also the delightful world of sexual intercourse. And when he does, everything is enchanted; the world takes on a soft pleasing sheen. When the poet traverses London now he doesn't sees how the chimney sweeper's cry appalls the church or how the soldier's sigh runs in blood down the walls of the palace. That (very accurate) nightmare vision has been replaced by the kind of soft delusion that Keats's knight at arms experiences in "La Belle Dame." Both are reveling in what Freud would call "the cure through love." Both are being caught in delusional, pleasure-loving Eros. But Freud does not admit to there being any other kind of love. Keats senses that there is, and Blake boldly asserts it.

To the Romantic poet, love has a double power. It is that which inspires, but also that which deludes and oppresses. Says Blake

> Let us agree to give up Love
> And root up the infernal grove

Then shall we return & see
The worlds of happy Eternity

& Throughout all Eternity
I forgive you you forgive me.

(477)

By "love" Blake here means jealous love, possessive love; he aspires to forswear the love that exists as an alluring counterfeit to the true love that brings freedom—and is an inducement to more arduous and valuable creative labors.

Love is not the only resource the Romantic imagination draws upon to attain full strength. The Romantics, as everyone knows, are also infatuated with childhood. Following Rousseau, they are inclined to see children—and especially their childhood selves—as sources of authenticity. And of course, almost all Romantic poets are inspired by Nature. They take themselves to live in times when culture has become far too pervasive and accordingly oppressive—they seek the purity and vigor they can find in the natural world. Romantics are dreamers, too, or at least they look to dreams as likely sources of inspiration. Dreams weave through the *Prelude;* dreams frame Keats's *Hyperion* poems; perhaps the best known and most marvelous of the Romantic poems, *Kubla Khan,* comes out of a dream. An opium dream! Romantics often stimulate the dreaming mind with this or that sacramental substance—for the gates of paradise do not always swing of their own accord.

Dreams, childhood, and Nature: three sources of Romantic inspiration, all of which Freud seeks to discredit. Dreams, the great analyst says, give us nothing that is new. They are regressive and not inventive; no one ever had a genuine mental breakthrough in a dream. For a dream is, after all, merely a "disguised fulfillment of a repressed wish." Childhood? Children are unhappy creatures, blocked from having what they most desire: true conjunction with the parent of the other sex. Children, to Freud, want to be adults. They play only one game: they play at being grownups who can satisfy their desires (in displaced forms only of course). When Wordsworth sees a child playing at being grown he is sad, -for that child is, he tells us, "blindly with [his] blessedness at strife."

And Nature? For Freud, Nature is Darwinian Nature, red in tooth and claw. Freud is respectful of the natural—no doubt about that. We must not outrage Nature by renouncing too many of its impulses in the interest of civilization. But Freud never imagines that Nature could be a source of refining wisdom and moral guidance, as Wordsworth does when he proclaims that he grew up in the natural world, "fostered alike by beauty and by fear." Nature, childhood, dreams (and drugs): all feed the Romantic imagination. But what inspires the most original of the Romantic poets and (perhaps) brings a new ideal into the world is surely Love. "Release yourself from misery," the once-grand Peter Townsend once chanted: "there's only one thing gonna set you free." (Saint Paul is confirmed and turned inside out.) "And that's my love." (What else could it be?) "Let my love open the door, to your heart."

How many women and men have acquired only half the wisdom of the Romantics? They feel that falling in love and having their love returned will make them happy. But happiness, from the perspective of Soul, is a delusion of Self. Happiness to the common mind is all about beautiful stasis. Love that is taken up fully into the imagination propels the individual forward to more work and more works. True love does not rest in complacency.

The centrality of love to the Romantics has been surprisingly little remarked by scholars. There is much talk about subjects and objects, and about the Romantic image, and more recently about the gender politics of the poets. But little is said about love and the Romantic endeavor. The man or woman in the street who calls someone who is in love with love a Romantic is in some ways closer to the truth about Romanticism than the most esteemed professors of the subject generally are. The academy is often disposed to take the most humanly intimate and provocative works and make them as abstract as possible. It is part of the university's function, no doubt, as a protector of social mores. But in this case it is particularly debilitating. Those who are in love with love—whose erotic lives have become their spiritual lives—have a great deal to learn, and of a practical nature from the close study of the poets.

Western culture seems to have displaced or denigrated the ancient ideals: courage, contemplation, and compassion. But the culture does not seem to know quite what to make of the Romantic faith. Though many people, if not most, will at least for some period allow their lives to revolve around the quest for love, we still do not know how to value this quest. Wise therapists and bureaucrats of the imagination know that they cannot erase the Romantic strain from current culture. Instead they attempt to contain it. They declare that head-over-heels love is a passing stage in normal life. They say that, after the initial thrill, matters should calm down and the individuals involved learn that the hope for a Soulmate was a false one. Respect must replace fierce desire, maturity reign. Romantic lovers have in time to become friends, allies, and business partners, to navigate the rapids of middle-class life. The best of marriages are not ecstatic conjunctions but prudent mergers.

But many people will not have it so—and not all who dissent are young. People leave stable lives and stable marriage all the time, seeking that great love that will finally bring them joy. The quest for true love fires the teenager's life, but the man or woman passing into a sixth or seventh decade had best not assume immunity.

Few who take on the Romantic quest can readily claim triumph. It may be that the quest is contaminated from the start by being intertwined with desire and accordingly with Self. The thinker and the saint are often beyond Eros—for the warrior it is a secondary matter. Perhaps, for whatever reason, the erotic faith inevitably dwindles. Maybe it is simply a matter of age—young poets can write the Romantic poetry of their moment because they genuinely feel what it is to be possessed by the desire to complete being in the Soulmate. As desire dwindles, the passion for self-creation through love may dwindle in its intensity as well.

Shelley and Keats, the archetypal Romantics, died before they could wither entirely into erotic detachment. But in Shelley's last substantial effort, "The Triumph of Life," there is evidence of a souring—though who knows where the poem might have gone had Shelley lived to finish it? Whitman and Wordsworth (who is something of a post-Romantic even at his height), end their careers with decade upon decade of stale verse. Whitman goes on palely imitating the astonishing work of 1855 to 1865, sometimes moving into unconscious self-parody. Wordsworth is worse: he becomes a guardian of the established order, in time writing a sequence of sonnets in praise of capital punishment. In Blake's terms, he goes over to Urizen and he stays there. George Gordon, Lord Byron, whose relation to the Romantic is complexly ambivalent, travels to Greece to martyr himself in the Greek war for independence against the Turks. Byron hates and fears old age, which sets in for him, by his account, at around thirty-six years.

Hart Crane dies young—apparently a suicide. Though he never surrenders the Romantic quest, he cannot quite sustain it, either. After the amazing achievement of *Howl*, Ginsberg's poetry becomes flatter and more programmatic, though not without its flashing moments. His Buddhist mentor, Trungpa Rinpoche, persuades him that his first poetic thought is inevitably his best thought, a precept that does not always serve Ginsberg well. Despite his lifelong adherence to Blake and Whitman, one would be hard pressed to say that Ginsberg completes the Romantic quest, burning fully through the private and social Selfhood. One can sometimes fear that the harsh Romantic critiques of love—"La Belle Dame," "The Crystal Cabinet," virtually all of Byron's *Don Juan*—apply to all erotic life, not merely to the fallen modalities of it.

But there is Blake. Blake does not seem to fall to the Spectre of Selfhood. In *Milton* and *Jerusalem* he persuasively dramatizes the overcoming of Self, for himself and potentially for anyone who wishes to join with him. And he enjoys that overcoming. He died, we are told, a happy and fulfilled man. In a letter from his deathbed he wrote: "I have been very near the Gates of Death & have returned very weak & an Old Man feeble and tottering, but not in Spirit & Life, not in the Real Man The Imagination which Liveth for Ever. In that I am stronger & stronger as this Foolish Body decays" (783).

The Romantic quest is not over—its possibilities are incompletely explored, its validity far from decided. Is the Romantic quest ultimately an affair of Self or of Soul? We do not entirely know. But we still live within its dangers and possibilities. Though the greatest Romantic poems may have been written, we still need to discover what the possibilities are in life for the fusion of love and imagination. As the rock and roll poet says: "After the fire, the fire still burns."

6

Freud and the Ideal Self

Often throughout this study Self has been understood as the state that stifles Soul. The pursuit of power and pleasure and social ascendancy block the hope of achieving unity of being through contemplation, compassion, bravery, or the use of imagination. Self yearns to fulfill its own desires. It yearns to live as long as it possibly can and to gain all the enjoyment available to it and then (perhaps) a little more. Self hungers for the good things in life. There are satisfactions to be found in the Soul State, to be sure, but of a different order from those available to the Self. Soul lives not only for itself, but also for others. The acts of the Soul benefit suffering men and women. Exertions of Soul help deliver them from danger, hunger, and ignorance and sometimes, by example, from the sorrows of living exclusively within time. Soul lives (perhaps) above time.

Self often yearns for Soul. Those who live in the State of Self—the state that takes the fulfillment of desire as its ultimate horizon—understand, on a level often too deep for words, that their lives lack an essential quality. They do not create; they do not truly think; they do not care; they are not brave. They ache internally, and to assuage this ache they make, or participate in, a simulacrum of the world of

Soul. They spend as much money as would feed small hungry nations to create movies and video entertainments that celebrate heroism. They attend churches that profess allegiance to the poor but love only their own glory and their own gain. They replace the compassionate doctrine of Jesus with fundamentalist obsession with the law of the Father. They patronize so-called artists who are entirely devoid of imaginative power—which is to say, the power to conceive the world that we human beings might live in, if we tried. They attend universities where Truth is held in contempt and think themselves to be educated. They acquire the skills of the marketplace and call it learning.

In the current world, Self sometimes delights in its own desires; it celebrates its love for consumption and for pleasure. Self can worship its image. When this grows tiresome and the bad faith of it all becomes too clearly manifest, then Self often fabricates for itself a culture of Soul and inhabits it. The current version of Self is narcissistic, slight, aggressive, piping, and crude, and this is the case in part because it has no real competition. There is little thriving culture of Soul. There is no new Romantic movement. There is no revival of the Gospels or the Pali Scriptures. Self is victor, and therefore it does not need to explain itself; it requires no manifestoes, no reflections, no brilliant defenders. Pragmatism and deconstruction, the last two philosophies to justify Self, are no longer necessary. No one needs the complex undoing of ideals that deconstruction enacted—everyone knows that there are virtually no ideals left. No one needs to be told that pragmatism—the conviction that truth is the belief that gets you what you want—offers a better theory of truth than Plato or Kant or Schopenhauer. Almost everyone now is a pragmatist: everyone believes that the mind is an instrument to advance his own ends. What else could it be? Those who do not agree, as Nietzsche said, go voluntarily into a madhouse.

And no one needs Sigmund Freud anymore. For Freud took the Soul State seriously. He feared it and, in some measure, was drawn to it. With impressive integrity, he examined it as closely as he could and decided finally that the allure of the Soul was too dangerous for men and women to face. Aspirations to the Soul State did far more harm than good. What we have called the Soul is the seat of illusion for Freud, illusion of the most destructive sort. Freud spent his intellectual energies attempting to demystify the Soul, yes. But he did something else as well. He put forward a version of the Self that is, in a certain way, an ideal. He offered a vision of Self that eschews unity of being, dangerous joy, fullness, and existence outside time. He makes resistance to these states of being a major virtue. He makes living within the State of Self—which means living in the state of disjunction and the state of conflict—the goal of life. The ability to say no to the ideal, and to do so with awareness of what is being lost, is what makes the Freudian individual what one might call a hero of Self. Freudian man is the antiheroic hero. Yet, as Philip Rieff drily puts it, "To be busy, spirited, and self-confident is a goal that will inspire only those who have resigned the ghosts of older and nobler inspirations" (55).

Freud has been described in many ways over time: he is the discoverer of the unconscious, the founder of a new therapy, the archaeologist of the inner life. But perhaps the best way to think about him within the context of this inquiry is as a theorist of intoxication. Yes, Freud broods constantly on the ways human beings succeed in medicating themselves. He reflects on how we turn away from reality, or what he calls reality, in the interest of inhabiting another, less painful, state. Most of us are slaves to the pleasure principle, Freud says. And when we cannot find pleasure on our own—it is very hard to find—we do what we can to achieve the next best thing, which is the annulment of pain.

"Why do we not get drunk?" Freud asks in a letter to his fiancée, Martha Bernays. Why don't we follow the example of the masses and achieve whatever level of anesthesia we can with the usual means? We can consume alcohol until we no longer feel the pain of being. (Keats speaks of "the feel of not to feel it.") So why don't we get drunk? Freud answers directly: we fear the morning after. We cannot bear the pain that comes as a result of our temporary pleasure. (Freud, one might say, will become a philosopher of the hangover, as well as a philosopher of intoxication.) We want to go to work the next day—work being to Freud one of the first blessings in life. We do not want to exchange an intensity of pleasure—or at least a striking absence of pain—for prolonged incapacity.

Freud was never drawn to alcohol, but for a while he did have a drug of choice, cocaine. He gave it to his patients. He took it himself. He boasted to Martha that he was becoming a larger, stronger, more virile being, flushed with the powers of this vital drug. But coke did nothing for Freud's patients except stimulate them to some fresh heights and then drop them, hard. ("As high as we have mounted in delight," the poet says, "in our dejection do we sink as low." With cocaine, the dejection can be three times the ascent.) And cocaine did nothing much for Freud, except to make him boast to Martha and raise his ambition higher than it had previously soared. So there would be no drug-joy for Sigmund Freud and no alcoholic heights either—no Bacchus and no biting "mind of winter," no head full of snow.

What would there be instead? There would be—to stay with Stevens another moment—"the difficulty of what it is to be." Freud would affirm the harsh world that exists when one eschews intoxicants and faces up to the truth. And what is that truth? What is the fundamental state of being? What is the actual state from which men and women use intoxicants—and as we will see there are many intoxicants—to deliver themselves?

For Freud authentic character (nonintoxicated character) is conflict. Character is not essentially conflict with the external world, though such conflict is an inevitable a part of life. Character is internal conflict. We are all at war within ourselves. There is no authentic stability to the inner life, and the dynamics of the inner life's struggle are often beyond the reach of consciousness. We are, according to Freud, perpetually at internal civil war.

Why are we creatures of conflict from Freud's perspective? We are internally divided. In Freud's first map of the mind, which he unveils in 1900, we are split into two parts, which he calls the I and the It, or the ego and the id. The It is by far the most important: it is the seat of the drives. The id is the source of the wishes, aggressive and erotic, that the I does not wish to acknowledge or act upon. In Freud's second map of the mind, which he unveils in 1914, we are composed not of two but of three agencies: the I, the It, and the Over-I, or the superego. We possess (and are possessed by) not one but two inner forces of authority. The first, the I, is largely identical with consciousness. But the second, the Over-I, is about as available to the conscious mind as the It generally is. Freud says early in his career that a dream is the disguised fulfillment of a repressed wish. Had he truly revised his theory of dreams in accord with his later findings, he would have said that the dream is a disguised fulfillment of a repressed wish or the disguised fulfillment of a repressed (and often irrational) demand. What we call an anxiety dream is a dream of the superego; a dream of desire is a dream of the id.

Freud's is a vision of the Self—and nothing but the Self. That is, he offers us a vision of humanity as defined by desire. (Could humans be defined by anything else? The contemporary individual has a difficult time imagining how this could be.) Every component of the Freudian self is defined by what it wants—for itself. The id desires the immediate satisfactions of the appetites, yes. They are emphatically individual appetites. No one ever truly wants happiness for others, for strangers. No one ever dreams of the eradication of hunger or of peace in the world. But the Over-I too is defined by desire. It wants command, it wants to be right, it wants to be the ultimate impeccable judge. The Over-I wants to be stringent and to be strict, and it wants its judgments to be binding for all time. In short, it all too often wants to be God. The I, what does the I want? The I wants to survive. The I wants to go on living—though maybe, given the stresses upon it, the I does not want to go on living forever. The I, Freud tells us, feels the unending *pressure* of the It and its demands. Yet it does not always know what those demands are, due to repression. (Freud replaces the quest for compassion and courage with the quest for a certain kind of self-knowledge.) The I also feels the pressure of the Over-I, which is always judging it, almost always finding it wanting, always trying to raise its standards. And then there is the external world. To Freud the social world is a place of barely veiled hostility. We men and women do not, on the fundamental level, care all that much for one another. We are not compassionate beings. In a certain way, the paranoid's feeling is precisely the right one—the man walking toward him down the street does wish him ill. Freud is a Darwinian: Freud sees us as all striving against one another to feed and to procreate.

The ego, Freud says, in what may be the book that best defines his sense of life, *The Ego and the Id,* is "a poor creature" in thrall to three masters and accordingly susceptible to three kinds of danger: "from the external world, from the libido of the id, and from the severity of the super-ego. Three kinds of anxiety correspond to these three dangers, since anxiety is the expression of a retreat from danger. As a frontier creature, the ego tries to mediate between the world and the id, to make the id pliable to the world and, by means of its muscular activity, to make the world fall in with the wishes of the id. . . . In its position midway between the id and reality, [the ego] only too often yields to the temptation to become sycophantic, opportunist and lying, like a politician who sees the truth but wants to keep his place in popular favor" (*SE*.XIX, 56). And then there is the ego's relation with the superego, which often persecutes it harshly for small cause and from which it cannot flee.

For Freud, there is no authentically unified I; there is no justifiably cogent Self. (There is unjustifiably coherent Being, but that is another story.) Strictly speaking, one cannot answer the simplest of questions. "Do you like sex with your lover?" Perhaps the It does—though maybe it dreams of other, more forbidden "objects." Perhaps the I can be recruited to the program of momentary pleasure. Though maybe it is worrying about time lost, about obligations, about the risks to health, about contraception, about disease, about the atmosphere of the room, about the toxic quality of the precoital drinks, and finally about who will pay the hotel tab. ("You look so beautiful I can hardly keep my eyes on the meter," says Woody Allen riding a New York taxi with Diane Keaton.) And the Over-I? The Over-I presumably disapproves of almost anything that brings pleasure and creates no product. Where is the use in this? Where is the profit? You are *wasting time.* (The superego is in love with time as chronos: a sequence of undifferentiated moments that lead absolutely nowhere. The superego, one might say, can be the Selfhood intensified to a preternatural and nearly insane degree.) Thus the Church—one of our many exteriorizations of the superego—will proclaim that sex is only for procreation. Sex is the work of making new beings. Sex is labor. The superego loves work. Anything that can be cast in the idiom of labor has a chance to purchase its grudging acquiescence. "Are you still working on that?" the waitress at the upscale restaurant asks the eater lounging over an absurdly overpriced entrée. Could she ask if he is still enjoying it, still taking pleasure? No, not if the Over-I is to be included in the pleasure—if that is what it is—of the overpriced meal.

The fundamental condition of life for Freud is anxiety, the feeling that arises from conflict with the outside world and also from internal conflict. Aristotle said that the basic feeling of being alive is an ongoing mild unpleasantness. Freud can tell us why. The sense of unpleasant inner tension that we all feel most of the time is the result, according to Freud, of the conflict going on beneath the level of awareness. We are not one person, but three people, forever in a state of inner tension, though—if we are sane—not quite a state of inner turmoil. Usually the civil war within is something of a cold war: the id and the super-ego do their work quietly and clandestinely. But tension is the order of the day.

Still, at various points, the conflict of agencies produces stresses that are nearly impossible to bear. The inner being rebels; the subject dissolves in depression or is left incapacitated by anxiety. He develops a set of symptoms that disrupt everyday life: he cannot leave the house; he cannot sit down at the table without washing his hands again, then again; she is afraid of sex, and she is afraid of conflict, and she is afraid of herself. What has happened, from Freud's perspective, is often that one of the agencies has overwhelmed the rest. The superego has reduced the poor ego to a scared fraction of what it was, and self-hating depression begins. The ego senses that the id is reaching tidal-wave strength, so stay inside, stay confined— don't risk an explosion of desire out in the world. Face it: to be human hurts. We are always, even at the best of times, in a state of unhappiness simply because we cannot decide who we are (we are multiple) and what we want (we want too many things and at the same time do not want them).

Freud's solution to the problem of relative imbalance is, in its way, a moving one. He cannot do anything to help fix an absolute imbalance; when one inner force has overrun the others, symmetry is completely lost and the sense of reality (Freud calls it the reality principle) is overthrown. Freud cannot cure psychosis. Schizophrenia breaks his heart—this much is clear—but he can do nothing about it. For the psyche that has fallen out of balance with itself there is a solution. Talk. Words. Freud believes that expressing one's desires honestly (even if the desire at hand is the superego's desire to overwhelm or obliterate desire) can create partial liberation. Let us underline that word—partial. There is no full freedom in Freud's world of the Self—though there is the illusion of freedom, which is very costly.

But articulation brings a relaxation of tension. To know oneself, to the degree that one can, and to express that knowledge in words of one's own devising, can melt inner tension (a little) and unbind the energies that are caught in fruitless conflict. Why should this be so? It is not clear. Perhaps it is because expression brings some measure of compassion from ourselves for ourselves. Perhaps articulation, however uncertain and stumbling, can be a way of making art (however flawed) of our state and allowing ourselves the earned pleasure of detachment. Maybe someone (such as the therapist) hearing our words and believing them and sympathizing reminds us of a fundamental truth: all human beings suffer, all of us live in pain, there is no one who escapes. It is hard to suffer. It is harder to believe that one has been selected especially for suffering and that one suffers along. Expression breaks the barrier of aloneness—or at last so Freud suggests.

Where id was there ego shall be, Freud famously said. He meant that consciousness could colonize that which resists expression so the self can achieve some stability. From self-knowledge might arise the power to love and to work. We might add a corollary to Freud's famous dictum about ego and id. Where superego was there ego shall be. That is to say, with effort—and the well-timed relaxation of effort—we might allow the superego, which is most of the time unconscious, to be heard. There is a paradox here: Freud believes that the superego actually operates "through the medium of the voice," though by and large this voice goes undetected. But he also suggests that we may, at times, elevate the volume on the superego, hear its dictates, and respond to them critically. We may recognize in that voice the trace of the parent's voice—entirely adequate to guide the vulnerable child, but not fitted to the reasonably capable man or woman that we can now take ourselves to be. We might recognize the voice as one inflamed by the influence of overbearing figures of authority or of fire-and-brimstone religions. We may, to adapt some terms of Harold Bloom's, overhear the way in which we talk to ourselves and by virtue of that overhearing we may change.

But not a great deal; Freud does not allow for that. He famously said that the objective of psychoanalysis was to transform hysterical misery into common, everyday unhappiness. That is an extreme statement—sometimes Freud wants more than unhappiness, especially if the subject begins further along the road than in hysterical misery. But the point is clear: within the realm of being that Freud describes (and in some sense creates) one cannot ask for too much. Life can get a little better; the spirit (if one can use that word) may breathe a bit more freely. There might be a little more room to be productive and cultivate some awareness of others (to the Freudian self this does not come easily); one might even enhance one's capacity to experience a little pleasure here and there. Yet at Freud's back one hears Nietzsche: he has his little pleasures for the day and his little pleasures for the night, but there is always a regard for health. Yes, with Freud there is always a regard for health.

"The psyche must know how to make deals." This is not Sigmund Freud talking but rather Carl Gustav Jung, in what is likely the most Freudian moment of his life. Jung was interested in anything but deals for himself—he wanted everything. But Freud's is ultimately a pragmatic philosophy: he seeks to get a little more without losing all he has. Thinking of the ideal life, Marx said that a man would be a hunter in the morning, a fisherman in the afternoon, and a critic at night. The true Freudian must also divide his days. He must leave some time for the satisfactions of the ego, some for the id, and even some (of a judiciously limited sort) for the often-tyrannical superego. He must make promises. The agency held in abeyance during a given interlude should understand that in time it will have its satisfactions. To break a promise with the id or superego is perhaps like breaking a promise to a child. One is never wholly forgiven.

The psyche must know how to make deals. In other words, the *ego* must know how to make deals: it must understand how to give something to the other, more archaic forces that dwell inside and also to leave something over for itself. The ego, in the healthy individual, has to be the great negotiator, the grand broker, without ever losing the understanding that the agencies with which is does business can never really be pleased (or fully trusted). There is always discontent; there will always be troughs of depression; anxiety is a constant presence in the best-regulated life. The most adept broker of the psyche feels the strain—and perhaps, anxiety being the grinding constant force that it is, he eventually perishes from it.

Freud considers the riddle of being in terms of free and bound energy. If we bind all our energy, committing it to one end and another through the making of deals, we may feel a certain level of contentment. We might form a judicious budget of the psyche— allocating a certain amount of libido to love, a certain amount to work, a certain quotient to family and friends. We might carefully calculate the time needed to relax and recharge. We may, like a shrewd prime minister, try to satisfy all the constituencies of the Self. If we give every indwelling devil his due, they will perhaps relax their insistences.

But if we bind all our internal energy, there will be nothing left to respond to immediate life. There will be no present for us, because everything will already be committed. Free energy is the energy of freedom: it allows us to make new choices, take new branches in the path, even to have fresh perceptions. Making comprehensive internal deals binds free energy and renders us more quiescent. The price of sanity—fully and intelligently bound energy—can be staleness and inertia, which is a form of suffering in its own right. And because of the dynamics of repression, we can never do what Socrates commended and know ourselves. So even the most adroit dealmaker is likely to be deceived and humiliated time after time.

What then is to be done? Freud's implicit answer is simple but demanding. One must, finally, *live with it*. One must understand that tension and disunity are the essential conditions of life and that finally, as skillful as we may be as managers of the psyche, we will never feel very well for very long. People go into analysis, or pick up a volume of Freud, thinking that it might help them to become happy. But truly there is no such thing as happiness—at least not in any protracted form. Freud defines pleasure as the sudden release of tension. The stronger and the more prolonged the tension, the greater the pleasure. For we are creatures that can only note extraordinary changes, and even when they are for the better, we cannot enjoy them long. A human being, as Dostoyevsky suggested—and Freud would concur—is an animal who can get used to things. We ought to get used to the fact that, as Freud says in *Civilization and Its Discontents,* we are not designed to be happy. So we need to accept our unhappiness and deal with it. We need to get used to the fact that we are (at best) the animals who get used to things.

People come to Freud and his heirs wishing to be cured—wishing to be reborn, cleansed, made new, as John did for Jesus with the waters. But this is not a tenable wish. A Freudian individual lives within the borders of the Self and does not expect great things. He knows himself well enough to create some internal stability, though it will never take the form of harmony—too much of the Self is unconscious for that. He chafes inside. He aches and he does not usually quite know why. But he does the best he can—making his deals—and he lives with it.

And though living with anxiety and depression and unfulfilled desires may be arduous enough, it is distinctly unheroic. No one should receive the laurels of fame for bringing it off. It is simply what a middle-class man or woman must do. The paradox is that leading the Freudian life well is a true challenge, and generally we do not succeed in it. As he observes in "The Resistances to Psychoanalysis": Society is not "sufficiently wealthy or well-organized to be able to compensate the individual for the amount of his instinctual renunciation. It is consequently left to the individual to decide how he can obtain, for the sacrifice he has made, enough compensation to enable him to preserve his mental balance. On the whole, however, he is obliged to live psychologically beyond his means, while the unsatisfied claims of his instincts make him feel the demands of civilization as a constant pressure upon him" (*SE*.XIX,219).

But even succeeding in making psychological deals does not add up to very much, at least for some. Ultimately, all you do is live and die and provide for the same kind of life of renunciation and relatively meaningful work for your children. This is all, and it may not be very much. But Freud believes that to attempt much more is a serious error. The nobility of Freud's implicit view of life is muted. But, he repeatedly insists, the pain and sorrow that can come from seeking alternatives is anything but minor, anything but muted.

For there are ways to *solve* the Freudian dilemma, and Freud is aware of them. He recognizes that though we are divided beings, we pine for unity, and that there are ways to achieve that unity—or at least its illusion. Though we are tripartite creatures, we can make ourselves quite readily into composite wholes and enjoy the feeling of fullness, at least for a while. But these states of wholeness are potentially destructive, not only to the individual involved, but to the general social world—which Freud, to be fair, does not always care terribly much about.

Freud is no Romantic, but the intensity of his preoccupation with erotic life connects him, as we have seen, to the High Romantics. Freud's anti-Romanticism takes a simple form: he believes that only a fool is willing to make his erotic life into his spiritual life. Only a deluded man or woman—a Romantic—believes that he and his works can be made new through merger with a beloved. Erotic love, according to Freud, is best understood as "over-estimation of the erotic object." Why are we inclined to overestimate the beloved? One answer is that many of us have no god and no gods, and so cannot live without enchantment of some sort. We cannot bear very much reality. We are creatures who require our illusions. There have been many sources of illusion in the West, but the most pressing, because the most recent in vintage, is the idea that the sexual life can be the way to rebirth.

Aristophanes' myth suggests that we can find the beloved who is our other half and dwell in bliss, and generations of questing Romantics have concurred. Some forget a half of the quest: they do not know that love must produce renovation in all areas of life, and that if it does not do so, it is not High Romantic love. Others—the modernists—believe that imagination can get along perfectly well without the inspiration that Eros provides. And this may be true or it may not. T. S. Eliot is a remarkable poet, but whether he ever leaves the Waste Land or not—even in the supposed affirmations of "Little Gidding"—is an open question.

So what then is "over-estimation of the erotic object"? The line strikes directly to the heart of High Romanticism. For the Romantic estimates the beloved—he will never descend to use such a term as "object"—highly indeed. She is his other half; he is hers. They provide each other the lineaments of gratified desire. Together they achieve that unity of being that makes hope and creative energy flow again. Together, they might change the world, or at least deliver people from some measure of self-inflicted pain. The great hymns to renovation in Shelley's *Prometheus* are hymns to the possibilities that open when male and female forces, Prometheus and Asia, join together in love and mutual esteem. Blake's liberating polemic at the close of *Milton,* in which he declares his sanity and more than his sanity, rises from the unification of Milton and his Emanation and Palamabron and his. Even to a more susceptible spirit than Freud's, the polemic in behalf of heterosexual Eros that Blake and Shelley engage in could well be considered excessive. Yet—Blake might ask—what will take you to the palace of wisdom, if not the road of excess?

In every profession of love, Freud hears an echo. (We might say that in every significant utterance Freud hears echoes.) In a remarkably illuminating sentence, Philip Rieff says that to Freud there is little difference between the obsessive monogamist and the devoted sexual adventurer, between the drab, clutching householder and Don Juan. Both want to reunite themselves with what Freud likes to call the "primary object," which is to say the mother, or if we are speaking of a later stage in development, the parent of the opposite sex. Casanova proceeds by frantic pursuit. He discovers again and again that he has not found what he was looking for; the uxorious greengrocer grabs tighter and tighter, pulls the beloved ever closer, hoping to see and feel a primary satisfaction that never arrives.

To Freud, life is full of ghosts. Every figure who truly matters to us today is inhabited by the spirits of those we have loved and revered—and feared and worshipped—in the past. In Freud, who is sometimes nearly as Gothic a mind as Poe, there simply is no pure present. There is no moment where you encounter the possibility of something that is truly without precedent. The theory of repression, Van den Berg says, is entwined with the idea that everything is past and that there is nothing new. Yes, says Freud, everything is past and there is nothing new—except perhaps for his coherent and comprehensive vision of the strength and subtlety of the past.

Freud assaults love from multiple directions: he understands that Romantic Eros is a new force—comparable to compassion, comparable to courage—that makes dangerous promises. But history (and Shakespeare) have dealt with the myth of courage; history (and the Enlightenment) have dealt with the myth of faith. Love is Freud's primary antagonist among human ideals, and he attacks it from every plausible direction. The lover, says Freud, puts the beloved in the place of the superego. That is to say, the experience of love solves the crisis of the superego—it is no longer a rogue agency, overwhelming the psyche with fierce injunctions. It becomes benign—to the degree that the lover and beloved have joined with each other in what they value and what they aspire to create. The two people share ideals—the two, as it were, become one. Freud does not like this much. Every man should suffer under the rule of his own superego—this is part of Freudian authenticity of Self. But in saying that I and the beloved can merge, Freud is participating in the heroic story of Romantic love: he simply values it rather harshly, for he assumes that the beloved will always provide a flattering ego ideal. That the beloved might urge the lover on to higher creations and fiercer exertions—this possibility does not occur to Freud.

Freud believed he had been deluded in love. Early in life, he imagined Martha Bernays to be a potential Soulmate, when she was only an industrious and intelligent young Austrian woman who was amazed, but also often baffled, by her brilliant lover. When young, she was enough of a blank slate that Freud could make her much that she was not: he could impose whatever identity he needed on her. For a while, Martha was a walking goddess, the muse of Freud's creative life. With no little integrity, she insisted on being ordinary; eventually her insistence, and Freud's own perceptions, won out. Love, it turns out, was and is the overestimation of the erotic object.

Freud assaults love from every side. The objective of psychotherapy in its last phase is to expose and then dissolve the patient's erotic illusions. The patient believes he can be cured through the love of the therapist. He will be delivered from his misery by a figure of authority, who can also sate the desires: id and superego will be rendered content and wholeness achieved. But this is a lie. The patient falls in love with the therapist through the process that Freud calls the transference—and sometimes the therapist falls too; the counter-transference is almost always part of analysis. The patient asks to be cured, which is to say to be made whole, and this is what he does in life when he falls in love. He asks for wholeness, he asks for the unity of being that passes beyond the everyday disjunction he feels. But he is asking for too much. He is asking for the love that the parent gives the child. Frequently the therapist invites the patient to consider the perception that he is always demanding this sort of response when he falls in love, even in what is called adult life. He is a creature of need, not a creature of desire. A human being possessed by need is greedy, hungry for more, and prone to bitter anger, sometimes rage, when perfect love is not forthcoming. The human being who has moved on to desire hopes for understanding, reciprocity, and partnership, but also knows that even in the best of marriages those benefits will not always be available. The psychoanalytic patient must break his erotic illusions if he is to take up a sane and productive life.

If he does not, love will always be bitterly frustrating. To the Freudian way of thinking, a marital argument about the budget or the true location of the house keys often hides deeper content. You spend too freely is sometimes a coded version of an injunction: You don't love me enough. You are not my Soulmate. And for this I am enraged. You must be, must be. To which the Freudian patient has to learn to answer: You don't love me enough because no one can possibly love me as much as my regressed self, my childhood self, calls out to be loved. You are not my Soulmate, because there is no Soulmate. The idea is a rank illusion. When the patient knows this, he is on the way to being cured. But he has not been made whole as he hoped. He has been made aware of the inevitability of partial being, of partial presence (at best), and of partial love. The cure is not constructive but deconstructive. Freud, like Derrida and every cultural critic who believes that the art (or the life) in front of him refers inevitably to something else, is skeptical about the desire for presence. He detests—and perhaps he fears—unity of being.

And why should he not detest unity? To the Freudian mind, unity is always *forged;* it is a counterfeit that leads to overreaching today and to despondency in the future when all the illusions come to light. For Freud there is the forged unity of erotic experience, when the individual believes, as he puts it, that "I and you are one in the same." We eventually fall away from that dream, abandoned on the cold hillside, "alone and palely loitering." We thought we were looking for completion and inspiration; it was only the old Oedipal urge, combined with the hunger to leave behind our poor and isolated selves.

We can also seek unity of being by fusing ourselves with a group, under the auspices of a leader, who himself takes the place of the superego. We transfer to him our right of self-determination. He thinks for us. He takes over the faculty of judgment. What he assumes, we assume; what he derides and denounces, we abhor. The leader in the so-called civilized present is not at all unlike the leader of the primal horde, whom Freud describes in a few sharp strokes. Though the members of the group were bound by various ties of allegiance and love, "the father of the primal horde was free. His intellectual acts were strong and independent even in isolation, and his will needed no reinforcement from others. Consistency leads us to assume that his ego had few libidinal ties; he loved no one but himself, or other people only in so far as they served his needs. To objects his ego gave away no more than was barely necessary" (*SE*.XVIII, 123).

The importance of such figures in the history of mankind is very great, Freud says. We are drawn to leaders for many reasons, but one is that they seem to possess an assurance and authority that we do not have. They know what is true and false, right and wrong. We are tormented by having two sources of authority within: the ego and the superego. They constantly contend with each other, creating endless confusion. Individuals of the leader type appear to have merged their two sources of authority and to be at one internally on all worldly questions. This is a dramatically attractive condition, and we often wish to make it our own.

Whatever independent being we had we surrender to the leader, who performs a kind of hypnotism on us. He who makes himself into a beast evades the pain of being a man, the poet says, and to Freud the crowd is a sort of beast. The individual need no longer be tormented by his own internal disunity. The leader becomes the executive function: he can be both ego and superego to the individual. And if what he demands is in line with the rages of the It, then a complete fusion of inner agencies can take place and the individual be liberated from the disjunction that he finds so painful moment to moment. He attains unity of Self.

But the cost of this unity, which is manifest as a kind of inebriation, is often horrible. The members of the crowd surrender themselves to the great leader, who allows them to think of themselves as fulfilling high ideals even as they behave bestially. Hitler persuades his countrymen that by eliminating the Jews and taking their property, they are serving the grandest possible destiny. They are acting on behalf of Germany and the world. The guards in the concentration camps were told all the time how much they were sacrificing when they did what they did and witnessed what they witnessed. But they were functioning for a high purpose: they were being heroes. Hitler's crowds, Freud's thinking suggests, were leaving behind the disunited self and achieving sublime unity of being. They were transcending the pull of the past and living in the present. They were living with full intensity, and their lives were charged with meaning. "Why do we not get drunk?" The entire nation of Germany did, and then woke up, not to the continuation of a thousand-year Reich but to what may well amount to a thousand years of guilt and sorrow—the most horrible morning after in recent history.

The idea that one could pass *authentically and legitimately* out of the State of Self into the State of Soul is not available to Freud. To Freud, the crowd offers transcendence of mundane being, but at a high cost. In exchange for unity of Self, we regress into our least thoughtful, potentially most barbarous way of being. The leader is always at the heart of the crowd for Freud and, he implies, the leader becomes a leader through his ability to sanction regression. We become more primitive, more childlike, but thanks to the blandishments of the leader, we do so in the name of elevated ideals and so with a clean conscience.

Freud cannot readily imagine a crowd like the one Jesus creates when he asks the disciples to divide loaves and fishes. The members of that crowd, presumably, reach into their pockets and pouches and takes out what little belongs to them and they *share* it. What once was a crowd is now a community. Where id was there ego shall be? To Freud this is an ultimate goal. The goal of Jesus (and the Buddha and, in some measure, Confucius) is rather different. Where the grasping Self was, acting only in its own interests, there communal Soul shall be. This is the ideal of Jesus at its height. But for Freud such an aspiration is too high. The better, Freud never wearies of telling us, is almost inevitably the enemy of the good.

Jesus and Buddha and Confucius teach us that it is possible to remove oneself from the sorry provinces of the Self and join a universal being. This happens for the sages not under the sign of regression, but under the sign of compassion. Love God with your whole heart, your whole soul, your whole mind, the Savior says. And when he becomes most exultant about the figure he calls the Father (and Blake calls Nobadaddy), Jesus is often about to be most radical. For then he tells us, Love your neighbor as yourself.

Who is your neighbor? A man was beaten and robbed and thrown in a ditch. Two powerful members of his own tribe passed him by. But then there came a Samaritan, a man who had no blood relation to the poor man left like refuse on the side of the road. Yet the Samaritan hoisted him up and bound his wounds and took him to the inn and paid for his stay and for his care. Who then was the true neighbor to the poor man beaten and thrown in the ditch? Worlds of possibility (and risk) open when Jesus tells this tale. Just so, worlds open when Gautama responds to Mara—his Selfhood—after she tells him that when he unfolds the noble truths about life there are many who will laugh at him. (Aristocrats do not like to be laughed at.) "Not all of them will," the Buddha says. "Not all."

To which Freud replies: Jesus and Lord Buddha and Confucius and all the rest are asking too much of human beings. It is enough to create the basis for justice in this world, but all-encompassing mercy, that is beyond our capacity as humans. Asked to be compassionate in the way Jesus commends, people will fabricate compassion, or they will rebel against its dictates and become even more Self-centered than before. (There is only Self, Freud tells us. Everything else is an illusion.) How can we love our fellow men? Freud asks. Our fellow men, in general, have at best a mild contempt for us; at worst, they nurse murderous rage. That rage becomes more likely to manifest itself if we ask too much of the Self. There is only Self. Soul is an illusion.

We were once a courageous people, Freud said: once, but alas, no longer. The time was the late 1930s when the Nazis were persecuting the Jews in Vienna and Germany and Freud was about to publish his book, *Moses and Monotheism*. The book would be controversial, and Freud knew it. In it, he speculates that Moses was not a Jew but an Egyptian. To this he adds the possibility that Moses was killed by the Jews. His crime? Much like the crime of the creator of psychoanalysis: asking people to believe in a supersensory realm of being. For Moses it is the invisible Yahweh that the Jews must believe in rather than Moloch and the Golden Calf. For Freud the invisible world is the one composed by the psyche and the trinity of I, Over-I, and It.

Freud says that by and large the Jews have lost their courage—but that he has not. He will publish the book. The Jewish bravery he is thinking of is not bravery of an intellectual sort, however. It is the courage the Jews showed when, shortly after the death of Jesus, they rebelled not once but twice against their Roman overlords. The account provided by Josephus, which is not entirely reliable, chronicles infighting and competition among the various competing Jewish factions, but some ferocious bravery as well. Finally Vespasian and his son Titus were compelled to leave Rome with some of its best legions to put down the rebellion. The Romans ruined the city, killed and enslaved the resistance, and destroyed the Temple. On the Arch of Titus in Rome one sees Roman troops carrying the sacred Menorah, their booty and sign of victory over the brave and often reckless Jewish rebels.

Freud may have been moved by Jewish courage two thousand years before his own life, but he is not moved by martial courage in the present. Consider again Freud's topography of the inner life. It is a commonplace to say that Freud relies on the map of the spirit that Plato drew, and in this commonplace there is some truth. Both maps are tripartite: both men believe that the human spirit is divided into three parts, which can often be in conflict with one another. Plato's map is a major revision of the Homeric version of identity. What matters most to the Homeric heroes is spirit, courage, daring— which they call thymos. Knowing a man in Homer means knowing how brave he is: can he lead troops into battle; is he willing to risk his life; does he have what Homer's heroes call "staying power"?

When Plato redraws the map, he basically preserves thymos; spiritedness is still a major element in his model of the human soul. But in the best human souls, thymos is subordinate to reason, or nous. One thinks before one acts; one asks before the fight if the war is just. (Where thymos was, Plato might have said to describe his revision of Homer, there nous shall be.) Plato concentrates his views on this matter in a brilliant phrase. What is courage? he asks himself. To the Homeric warrior, courage means completely conquering fear; courage means rampaging through battle without being afraid of losing one's life. To Plato, courage means *knowing* what to be afraid of and what not to fear. For Plato, all experience must be brought before the judgment seat of reason.

Freud drops courage from the spiritual map. There is no equivalent of Homeric (or even Platonic) courage in Freud's three-part model of the spirit. In Homer, and even in Plato, to know a person is to know how brave or cowardly he is. What will he dare? How readily will he risk his life? This is not part of Freud's sense of human nature at all. Whether one can or cannot exhibit martial bravery may not be entirely beside the point, but surely it is not what is essential. To put it crudely but not inaccurately, an everyday man is his ratio of repressions, to Freud; a more civilized man is his capacity for sublimation—that is, for turning the primal energies toward socially approved goals. A man is his capacity to love (in the middle-class manner) and to work (in the middle-class manner). A man is also the strength of his superego and his capacity to respond to its demands. But a man is not his fighting strength. Courage may occasionally be an admirable quality to Freud, but it is not central to the struggles of Self.

To Freud, what is called courage is usually based on illusion. Why do men rush over the trench toward emplaced machine guns, ready to meet death? Freud, like every civilized person, was shocked and horrified by the First World War. No one understood its cause when it erupted—and a survey of current historians suggests that no one knows its origins to this day. What George Steiner called Europe's long Sunday afternoon—civilized, calm, decorous, and (alas) rather boring—turned rapidly into hell on earth. Why did the men leap up and over the trench? Freud has an answer: the narcissistic illusion. They believed that they, unlike all the men around them, would never die. All of us are convinced, on some level below the reach of reason, that we are extraordinary and will never leave the earth. "We know no time when we were not as now," as Milton's Satan says. The individual knows of no time when he was not present, on the scene, and, for all purposes, the center of the world. The idea that we will in time not be "as now" is untenable to us, to the degree that we are ruled by our narcissism. And when is self-love as strong as it is in youth, when the soldier goes off to war?

As Freud says in his "Thoughts on War and Death": "What we call our 'unconscious'—the deepest strata of our minds, made up of instinctual impulses—knows nothing that is negative and no negation; in it contradictions coincide. For that reason it does not know its own death, for to that we can give only a negative content. Thus there is nothing instinctual in us which responds to a belief in death. This may even be the secret of heroism." Freud goes on to say that in the commonplace view of heroism, the individual takes in the dangers manifest before him and overcomes his fear. He is willing if need be to sacrifice himself for the general good. But really, Freud says, most so-called heroes defy danger under the belief that "Nothing can happen to me" (*SE*.XIV, 296).

For Freud it is not only self-love that can inspire what we commonly and (he believes) mistakenly call bravery. It can also be something much like the opposite. We are all subjects of and subject to what Freud called the Death Drive. Every living creature wants to end its own being: The aim of all life is death, Freud famously said. Freud refuses to associate the Death Drive with the gathering strength of the superego, as he perceives it in his later work. The Over-I gathers force as civilization gathers force, and it oppresses the individual more this year—or at least this decade—than it did last. The Over-I can provoke despondency, depression, even suicide. And Freud does once say that an enflamed and punitive Over-I can create a "pure culture of the death drive." But by and large the Death Drive is an independent force that has no real cultural affiliation. The aim of all life is death, Freud says, but every creature wants to die in its own way. The Death Drive, according to Freud, manifested itself in trench warfare: the men who jumped over their own wire and ran toward those guns were, in effect, being directed by a force stronger than their own wills: the aims of their lives became death.

But which is it? Does what is erroneously called courage come from loving oneself (and accordingly one's life) too much or from detesting life at something like a cellular level and hungering to die? Freud is pleased to offer both purportedly debunking speculations. The fact that Freud is willing to call forward two opposed explanations for the same behavior suggests a rather high level of unease. Courage must be undermined, even at the cost of logic. Anything that promises unity of being needs to be reinterpreted in Freud's transvaluation of heroic into bourgeois values. Where Soul was, there Self must be.

But Freud is a thinker, a quester after Truth, is he not? In a manner of speaking, yes, he is. Freud has something of genuine interest to say on every consequential human subject. Freud is always provocative and, given the limits he sets for himself, frequently quite accurate. That is to say, he is accurate about life under the aegis of the Self. Freud detested most philosophy, which in the immediate sense he associated with Kant. He found the thinking of the philosophers hopelessly arid, in that they did not give enough attention to sex. For Kant and for the other idealists (with the exception of Schopenhauer, whom Freud admired and—let us say—borrowed from freely), life was all about the deployment of mind. Freud believed that thought was almost always yoked to the sexual past; most intellectuals, he said, were preternaturally curious about erotic matters when they were children. Most of them never managed to detach their thinking from its sexual origins, which is to say, their reflections were almost always a form of wish-fulfillment, even if the wish at hand was to free the Self from the claims of the instincts. "The patient," Lacan often found himself saying rather wearily, "desires to have no desires." He probably said it to intellectuals or aspiring intellectuals more than to other types of patients. Freud seems to have believed that he had liberated his own thought from erotic longings and from anything that could qualify as fantasy. He had withered, as Yeats says, into truth.

On love, government, culture, art, history, aggression, money, sex, and a span of other subjects, Freud has much to tell us; as much, one might say, as some of the great philosophers. But Freud is distinct from the philosophers in that he offers no ideal. There is no "major man," as Stevens might call him, who emerges from Freud's thought. The figure who can successfully balance the drives—the certified public accountant of the psyche—is no major man or woman. What psychological man has over the everyday middle-class individual is a higher level of self-awareness. He knows why he does what he does, desires in the measured manner he does, holds at bay what he holds at bay. He hops and blinks and has his little pleasure for the day and his little pleasure for the night, Nietzsche might cruelly say, but he knows exactly why he hops as he does (and never leaps), and why his pleasures are of the moderated sort they are.

The Freudian subject is nothing if not pragmatic. He lives in a perpetual condition of chronos—time is grinding, uniform, inexorable, and moves inevitably toward death. Every second tastes of mortality. The Over-I, Freud tells us, is the seat of the time sense, which is to say that temporality will always be invested with the force of authority, demand, and the iron laws. There is no kairos for the Over-I or for the Freudian subject. We never can live in the fullness of being. There's no breaking into a clearing, no sudden descent of the angel, no perception of the bridge as "harp and altar of the fury fused" as Hart Crane calls it: a bridge is a transit from one place to another. Space is a secondary matter to the Freudian subject, for in Milton's fashion, the mind makes its own place and can create a hell of heaven, a heaven of hell, though usually what it does is create nothing so melodramatic: it creates and affirms a purgatory.

Traveling is a fool's paradise, Emerson says. My giant goes with me where I go. By the giant, Emerson means the force of repression and regret that we all carry because of the interior compromises we have been forced to make. In Freud, interior reality always trumps the exterior condition, be it ever so benign.

Is there any way to emerge from this state of highly tempered balance? Might one actually achieve some kind of joy before one's days are done? Is there even happiness, rather than simple balance, to be found in the Freudian universe?

"Psycho-analysis," Karl Kraus famously said, "is the disease of which it purports to be the cure." There are many ways to take this rather unpleasant observation. But perhaps the most germane is this: Psychoanalysis, and the life philosophy that emerges from it, assigns men and women to a world of carefully balanced inner accounts and restrained pleasures. But Freud also assiduously denies the alternatives. Anything that could conceivably change the life of renunciation into the life of joy is an object of Freud's debunking drive. You might save yourself through love; you might save yourself through creating art; you might save yourself through compassion; you might do so by exercise of courage or of idealistic thought. But all these activities are out of bounds. Embracing them, for Freud, causes only trouble.

It is possible that to deny human beings these primary satisfactions makes them sick. It causes a disease, it does not cure it. If you live life without courage, compassion, the true exercise of intellect and creation through love, then you will not feel very well. You may even get quite ill. When you cordon off the great sources of human meaning that have arisen through the centuries and say they are all illusory, then you will have contributed something to creating an ill and worried herd. There will be no chance to redeem the inner State of Self with its divisions that Freud so ably describes. Freud, in other words, is right about everything once you have joined him in shrinking the world to certain dimensions. No one can tell you more about Self, and this knowledge becomes a form of absolute wisdom when you are persuaded that Self is all that there authentically is. Then, when the banishment of ideals has made you ill, Freud can show you, through psychoanalysis and through the ethical program of his thought, how to feel a little better than you do. Psychoanalysis helps the culture of Self create disease. And this disease psychoanalysis will happily help cure.

One will be told that there have been many developments in psychotherapy since Freud, and this may be true. But it will not be easy to find any therapeutic form advocating creative Eros, or the quest for unconditioned Truth, or risking one's life in a just cause, or selling what one has and living for the poor. Anyone who does such things, or even contemplates them, has left the regions of modern psychology behind. Any so-called therapy that enjoins ideals is no longer therapy. Therapy can have many values, but they will never be idealistic. All therapies are about learning to live with half a loaf.

Freud fights ethically. He shows you exactly what he is doing and he tells you why. The Soul State is not worth the risk it entails. Religion and love create more grief than good, and Freud can tell you why this is so. His values are overt. His conclusions are there to be proved on the pulse, as Keats would have it. Freud engages in open mental fight with the culture of Soul.

In our current state there is no such open struggle. Self has won the battle and does not need apologetics. It does not require complex philosophical justifications. Freud is irrelevant because Freud has won—though the terms of the victory would no doubt fill him with loathing.

Freud commended a self-aware, literate, and deliberative life beyond illusion. But to have any measure of depth, it turns out, a human being must take "illusions" like compassion and courage seriously. One must work through the blandishments they offer and then decide to live without them in a life that may be severe but is full of integrity. The modern—or are we now to call him the postmodern?–individual has figured out matters differently. He does not have to live beyond courage and compassion in a life of difficult renunciation. He can possess these ideals almost as fully as his predecessors could, but without the risk. The world of TV and entertainment and other media can provide him with the illusion of possessing Soul. But the possession comes without risk. He can have the satisfactions of the Self in relative safety. He can risk little and live a long time. But he can also, in his displaced way, possess the life of the Soul. He can have his cake and gorge himself sick on it too.

Polemical Conclusion
In the Culture of the Counterfeit

Critics have often identified current Western culture as a culture of the image. We live, it's been said, in a culture of simulation. Guy Debord may have been the first to recognize this situation when he conceived *The Society of the Spectacle,* but by now the perception is pervasive. Jean Baudrillard, among others, has insisted upon it for the past three decades at least. The idea that our society is geared to simulacra is anything but a new one, though few seem ready to ask and answer a simple question: Simulacra, precisely, of what?

The answer that arises here is that current popular culture (as much adored now by the elite as it is by the populace in general) is largely a culture that simulates Soul. What passes for current-day culture is often the fabrication of the Soul States. An enormous, complex, and stunning technological force, which might be put to use to feed the world or to rid it of disease, is instead devoted to something else. It is devoted to entertainment—to delivering experiences that fabricate States of Soul. This technology of simulation was not available in Freud's time: his escapist patient might read wish-fulfilling novels; he might attend a movie or two; he might go off to a play. Mostly he had to live with the disjunctions that middle-class life can bring. He had to live with his distance from

Soul. There was nothing like today's technology of diversion at his disposal.

The primary appetite of the Soul—or the one most often suppressed by current life and so in need of feeding—is not hard to guess from the state of current culture. The shape of that culture may suggest to us that Homer (as equivocal as he may occasionally have been) and his warriors were right: human beings are desperate to enter the State of Soul defined by courage.

The simulation of the martial world is one of the largest businesses in current consumer culture. The elements of this world are almost too tedious to enumerate.

Corporately mediated sports are probably the primary vehicle for contact with simulated, safe, and sanitized Homeric virtues. A televised football game is an irony-free zone, where the commentators can talk openly about courage and daring and the will to victory. Football is not simply football—it is a packaged, mediated, and controlled experience. The announcers, acting in the interest of the corporate sponsors, take a boys' game and turn it into an epic quest. The players are warriors; the line of scrimmage a battle line (its zone is referred to as the trenches); on comes the blitz—beware the impending quarterback sack. (The vocabulary of war has effectively been diverted to the game of football.) The game's an absorbing one for many and maybe sometimes an inspiring one: there are amazing feats of athleticism; there are remarkable plays. These feats are *not entirely unlike* the feats of the battlefield; they share a vague but true kinship. Yet to force them together and to suggest that heroics in corporate sports are equivalent to battlefield heroics is delusional. On football fields, players suffer concussions and that is too bad; on battlefields soldiers commonly die, often with great bravery. Such deaths are the true subject of epic and of tragedy.

A highly produced, highly mediated televised football game is an impressive simulacrum of heroic culture. There is usually even a military presence: soldiers hold flags, march, stand on guard, and play the national anthem. Navy jets flare overhead. So strange has the world become that the soldiers believe they are being exalted by their presence near the game. They are being raised up through their contact with authentic professional athletes.

Real exercise of courage is dangerous. We want to hop and blink and live a long time—live forever if possible. When Nietzsche says that bourgeois man is good at inventing happiness, he might well be prophesying the present (and probably the future): middle-class happiness is living the life of a Self that can possess the persuasive illusion of Soul. We have become stunningly good at doing this. Instead of going to war we (and our children) go to the TV screen and watch the Sunday pseudo-carnage. Or we repair to the computer screen to act the part of world-class warriors, pocket-Achilles and Hectors. Video games make heroes of us all. (What renders someone an adept slayer of his virtual enemies on the screen is dexterity with a stick and some buttons—something akin to typing skills.) We catch an action movie; we watch another installment of this cop show or that; we read a mass-marketed corporate thriller and put ourselves in the place of the daring hero. But the book is an old technology of pseudo-transcendence, now nearly eclipsed by the electronic juice and jolt that comes off the screens.

In current culture, where is wisdom to be found? If wisdom is a hunger in the Soul, as Plato said, and if we are transfixed with true figures of wisdom—the man who has had time to think enough, the woman who has the chance truly to reflect—how do we now slake the need? It turns out that the problem of wisdom is an easy problem to solve. For acquiring wisdom, as we saw, is dangerous. The individual who pursues true insight is, to use Nietzsche's phrase (though the perception goes back at least as far as Plato), un-timely. That is, he strives to be ahead of his own time in his perceptions, albeit sometimes basing his thoughts in the intellectual achievement of the past. He is out of joint with his moment, and the result of being so dissociated is often the enmity of others. People do not like his ideas, which seem to be an indictment of the way they are living. The thinker is a walking criticism of the lives of the rest, as Socrates showed. And Socrates paid for the demonstration.

But still—one wants to *know*. To possess the Truth may, as Aristotle suggests, be something not unlike a human instinct. One desires to know, and one is even willing to extend admiration to those who appear to possess knowledge. Yet all of this must be safely done. One has a regard for health, as Nietzsche says: one's own health. How are we to slake our hunger for contemplation and for its (possible) result, wisdom? It is not hard. Let the acquisition of *information* replace thought; let the *well-informed* individual, brimming with opinions, replace the man or woman who might actually be wise, the philosopher.

For information is valuable: information helps the Self successfully navigate the current world. What portable wireless device shall I buy? How shall I finance my home? (And what lending-thieves must I avoid?) Where is the optimum place to vacation? How can I get the best-priced transportation there? (And once there, how can I best ignore the plight of the indigenous poor?) Where shall I send my children to school so that they can have the best possible careers—make the most money and be the most secure? Whom shall I vote for in the next election—which is to say, who can best serve my interests? Plausible answers to these questions qualify as authentic knowledge in contemporary culture, and there is no end of sources to provide them: turn on the TV, the radio, pick up the newspaper, enter the world of the Internet. That there could be any other kind of knowledge is anathematic to the faith in information. One knows in order to consume. One knows in order to succeed. One knows in order not to be made a fool of. But one does not learn in order to do the only things that real learning offers: to acquire virtue and wisdom.

There are other kinds of "knowledge" that current culture pursues: there is "the news" and knowledge of "the news." We are constantly bathed in flashing images of events from around the globe; where there is war, famine, revolution, religious upheaval, there the camera goes. We are briefed on the international situation as often as a head of state—or we can be, if we wish. We are regal in our need to know and our power to be informed.

What is the covert message of this flood of news? Perhaps the most significant is that everything is changing constantly and that nothing stays the same. We live in a vertigo of wars and devastations. Since this is so, since change is constant, there is no reason to stop and to think and to try to arrive at values that will transcend the pressure of the moment. It's OK not to think too hard, the news tells us, for no complex thought could possibly keep up with the flood of change—it would be obsolete the moment it was articulated.

The spray of events the news shows us demonstrates that we need to think in a manner that is mobile, strategic, pragmatic; we need to "deal with the situation." And then move on to the next pressing matter. Things are so different from moment to moment and place to place that we could never arrive at a theory to encompass all of human life. So drop that wish—replace it with the desire to be informed, to be in the know. We must be aware that what counts as knowledge today will probably be irrelevant tomorrow. Tomorrow it will possess the value of yesterday's paper, but today the current information is all in all. One said once that the great cultural quarrel was between philosophy and poetry. If so, the quarrel was rich. The current quarrel is between authentic thought (which barely exists, if it exists at all) and journalism, which is everywhere. Journalism has all but won. The idea that any form of writing or thought can be, as Pound put it, news that stays news, is an absurdity.

The newspaper sells the news. But the newspaper and the many organs of information sell something else as well. They sell *the new*. When you buy a newspaper, scan one online, flick on a news station on TV or radio, what you are purchasing (in one way or another) is newness. You are committing yourself and your resources to the idea that things change so rapidly and dramatically that one must constantly "keep up." If you slacken, if you ignore the various outlets of information for a week or a month, the ground of reality will slip from under your feet. There will be no more there there.

Lodged within the insistent onrush of information is the implication that no form of knowledge could possibly have anything but a transient status. What is true, or current, today will be gone by tomorrow. Thus we guard ourselves against the pressure of finding unconditioned Truth—finding a good and true way to live individually and collectively—by committing ourselves to sensation and information. In this way, we both evade our hunger for Truth—for the discoveries of the true scholar—and satisfy that hunger in a displaced form. Stuffed full of pointless information, we can consider ourselves wise. With a sack of minute, ephemeral truths on our backs, we can imagine that we possess the Truth. We feed ourselves incessantly and are still starved—which only makes us more insistent to consume.

What about art? What about imagination? How have we dealt with the Soul's hunger for the transforming artist?

Surely our culture is much in favor of art. We have all been told repeatedly how important it is to live in a world rich in creations of the human mind. The problem is that the Self does not like those creations much. Authentic art is always in some fundamental way Utopian. It looks out on what we have made of the world—as Blake does, as Shelley does, as Wordsworth does—and it exclaims at what it sees. "The world is too much with us; late and soon. / Getting and spending, we lay waste our powers." The true artist always begins in some version of protest. What is before us is not good enough. The world as given is not adequate to the needs of the Soul. True art always begins in rebellion against what is, in behalf of what might be. True art is what Matthew Arnold said it was: a criticism of life.

But to us now, such a vision of art is not acceptable. The world as given is a marvel—particularly in its technological attainments. There is really nothing like it. We have computers; we have an Internet; we have consumer goods at our disposal unlike any the world has seen. Anyone who suggests that this is not the very best of times to be alive is a fool. He has fallen victim to nostalgia. Granted there are problems. Some people are not as rich as they should be. Some people are alarmingly overweight and unhealthy. But still: this is a fine and even a fabulous world. To suggest, as Blake surely would have, that the Self, also known as Satan, rules, and that greed, self-ishness, and self-seeking are rampant, is beyond the pale. No one can say such things without being jeered.

And surely the artist's next strong move—the creation of a paradise for the mind and heart—cannot be allowed. We do not need that. All we need is a larger quotient of resources so that everyone can be as greedy and happy as we are. The poet who seeks through love to penetrate beyond the illusory world of Self is not to be borne. He could make us hate ourselves—and that would be far from agreeable.

Still, there must be artists. A culture without art is a morally depraved culture. We all know this. So what is the solution? We will make everyone an artist, or at least everyone who half-wishes to be. Anyone who chants an agreeable song that is in tune with the overall music of Self may now be considered to have joined what Keats called "the immortal freemasonry of intellect." Thug rappers who chant about power, pride, and acquisition are artists; a man with a pencil who can juggle words is a poet, despite the fact that he has nothing to say, only some semi-agreeable sounds to make; put an archly conceived cartoon on a canvas, sell it to a millionaire, and you are a painter dangerous with subversive intent. (People do not care what it is you have painted or how; they care what the painting sells for. We speak of a thirty-million-dollar Picasso—and forget the subject and title of the painting.) As long as you do not evoke the needs of anything higher than the Self, and you can proceed with some polish or some eloquence, then an artist is what you are. Congratulations.

Anything that possibly can be called art is. Constantly we are pushing the boundaries of art in the interest of what seems to be an aesthetic populism. The latest noise from a suburban garage band? Art! An animated Hollywood-made romp for children and for adults who have decided that growing up is not in their interests? Art! A novel or book of poems by a celebrity with high name recognition? Of course: art.

Much of what we are willing now to call art is inevitably fully compatible with the status quo. It does not really evince dissatisfaction with the way of the world. In our so-called art, the (purported) artist may express grief or sorrow, bemoan his own state, trouble deaf heaven with his cries and all the rest. But he does not indict the world and worldliness. He does not challenge the reign of Self. Anyone who has doubts about Self is understood to be pathetically naïve. We all know that Self is all there is. We all want status, money, and health. Anyone who seems not to desire these things is clearly dissimulating. He must be exposed for the fraud that he is. Or he is a total fool—so naïve as to be below one's notice.

Art is everywhere: art is omnipresent. Yet there is a problem. Almost none of it is art.

Where is compassion in the current Self-obsessed culture? Part of what is most startling in the world that we have made is that we have abjured the virtues of the saint. We have collectively turned our backs on most versions of loving-kindness for all. And we do not feel a very pressing need to forge a counterfeit culture of compassion. Surely there are the church drives and the benefits and the charities and the collections and the various forms of organized pity—but many if not most of those are merely forms of self-congratulation. "Pity would be no more," says Blake, "if we did not make somebody Poor." We are rank with voyeuristic kindness.

But the main event in American Christianity over the past decades has been a usurpation. More and more, the faith of American Christians is not the faith in the compassionate and merciful Jesus, but faith in God the Father. When fundamentalist believers talk now about Christ, they are often talking about Yahweh. They have forgotten the figure who was mild and sometimes humorous and endlessly kind. They have little interest in Jesus the poor vagrant who was not well disposed to any forms of worldly authority, who liked to spend his time with publicans and whores, and who despised money. The true Jesus was what Whitman said he was himself: perennially on the side of those that the others are down upon. Many American Christians have forgotten this figure. They've recharacterized Jesus as a bitterly judgmental father in love with punishment and retribution.

The complexities of Christianity (and to be fair the complexities of Jesus' own teaching) make this possible. But trading Jesus for Yahweh is not desirable, if what you care about is the welfare of the world, and in particular the plight of the poor. The Jesus of many American fundamentalist churches now has nothing more against getting rich and powerful than Yahweh does. Christianity always hangs between being the religion of the poor and the religion of Rome. It is now very much the religion of Rome, at least in America.

We seem to have come to an agreement that life is every man for himself, and every woman too. We have created a war of each against all, and revel in it. To be sure, culture occasionally throws forth a displaced version of the compassionate ideal. Rather than the miracle of the loaves and fishes binding the crowd together into one, we have the miracle of the soft drink, drawing every race, creed, and color into collective consumer bliss. Nothing, it seems, is more conducive to the love of one's neighbor than the sharing of identically branded products.

But by and large, the compassionate ideal is so dangerous to the Self that is it not even safe to put it into displaced or sublimated form. Pressed to the wall, we affirm the faith in individualism, and that is that. Jesus the preacher of universal brotherhood—"Who is my neighbor?" the lawyer asks, and the Savior tells him so that no one is likely to forget—that Jesus is all but gone, and it is best for our comfort and our entertainment that this be so. In Africa and Latin America, one finds bold priests and nuns and brothers who stand up for the poor and who defy Rome. All honor to them. They have brothers and sisters in America and Europe, a few, but by and large the rich Western churches have gone over to relative quietism. Let us take the Buddha and Confucius and the Hindu Sages off with this Jesus, too, and have done with it.

One could pursue the critique of the current culture of Self through many pages—it has as many turns and twists as Satan's tail. But this is not time well spent. The culture of Self is the god Proteus; it is a shape-shifter. Today it percolates through the Internet and shines and flashes on the flat screen. Tomorrow it will have another form. Self and its works are legion and infinitely variable, but we humans have created them all and will continue to do so until our race on earth has been run.

But the ideals have their strength too: Plato, Homer, Jesus, Buddha, Blake. These figures will not readily die, and we will not let them. We simulate (or suppress) their visions now in ways that are almost laughable, but those simulations testify to our need for ideals that transcend the Self. Someday we will perhaps get tired of living among shadows in a cave.

At a certain point it will again become clear to young people that they have a choice in what they make of their lives. There are ideals of the Soul and there are desires of the Self, and young people will once again have the chance to decide which they will pursue. Some will be drawn to Soul, but they will see that they cannot commit themselves all the way. Some defense, some carapace of Self, will be necessary. So Walt Whitman, greatest of American poets and a true High Romantic, cultivated the persona of one of the roughs. He presented himself as a worldly man, full of desires: "disorderly fleshy and sensual, eating drinking and breeding" as he puts it. Without that tough shell of masculinity—that shell of Self— Whitman's Soul might have perished early. For one sees quickly how delicate and tender the poet was. "Apart from the pulling and hauling stands what I am," he says.

> Stands amused, complacent, compassionating, idle, unitary,
> Looks down, is erect, bends an arm on an impalpable certain
>   rest,
> Looks with its sidecurved head curious what will come next,
> Both in and out of the game, and watching and wondering
>   at it.

If this being, neither man nor woman, neither child nor adult, had been exposed fully to the world, it would probably not have survived.

Whitman's Soul is a being of amazing delicacy, and Whitman needed to do all he could to protect it. He needed to surround it with a potent armor of Self, and then his Soul could expand into the poems and into American life. Socrates and Jesus seem to have been beings without Self—they were undefended in the world. It is a miracle that Socrates lasted as long as he did; it is rather a shock that Jesus could preach even for three years, given his absolute Selflessness.

Young men and women may come again to understand that Self at its best is a protection, and only a protection, for the life of Soul, and that when the moment comes for Soul to exert itself—Whitman's moment came in 1854 and 1855 when he wrote and published the stunning poems—Self must stand aside. It's said that when Wallace Stevens stepped into the room wearing his three-piece suit and his insurance man's frown, the temperature dropped twenty degrees. How much strength of Self was necessary to defend the Soul who wrote "Sunday Morning" and *Notes toward a Supreme Fiction?* Clearly a great deal. It is always dangerous to invoke Self to protect Soul, as Whitman and Stevens did. Self, given freedom, can consume Soul, or counterfeit it. But in a world as greedy and violent as this one, Self's tough guidance and protection may be a necessity.

The young who wish a better world will also see that what appear to be tensions among the ideals are only apparent. Is the warrior the exclusive inverse of the man or woman of compassion? To everything there is a season. There will always be a time when we need defense from our enemies, our real enemies, and then Hector is the figure we will not be able to do without. Compassion may be our central ideal in the time of peace, but peace is not forever.

There are seasons too for the individual. She may find herself at one time an aspiring thinker, at another a fighter, at a third a creator. And she will judge herself not only on the feeling of fullness that these ideals create within but also on what she contributes to other people by virtue of engaging her ideals. Hope will replace desire and for a while she will feel free. She may at times feel consumed by Self. There will be a family to feed and protect, aging parents to tend; there will be the push and toss of daily life—the "pulling and hauling" as Whitman calls it. But in every act of courage or compassion or true thought, she'll feel something within her begin to swell, and she'll feel a joy that passes beyond mere happiness. She'll feel intimations of a finer and higher life and she'll begin, as well as she can, to move toward it. What she'll feel then will be the resurrection of her Soul.